# Shot and Shell
# The Road to Rebellion

Robert K. Lytle

# DEDICATION

To the Officers and Soldiers of the United States Army that served in the times the Nation did not feel the need to have them.

MAJ. GEN. H. J. HUNT.

# CONTENTS

Model 1857 12 Pound Light Gun

# FOREWORD

Having been raised in the South, the history of my family's involvement in the American Civil War was part of my identity. I remember hearing family accounts of heroism and suffering as it related to who was related to whom and how the families had interwoven through history together. On my office wall hangs the original letter written by a distant cousin from the Federal Prison Camp at Point Lookout Maryland. The soldier was J.D. Weeks of the 4th South Carolina Cavalry who had been captured by the Union Army at the Battle of Trevillian Station in central Virginia. The young man wrote to reassure his father of his good health and to pass news to other families of soldiers who had been captured with him. Approximately 30 days from the date on the letter, J.D. Weeks died of Typhus in that same prison.

I have throughout 30 years of military service, pondered on the motivations and beliefs of these simple soldiers who fought so determinedly despite huge numbers of casualties, sickness and suffering. In our modern age, it is difficult to understand how the previous generation dealt with the separation, bad rations, sicknesses and horrors of that conflict.

From my research I have discovered aspects of the age that lead me to consider that this was a generation of Americans who lived in closer proximity to death than we do in this age. If close kin or a baby died, the dead were washed and kept in the house. Wakes were a family affair, and the victims often were buried in the yard. Only the very wealthy had the means to distance themselves from the tableau of passing. This closeness to death, often brought on by epidemics pushed a helpless population to seek refuge in their faith. Going to Church was a social highlight of the week, a good sermon was the entertainment of the week, the music of the service might be the only music to be heard for the week. Conversations with each other were the other prominent form of entertainment, reading aloud or singing together might be an evening of joy. The very business of life was complex and lacking many conveniences that we today take for granted. If you needed soap you made it, if you wanted vegetables you grew them, and if you wanted meat you killed and butchered it.
A gentleman named Elliot Wigginton and his students, researched the ways of life in Appalachia and published a wonderful series of books known as the Foxfire series, which describe in intimate detail what the people in the remote mountains, made for themselves to answer the necessities of life and daily living. Having read the series and having spent time among the people there I feel I have an understanding of the nature of the people of the time.

For the south slavery represented a way to have others do the myriad of those tasks for you. While an evil institution, I understand the reluctance Southerners had towards losing it. Slavery enabled the pursuit of "greater" things, without the risk brought about hard and dangerous work. In many parts of the South, just being outside and exposed to mosquito infested swamps and wetlands soon resulted in contraction of lethal disease. Slavery transferred the risk to the slave allowing the rich to shelter elsewhere to the same economic result for having worked yourself. Industrialization brought about the death of Slavery, but it took a war to eradicate the institution irreversibly. The soldiers on both sides fought with skill, determination and conviction. Each side stood firm in their beliefs with religious fervor. That fact alone made for a bloody and drawn out conflict.

I clearly remember an Army Staff ride at Gettysburg while attending Army War College. The dominant question as we walked the ground of Pickett's Charge was, "Why did they do this?" The answer in my mind was faith. The men of the age were not afraid to be publicly religious. It was what held everyone together. The civil war soldier maintained a firm belief in the infinite and fought with a faith that steeled most against the horror of the war. Yes men broke and ran, but more than less came back to face the horror again and again.

The men of this war believed in their own destiny and acted with a freedom of mind that enabled them to achieve it. For many that destiny was death, but for others it was high responsibility and fleeting glory.
I stumbled onto Henry Jackson Hunt and his history for this story. The decision to pick M Company, 2$^{nd}$ United States Artillery was made due to its battle history, which closely coincides with the campaigns of my Southern relatives. The more I researched this officer's history the more fascinating it became. Hunt, born in Detroit Michigan, educated at West Point and determined to make a career in the Army is illustrative of the man of the age.

It was men like him, on both sides of the war, that made the event so tragic and so decisive. Also illustrative of the time it proved that men like him were what was required to knit the nation back together when the war ended.

This book is intended to share details of these people and their stories and it will take more than one to do them justice.

# 1 MACBETH SOUTH CAROLINA 1855

Joshua appreciated the cool of the September morning air, yet he was beginning to sweat as the sun rose. The horse's flank twitched in response to a fly and the rich musty smell of its sweat filled Joshua's senses. He quickly lifted her front foot and clamped it between his knees, without hesitation he quickly trimmed the frog of the hoof and scooped excess pad from the sole. Reversing his trimming knife he cleaned the frog between the sole, removing the foul smelling mud and fungus harboring there. Deftly pocketing his blade, He retrieved the nippers from the wooden box behind him and rapidly cut away the spare hoof bringing the foot to a rough level. He then tossed the nippers back to the box and found the rasp without a glance and proceeded to file the entire foot flat. Dropping the mare's foot he found his wooden protractor and checked the shape, satisfied; he moved to the other front foot and repeated the process.

Joshua remembered how he had been fascinated by the shoeing of horses as a child. He often would wander across to the smithy operation on the Markley Plantation across the creek to watch an older gray haired slave known as "Old Mose" expertly attend to the dozens of fine hunting ponies used so frequently by the Markley men in their weekly Fox Hunts. Old Mose tolerated the small tow-headed boy, so fascinated by his labor and began to give him small tasks to assist him, being it fetching tools, or adding coals to the forge; but always with a whispered enjoinder that should a Markley approach the shop, that the boy should hide lest a "white man see a white boy helping a slave". Mose knew that Mister Markley, while a kind gentleman; would take offense at such.

Remembering his secretive lessons well, Joshua had all four feet trimmed and fit in a little over an hour and proceeded to the forge. Giving the bellows a few pumps resumed the red hot center of coke and he selected a short bar of iron and placed the end into the glowing coals. He returned to the mare and sized her right front hoof with a piece of string from his pocket. With this measurement he moved to the bar of iron on the anvil and marked off the length of string with a slate chalk mark to know the circumference of the shoe to be made. Again he pumped the bellows to keep the heat up.

Mister Markley had finally caught Joshua at the smithy and instead of anger he beamed and instructed Old Mose to "learn the boy to make shoes as well". Edward Markley had started rough himself, despite his standing in Old Berkeley County as a member of the planter class. He appreciated how Norman Timmonds raised his boys to master labor that was required to tame the low country and farm. His eldest son EJ was soon destined to run the Markley estate and yet his sons favored employing slaves to do the work and they viewed all future work to be the task of more slaves. Reflecting on this, the old gentleman fleetingly wished his sons had displayed such fascination with hard work.

Joshua noted the yellow heat of the iron and swiftly cut the rod to length against the anvil. He then quickly fixed the edge of the rod and started to flatten the heated end. Returning to stock to the coals, he again pumped the bellows and returned the stock to the flat of the anvil to flatten it uniformly transforming the dull red iron rod into a long narrow bar. Pausing, Joshua then compared the length with his slate chalk mark and returned the stock to the forge.

Edward Markley had sold Norman Timmonds the parcel that Joshua grew up on. Timmonds had impressed Markley with his acute interest in the economic potential of the area. Saint John's Berkely Parish in the Santee was rich in lumber and the lowlands provided abundant fertility and water for crops. Its proximity to Charleston and the Santee Canal provided an ideal means to link crops and lumber to market. Norman Timmonds established his 300 acre homestead after paying 1000 dollars in gold to Markley from his inheritance from his Father in Charleston. Markley also offered up crews of slaves to assist in clearing the homestead location of the gum and pines covering the site to facilitate the erection of a home. The two men shared the profit of the cut lumber and the beginnings of a respectful partnership began.

Joshua pulled the stock back out of the fire and noting the good color dead-center of the stock rapidly bent it with swift blows to form a right angle first then before losing heat and color formed one curve on the horn of the anvil. Shoving the half formed shoe back into the fire, he began to think of his father.

Norman Timmonds, in his frequent discussions with Markley had begun to form the vision of establishing a mill to enable local farmers in the parish to grind corn meal, sorghum and sugar cane for molasses. Norman had determined that, like the Macbeth Sawmill, a small steam grist mill would enable Macbeth to supply local goods to the growing population of Macbeth and Moncks Corner and good profits could be made by this operation. Norman's business contacts in Charleston had provided him with advertisements that marine steam plants were available in Norfolk, Virginia for Chesapeake vessels that would be ideal for a smaller operation. Norman's mind was beginning to be fixed by the idea of this engine and he speculated that he had sufficient reserves to procure one.

Joshua and his brother Jacob had been minding the Timmonds household since early July and they had yet to hear word from their father. Sadly the boys had been orphaned from their mother Elizabeth since 1851, shortly following the completion of their house. She had contacted the fever in Charleston and quickly died after contacting it. Joshua was 14 years old and recalled how he had to comfort Jacob, then 12. Following her funeral and burial Norman Timmons buried his sorrow in increasing improvements and business negotiations. He rarely spoke of her and quickly rented an older house slave from Mr. Markley to attend to the boys. "Anna" was a stout and jovial soul who enjoyed being the "Boss of the Kitchen" as she would proclaim. Mr. Timmonds was always far too preoccupied with his dealings to be finicky in regards to her services, and she thoroughly enjoyed the freedom of action such preoccupation allowed.

Joshua retrieved the half-shoe from the fire and shaped the other side, with a quick glance he closed the width with a blow on the anvil and clutching the shoe in the tongs moved over to the mare and lifter her hoof to compare it shape with the overall rough shape of the shoe. He returned to the anvil and made several small adjustments. Then he returned the shoe to the coals. As he pumped the bellows he started to collect up his punches and a fullering chisel he kept in his box, laying them neatly on the stump of gum tree that supported the anvil.

Old Mose had apprenticed Joshua for four years from his 12th year until last year in shoeing and the nature of horses. The Markley family raised and hunted a peculiar breed of ponies known in the Low Country as "Marsh Tacky" horses. Smaller than most horses, they usually featured a distinctive dark coloration with a line of dark hair from the withers to the tail. They were energetic and eager spirited horses who were very sure of foot in marshy and swampy terrain.

So hardy was the breed that it was said that General Marion favored them for operations in the Low Country against the British in the revolution. Edward Markley's father had fought with Marion throughout the Parish and beyond on these mounts. Joshua recalled how thrilled he had been when Mr. Markley had allowed him to brandish the family saber that hung over the mantel of the Markley house when he had visited with his father.

Shifting the shoe to obtain an even cherry red, Joshua pumped the bellows until he got "dat ready color" to quote Old Mose; pulling the shoe out he laid the shoe over the anvil with the round punch hole underneath and placed his sharply beveled square punch at the right position and punched the first nail hole clear through the stock. Moving quickly he got one more hole punched prior to losing sufficient heat to punch another. Grinning to himself he recalled how Old Mose could get one full side done on one heat. Shaking his head he returned the shoe to the forge.

The younger Jacob had not embraced the labor of the farm like his brother. Every chance he got he would be off to visit the more idle Markley boys to socialize and continue the adventures they dreamed up at the schoolhouse in Macbeth. His father tolerated this behavior as he realized that of the boys, Jacob had the potential for a more learned destiny as he was not as handy as Joshua. Like his mother had been Jacob was gregarious and fun loving and always preferred being in a crowd.

Pulling the shoe back out of the heat of the forge Joshua finished the other side of the shoe with his nail punch; quickly he returned the shoe to the forge and secured his fullering chisel. Old Mose had taught him multiple times how to cut the fuller into the shoe to preserve the head of the horseshoe nail but Joshua despaired of ever cutting the even and artful curve of the work of the old slave. He retrieved the shoe and using the nail holes as his guide he pounded in a short fuller grove along each of the three holes, remembering to solidly strike the head of the chisel to get an even depth. At the next heat he would draw clips on each front quarters of the shoe, which would result in a shoe that would not quickly pull off in the swampy backwoods.

The midmorning heat was starting to make itself felt and Joshua hurried with his task as he wanted to be done with the mare by mid-day. He stepped out to get a dipper of water and looked out towards the house, Anna, seeing him emerge came out on the back stoop and announced "Mister Josh, I will have some Hopping John with Okra ready directly, and I don't imagine to be seeing that brother of yours so it is just you and me dining today!" Joshua nodded and appreciated having her mothering them.

Returning to his forge, Joshua withdrew the heated shoe and made a quick punch on each front quarter to push extra iron off the two front edges, he then quickly formed the clips on the anvil to overlap the front of the horses hoof, hammering lightly and then eyeballing the angle to match the hoof.

Thinking of the angle caused him to remember working for Edward Markley Jr, two summers ago surveying the southern boundary of Somerset Plantation on contract for the Dupre' family. He was paid 10 cents a day to pull surveying chain and hold the Jacob's staff for Edward junior, or EJ as everyone knew him. EJ like his father was a patient and kindly man who was eager to teach his helpers the art of the survey. EJ made a game of the task of running Joshua out with chain and staff through the tangled low country overgrowth and would challenge him to "guess the distance". Joshua knew that the chain was 66 feet and remembering his lessons in multiplication from Macbeth school he started to see the world in 66 foot divisions. EJ had demonstrated when they lunched on the tailgate of the wagon with chalk on the boards and showed him the art of triangulation and the law of sines. His dull geometry lessons from the school house started to come to life on those busy days of surveying. He recalled his fascination with the finely made brass English transit and the sturdy tripod. EJ would let him look through the telescope but would not permit him to handle the fine instrument, "too hard to find another, young'un", he would mutter in a good natured way.

Joshua took the completed shoe and dropped it on top of the coals for a brief moment to enable it to come to a blue heat, then he raised the mares front hoof between his knees and with his tongs first set the shoe on the anvil then reversed the tongs to insert the pointed handle ends into the nail holes and brought the hot shoe in contact with the freshly trimmed hoof. Now he had the mare's attention and he clamped his knees tighter as she tried to pull the hoof away, he pressed hard, blinded and choking on the acrid stench of the smoke billowing off the melting hoof and then he pitched the shoe off the hoof into a bucket of water nearby. Looking at the hoof he approvingly noted a good level set.

Looking to the bench he found the box of English horseshoe nails and his hammer and clinchers. It was time to put one shoe on. Working rapidly he returned the mare's hoof to his knees and in a quick motion drove two nails, one on the left and one on the right, taking care to bend over the needle sharp points protruding from the hoof walls, lest the horse decide to have her hoof back and drag the razor sharp points along the inside of his thighs. Old Mose had told him that he saw a man die that way as cuts inside the thigh bleed a lot and are hard to stop.

Joshua repeated the process until all six nails were in then he returned to the bent over nail shanks and nipped them off almost level; then using the clincher he bent the nails tightly over towards the shoe, tightly clamping the shoe to the living hoof. Joshua then lightly rasped the front wall of the hoof, evening the iron of the clinched nails with the outside of the hoof wall. He always loved to see a well shod hoof and felt proud of his work.

Moving to the next shoe, he began to worry about his father.

Joshua and Jacob had been watching the house with Anna since the beginning of July. After months of reading Charleston Mercury advertisements and discussions with Mr. Rivers at the saw mill, Norman Timmonds had his mind set on a horizontal beam Watts steam engine to run a grist mill on his place. Mr. Rivers had advised the shipyard at Portsmouth, Virginia due to the shipbuilding that occurred there as Portsmouth supported the U. S. Navy and had become a collection point of all the latest steam powered machinery. Norman mused that he might be so lucky as to secure railway shipment of his engine back somewhere close to Macbeth and he figured he would accompany his purchase to insure its delivery.

He wanted also to be able to discuss the operation of such an engine with the mechanics there who worked on them to obtain a first-hand understanding of their function in order to properly operate one. He calculated that by shortening the distance to local farms and milling corn flour at Macbeth, the engine could pay for itself in a little over a year. He reasoned that with Joshua being nearly 18 years old and with Anna watching the house that he could affect the trip and return in time to build the mill house in time for winter processing of crops.

Joshua watched his father board a barge on the Santee Canal bound for Charleston and then a steamboat to Norfolk. Waving goodbye, he suddenly felt very alone. Driving the wagon back the 6 miles to Macbeth, he noted that Jacob seemed completely undisturbed by his father's departure.

As they trundled down Black Oak Road he stated to his brother, "Jacob, now that Pa is traveling you are going to have to help more on the place, I ain't doing everything by myself!"

Jacob, looking off towards the moss laden live oaks muttered, "I've been doing plenty, and Pa did not say you was my boss, Joshua!"

Jacob knew he would now have to explain to his brother where he was going and what he was doing and he did not like it in the least.

Joshua decided to let it go. He knew he would be pressed into helping build the mill once father had returned and he knew, deep down that he would have to constantly chase Jacob down daily to get the least amount of chores out of him. Fortunately Anna attended to most of them anyhow.

After another hours labor Joshua finished the shoeing job on the mare. Standing back with her out of the stall he admired the solidly shod hooves, "she will hunt well" he said to himself and after painting some turpentine on each hoof face to seal them he led the mare to the barn. He wished it was his horse but this one belonged to Charlotte Markley, whom everyone called "Lottie". She was two years his junior and she always made a point of asking favors of him in school. Joshua saw her often at the Markley place but never thought too much about her because his mind was always on something that had to be done.

It never occurred to Joshua that Lottie greatly admired the studious "Charleston Boy" as she referred to him. Despite her mother's admonishments, Lottie was none to impressed with the distinctions of class. She also knew that Joshua was bound for greater things and listening to her father and oldest brother praise his talents and drive to achieve things, only caused her to admire him more. Shoeing her pony was simply another chance to see him and make him do things for her.

With the mare taken care of he washed in the water barrel and put away his tools. It was mid-day now and while very warm outside he noted that low clouds were gathering between the branches of the giant Live Oak that sheltered the barn and smithy. It was sure to bring a thunderstorm later in the afternoon.

Anna met him on the back porch door wiping her hands on an apron and greeting him heartily, "I got you something to eat Mister Josh, it's hot on the table."

Joshua smiled and replied "Thank you Anna, I'm truly sorry Jacob don't appreciate your cooking".

Anna just smiled and laughed, observing "That boy gets much better food over yonder with them Markley folks, plus he gets to look at that girl from time to time".

Joshua felt a twinge at the comment, knowing she meant Lottie.

Joshua ate the rice and peas hungrily, downing two plates before pushing away from the table. He got his cap and jacket on and announced to Anna,

"Thank you for the lunch I am going to take this pony back over to the Markley's summer place at Pinopolis so I will be late for supper."

Anna sensing his preoccupation asked "Have you heard word of your father?"

Joshua thoughtfully replied, "Anna, no I have not and I am greatly concerned that I have not, I would have expected at least a letter by now."

Anna shook her head and was worried as well for some time. All the slaves at the main plantation house talked about him leaving the boys and some crudely joked that "he had run off." She sharply defended Norman Timmonds among them knowing his drive to build something on the place that might promise less backbreaking labor.

She called out to Joshua as he went out to saddle the mule, "You should talk to Mr. Markley about your father".

Joshua calling over his shoulder said "That's what I aim to do".

Joshua felt slightly awkward riding a mule with a fine hunting pony in tow but felt that he should not ride a horse that was not his, the jacket was hot but his shirt being dirty would not do when calling on the Markley house. Even at the smaller summer cottage.

The Markley's like all the larger planters kept a house at the higher elevations in the Pinewoods areas of the parish to escape the mosquitos and the fever season. No one had yet to associate the two as linked but summering in the Low Country brought the fever and the fever brought death. The low country fever had claimed his mother and everyone lived in fear of contacting it.

Joshua pondered as he rode the six miles to Pinopolis in the heat, in the distance he heard the first thunder of the afternoon storm that was surely coming but he needed some advice on what to do.

The hunting dogs greeted him noisily as he rode into the yard, and Mrs. Markley shouted out to him from the front porch to come in for some lemon water.

Lottie came out of the front door and happily called out to her horse, "Marcie, you have such beautiful new shoes!"

She gave Joshua an adoring glance as she took the lead from him and led the mare around the back to the barn behind the cottage.

Joshua felt very uncomfortable in his dirty sweaty shirt and as he climbed the steps he removed his cap and asked "Ma'am is your Husband home?"

She replied, "Why certainly young man, he is on the veranda in back with EJ, have you heard news of your father?"

Joshua stiffened and replied, "No Ma'am I have not and I need advice."

Elizabeth Markley was astonished and worried at the same time, thinking the worst she led him by the hand to the back of the house exclaiming as she exited the back door onto the veranda, "Edward! Please take a moment to talk to Joshua his father has been gone all this time and these boys have heard no word from him!"

She pressed Joshua out towards the men and said, "you go ahead and talk I will bring you a cool drink."

Edward Markley looked at the Joshua and exclaimed "Damn boy! You mean to tell me you haven't heard from him since July?"

Joshua nodded, "Yes sir."

EJ shook his head and said "Norfolk is a long way off, at least a week by road and a 3 days by steamer." Edward had heard in town some news that Norfolk had a ship in quarantine for the fever but had thought nothing of it at the time.

Joshua stated, shaking his head, "My father took close to 1,500 dollars in gold with him to buy a Steam Engine and I had hoped him to have returned by now, I intend to go to Norfolk to find him."

Edward shook his head, "Son that would be foolish at best, what if he is enroute back as we speak, he departed by steamer and would be likely to either return by freight wagon or on the train to Goldsboro, you could miss him on the way!"

Joshua shook his head, fighting tears, "My father told me he would telegraph me of his plans once he arrived!"

"I have stopped by the telegraph office every week since he left in Moncks Corner without a word of news!"

Markley pondered and seeing his logic asked, "What can we do for you, Son?"

Joshua had thought this out on the ride over and replied "Can you keep an eye on Jacob and the place for me?"

Markley quickly responded, "Young man I would be happy to do that, but explain to me how you intend to get to Norfolk?" "Do you need money for passage on a Steamer?"

Joshua quickly replied, "No Sir, I have enough to do that from what I have collected from work, I can manage fine."

Markley knew better but sensing the young man's pride and admiring that pride stated "If you go to Jamestown there is a man called Abner Cross there who runs a freight wagon. He normally goes up the coast with Mercantile loads from Charleston once a month, He goes to Wilmington port most of the time but he might go further if he found a lucrative load to bring back, he would pay you to help him off-load and to watch the wagon."

Edward added, "I would be happy to get in touch with him for you."

Joshua, nodding, realized this was a better plan that what he had in mind, quickly responded, "Yes sir! That would be smarter than spending all my money just to get there."

Edward Markley at that moment wished this young man was his son, like EJ; here was a young man that did his own thinking and planning and who stayed busy learning to do things.

Digging in his pocket, he produced a 5 dollar gold coin and handed it to Joshua, "here is the wage for the shoeing of my daughter's pony, I don't have to inspect your work."

He added in a fatherly tone, "You need not worry about your father's place or your brother, I will see to it while you are gone."

Joshua nodded and pocketed the coin quickly.

He started to turn to leave but Edward looked out from under the veranda, noting the gathering storm clouds and stated, "Have a seat with us, son, we will have a drink and talk some and then you will have dinner with us this evening."

Joshua although agitated by his decision to go nodded in agreement and took a seat.

Mrs. Markley brought the drink and having overheard reinforced the invitation, "You relax a spell, and sit with Father, you can wash up later and we would be honored to have you for supper."

Joshua missed the feeling of family and sadly remembered his mother's voice as a child.

Edward turned to EJ and directed "Get Mr. Baker up to the house after supper, we will get him to send the carriage driver over to Jamestown tonight and determine when Mr. Cross wants to go. Tell him I have a load for Norfolk." He sipped his lemon water and winked at Joshua.

Following a simple supper of cold Ham, rice and beans the Elder Markley and his eldest son invited Joshua out onto the veranda, it rained heavily and was growing very dark outside, and the rain was punctuated with loud cracks of lightning that lit the porch.

Mr. Markley discussed the day's business with EJ and seemed disturbed by the diminishing returns of rice and cotton in terms of the cost of maintaining enough slaves to profit from the crop. EJ repeatedly would mention that cotton was the future and Edward Markley would counter with the cost of purchasing slaves and maintaining sufficient hands to harvest the crop.

"A good field hand costs nearly 1200 dollars in this day and age and working children was not efficient enough," remarked the old man. "I wish I could scale back and return to Indigo".

EJ shook his head sadly and observed "Father those days are long gone!" he added, "I hear the English import the dye from the India colonies and will not even buy Carolina indigo for any price."

Edward Markley suddenly was struck with an idea. Looking at Joshua he leaned over conspiratorially and asked, "Son, how would you like to act as an agent of sales for me?"

Joshua asked, "Sir, what do you mean?"

The elder Markley proposed, "Son, once we locate Mr. Cross, we will load him and his freight wagon with my remaining bales of indigo dye. I have maintained a stockpile since we harvested our last crop 10 years ago. I intend to send you to Norfolk under hire and see if you can find a buyer!"

EJ listening, and knowing his father's stubborn desire to keep the old ways alive observed diplomatically, "Father, maybe you are on to something."

The older man nodded vigorously, and added to EJ, "in the morning, You and your brothers go down and label each bale with the Somerset Plantation mark, put my name and "Charleston District, South Carolina" on each one."

As he rocked and watched the storm he added, "Each of those parcels marked as such, could result in a demand, like small ambassadors advertising the wares of the Low Country, you just never can tell."

Joshua willingly agreed now that the trip would have a double purpose. He replied "Sir, it would be my honor to represent you!"

Joshua noted the rain slowing and begged his leave to return to the farm.

As he stood to leave Mr. Markley touched his arm and said "Joshua, I am going to pray you find your father sound, Mr. Timmonds and I have plans for this parish. He sat many a night with me and we discussed it. I will collect some papers for you to read on your way there that may indicate who he contacted, that at least may help."

Joshua did not understand why this family was so willing to help what was left of his family but he now understood why people in the parish held the Markley family in high regard.

Mr. Markley told him as he walked down the steps into the night, "When Cross and his wagon get here, I will send a rider for you, I expect it will not be until a fortnight but be ready to go!"

Joshua replied "Thank you sir, I will be waiting."

Norman Timmonds was happy to be finished with the sea leg of his journey. He had spent two days of negotiating with the Farmers and Exchange bank in Charleston; he shook his head at the memory of the haggling required to withdraw 1200 dollars in gold from his account, following the market crisis of last year no banks wanted to release gold. Norman knew enough from his time in Charleston with his father that no agency outside of Charleston District would accept a Farmers and Exchange paper note.

At the harbor he had booked one-way passage on the fast Postal Steamer "Isabel" to Portsmouth, Virginia. This sleek and modern vessel stopped at Wilmington and Portsmouth before turning south bound for Cuba. Edward Markley had discussed possibilities with acquaintances at the Customs House and calculated that the Page and Allen's shipyard in Gosport, Virginia would be the best concern to engage in regards to marine machinery. Shipping agents had mentioned that this firm did major repairs and shipbreaking as well, offering plentiful sources for salvage.

He had spent hours on the 2 day voyage looking at the engine room and talking with the stokers and mechanics and enjoyed feeling the powerful vibrations on the deck as the powerful vessel drove its way across the sea. He worried at times about the boys, but felt comfortable with the assurances Edward had given him about keeping an eye on them. Since Jacob spent the majority of his time with the younger Lewis and Thomas, hunting and riding and Edward's eldest, Edward Jr. kept Joshua in paying work he was confident they had a second home. Annabelle, whom all called "Anna", kept the house as nice as Elizabeth had before her death, so he felt he had provided all a man could reasonably do.

It was the day after Independence Day, the ship had toasted the event last night at dinner among the limited passengers and officers, and it was a fine day at that. The weather was mild and the arrival of the gulls overhead screeching and diving showed that the Isabel was closing in on Hampton Roads. Shortly white sails hove into view and in the distance to the right old Point Comfort and the menacing granite and masonry bastions of Ft. Monroe were visible. For the observance of yesterday perhaps, the fort had aloft perhaps the largest flag he had ever seen and it became a topic of excitement among the passengers topside.

Isabel cruised into the harbor channel and hugged the southern bank of the Roads nearing the mouth of the Elizabeth River but then inexplicably came to a slow halt short of the inlet entrance and the crew dropped anchor. The passengers seem dismayed and started to ask one another why the vessel stopped short.

Observing the commotion, a deck officer announced briskly to the assembled passengers, "Not to worry Ladies and Gentlemen we must await a harbor pilot and the City Health Officer to inspect the ship, we should be underway shortly."

Norman hated the delay, he had much to do.

Soon a small steam lighter with a white canvas top could be seen approaching the Isabel and after a half an hour it pulled alongside her and two smartly dressed gentlemen in naval dress ascended the gangway steps of the steamer. The younger of the two, the harbor pilot shook hands with the Captain and departed with the first officer to the wheel house with much discussion and pointing about the harbor. The elder man and the Captain stood and talked for a moment and the Captain seemed to have a concerned look on his face. The two departed towards the cargo holds talking the entire time. As Norman watched, fascinated by the clearly important naval business underway; he mused about the exciting life it must be to work on the seas.

Captain Clements, who commanded the Isabel, rightly was concerned to insure the City Health Inspector; Dr. Morse would find no pestilence aboard his ship. The Isabel was 5 years old and only carried freight and mail, passengers were always a worry but he had no reported illnesses noted among the passengers by the ship's Doctor.  Dr. Morse was clearly agitated and inspected far more carefully than Captain Clements felt was warranted.

As they walked the passageway below decks he assured Dr. Morse, "she's nearly new and tightly run, Sir, I assure you we are easily ready to dock."

Captain Clements was on a tight schedule and wished to be clear of Portsmouth by tomorrow.

 Dr. Morse shook his head apologetically as he replied, "We have had a recent and very disturbing arrival, the Harbor Commodore and the Mayor are insistent that no ship docks until thoroughly inspected."

He continued as he walked to the galley, "The Benjamin Franklin got placed in harbor quarantine last month, with at least one seaman sick with the Yellow Jack!, another 6 seamen jumped ship during the quarantine and we found 2 drowned, we have yet to find the other 4."

Captain Clements now understood, the fever was bad business and he was now intent on clearing the harbor even more quickly, once he had picked up the mail bags.

Doctor Morse carefully inspected the food stores and, noting the modern and clean storage areas was relieved, idly remarking, "We made the Franklin dump the food stores from her holds into the harbor, Fruit it was….took two tides for it all to clear off, lemons and oranges and such…floating about."

Captain Clements gave an insincere laugh, newly nervous about where he was and asked, "Is there sign ashore?  Should I notify my passengers?

Dr. Morse quickly stated "no, not at the moment, the one sailor was put into the hospital and he still lives so we think it was all."

Dr. Morse then turned and asked, "Might I see your bilge, Sir?"

Captain Clements turned and strolled back to the galley and returned with an oil lamp which he paused to light with a Lucifer match and stated, "Follow me Doctor."

They paused a moment and the Doctor dipped his palm in the water and smelled it, he then observed "Very well Captain, If I could talk to your ship's doctor a moment we will be on our way".

Norman watched from the deck rail as the Captain and the Health Inspector came topside.

The Deck Officer noting his interest explained, "He is looking for sickness and disease or signs of a pestilence," he paused and added, "He was pretty quick about it so it looks like we will be on our way."

Norman felt better about that. He had business to attend to.

The Health Inspector returned to the lighter and the Captain returned to the wheelhouse. The passengers became more cheerful and expectant as the steam engine was stoked and the familiar rumble of the paddlewheel shafts returned to the deck.

Isabel docked at Portsmouth at 4:00 pm on the 5th of July 1855, Norman Timmons eagerly departed as soon as the gangway was opened clutching a rather heavy satchel case. He was anxious, happy and expectant at the same time. Unknown to him, he had just entered Hell.

Norman briskly strode across the quay to the nearest ticketing office and queried the clerk for the location of the Page and Allen's Shipyard.

The young man looked up from his penmanship and pointed West, replying, "Sir, walk one block North until you hit Cranford Street, the shipyard lies about two miles west."

The clerk added, helpfully, "if your business is with them today you might want to hail a cab as they close the front office at 5:00 pm sharp."

Norman paused thoughtfully and looked at his pocket-watch; it read 4:20 pm.

He quickly snapped it closed and pocketed it, and asked, "Is there a decent Inn nearby?"

The young clerk smiled and explained, "Yes sir, follow the same directions and it is about 2 blocks west from us on Cranford Street. Look for the Westbury House."

Norman thanked the young man and strode into Portsmouth.

Plying the busy street full of seamen, townspeople and freight wagons leaving the docks, he soon found and turned onto Cranford Street. Precisely two blocks down, he saw the wooden sign of the Westbury House with a smaller sign below it reading "Lodgers Welcome".

He clanged the knocker on the street level door and after a lengthy pause a washer woman opened the door. "Excuse me Miss, but do you accept lodgers?" Norman asked tipping his Hat.

The wash woman was flustered but replied quickly, "I am sure sir, however there is no need to knock we have a desk, please do come in."

Norman followed her through the foyer and saw the proprietress, Mrs. Westbury; at a desk in the sitting room.

She looked up from her ledger and asked "Good afternoon Sir, are you seeking room and board?"

Norman removed his hat and replied, "Yes Madam, namely only a room, I will seek board about town, I am here on business and I will likely leave early and possibly arrive late."

Mrs. Westbury replied "Very well sir I have two single rooms upstairs, a room without board will be 50 cents per day board is another 25 cents with meals at 7, noon and 6 pm if you change your mind."

Norman thanked her and gave her a dollar coin, adding "Room will be enough Madame and I will pay for tonight and tomorrow night for now."

She took the dollar and replied, "Sir I must impress upon you that we are a Christian establishment, we will brook no drunkenness and absolutely no callers are permitted. We also lock the front door at 1100 pm so I will ask you to remember these rules."

As she handed him a key on a chain with a brass tag indicating his room number 206 stamped on it, he thanked her and acknowledged her rules, "I am most glad to oblige Ma'am, honest business will be my only concern while here."

At 5:00 pm the work gangs and the sailors left the grounds of the Page and Allen's Shipyard where the Benjamin Franklin lay in the repair slip. The Captain had secured lodging for the portion of the crew displaced by the repairs in cheap boarding houses adjacent to the yards and had advanced partial pay to the Tars upon condition that they returned to the yard every morning to help with repairs. The Captain was in a foul mood having lost his cargo, 6 seamen, and almost sunk in the harbor with the damned quarantine. With luck he could pick up a cargo here following the repair to his hull that the storm they had encountered enroute to New York from St. Thomas, had damaged. The leak overwhelmed the pumps by the time they passed Old Point Comfort so he had decided to stop. Now he grudgingly accepted the reality that he would be laid up here for at least two weeks. He advised his 6 paying passengers to seek other accommodation for travel and sadly refunded the unearned portion of their passage.

Unbeknownst to the good Captain his other unintended passengers decided to disembark as well. In the bilges and damp timber bottoms of the Benjamin Franklin a unique species of Mosquito, namely the genus *Aedes aegypti* emerged from their second hatch of this voyage and slowly began to depart the ship under repair; flying in the hot calm to the tall marsh grasses that bordered the shipyard. In the later evening still they would emerge to feed; following the same pattern as in their native South America.

The sailors made a beeline for the nearest public houses in Portsmouth, glad to be off the sea for a while and off quarantine. Several had been taken ill with fever as well as the one who had been hospitalized but the fever broke and they felt better. They hoped to find their comrades who had jumped ship so one group decided to go across the bay on the ferry to Norfolk to see if they could find them there. They would not be hard to find, all one had to do was visit the pubs and public houses on Barry's Row.

Norman, quickly unpacked his satchel, hid the bag of gold coins under the mattress and securing his room key, exited the Boarding House and impulsively decided to take a late afternoon walk to survey the Page and Allen's ship yard. He hoped he could ascertain when they opened the front office. As he strolled down Cranford Street he began to notice the sailors and mechanics moving into town from the yard in groups, they moved with a purpose seeking pubs and public houses. It reminded him of Charleston when the ships came in.

Soon he could see the masts of the ships docked at the yard which lay in a spit of the Elizabeth River that separated Portsmouth from the Navy Yard in Gosport. Soon he had found the yard and within was a large and untidy shed, on the front corner were windows so he surmised that was the office. Walking up to the structure he noted that there was indeed a small wooden sign by the door that stated "Office hours 8:00 am to 5:00 pm". He poked about the building to see if any engines lay about the premises but it blocked access to the rear being surrounded by salt marshes. While he investigated he began to notice a humming noise and suddenly sensed a burning sensation below his ear.

Swatting the side of his head, he looked at his hand and noted a spot of blood, "Damned Mosquitos!" he exclaimed and waving his hands about his ears he quickly sought the safety of Cranford Street.

Feeling suddenly hungry; Norman, began to pay attention to the establishments that lay on the walk back. Seeing one with a nice sign, The Boars Head, he removed his hat and ducked in for a bite to eat and perhaps a snifter of Port to celebrate a successful start.

Norman returned to the Westbury House by 9:00 pm and decided to turn in, it had been a long and tiring day and he wished to get an early start.

Two sailors returning to the boarding houses near the shipyard were having difficulty, due to vast quantities of Ale, in finding the cross street off of Cranford Street where their lodgings were. Frustrated, they entered the Boars Head for more ale, hoping perhaps to encounter their fellow crewmen. They waited and drank another two hours to no avail so decided together to try again. By this point they were hopelessly lost and so they simply returned to the yard and sat against the side of the building and passed out, at least they would be at work in the morning.

Norman awoke at 6:30 pm and felt thoroughly refreshed he quickly washed in the basin and shaved. He changed into a new shirt and then recovered his gold from under the mattress and trotted down the stairs. The smell of breakfast almost caused him to change his mind on board but he really was not hungry and did not want to unnecessarily increase his expenses until he determined what the engine would cost. He took his time walking down Cranford Street and arrived at a quarter till 8:00 am at the shipyard. Mechanics and Sailors were gathered about awaiting the opening of the warehouse doors that led to the quay. He noted several standing off to the side of the building attending to two obviously drunk comrades slumped against the building. He chuckled at the notion of this scene repeating itself all over town.

At 8:00 am the doors were opened from the inside and the workmen and sailors streamed in. Norman waited for the pack to clear the entrance before entering and then proceeded to the office.

Seeing an older man there, he quickly introduced himself, "Good day sir, my name is Norman Timmonds of Charleston, South Carolina, I have received the highest recommendations in regards to your firm."

The old gentleman looked up and smiled replying, "and a good morning to you sir, I am Charles Allen, part owner to the yard, How may I help you."

The two men quickly realized they were fortuitous in meeting, Mr. Allen had a salvage motor, recently removed from a heavily damaged fishing boat, and Mr. Timmonds had arrived to purchase such an object. The two men walked past the quay into a flat area where vast stores of timber and copper sheathing lay stockpiled and looked over the steam engine. As Norman explained his concept for its use, Mr. Allen helpfully suggested a visit to another concern in Hampton, across the Roads; that had milling appurtenances that could be mated to the power plant and made to function for his purposes.

Returning to the office, the two men settled into a two hour negotiation of price. The final agreement was 900 dollars in gold and arrangement for shipping to Macbeth, South Carolina, payment upon delivery. Charles Allen being a kindly sort assured Norman that he would be happy to arrange shipping. He was accustomed to this aspect of the trade and he knew he had one east coast steamer sitting in his yard desperate for cargo.

Norman was elated and he took the clear ease of this transaction as an indicator that vision would succeed. His mind was already on the construction of the mill, he was anxious to discuss his purchase with Edward Markley, but first he must investigate the lead on the milling attachments to see if Virginia had more to offer.

The two men were interrupted in their parting by the Foreman, who leaned into the door and briskly said, "Mister Allen, sorry to bother you sir, but we got us a problem..."

Norman quickly rose and asked Charles if it would be alright to return to look at the engine again in a fortnight and he quickly assured him that it would be no problem. Norman then left. He intended to pay for board in the evening after he had determined how to get to his next destination.

"This one is dead, the other is near dead! That's the Yellow Jack clear as hell, Mr. Allen!" exclaimed the foreman as the two looked at the sailors slumped against the building.

One was unresponsive and his skin had a ghastly yellow color. The dead man was covered by black vomit on the front of his shirt and on the dirt around where he lay.

George Allen did not need this. Not now, turning to the foreman he directed, "Get a crew together and bury them out beyond the lumberyard, and not a word to anyone of this, do you understand!"

The foreman nodded quickly and quickly dashed inside to find a tarp to cover the two.

Norman found a nicer restaurant that evening and enjoyed a gentleman's meal that evening. Returning to the Westbury House by 7 pm he found Mrs. Westbury and arranged for lodging again in 3 days from tomorrow.

She asked where he was bound and he informed her, "To Hampton across the Roads" She recommended the ferry that served Hampton direct and explained that it required taking the ferry "Gosport" to Norfolk, then a cab to Willoughby Spit, she explained that he could then obtain the most direct route to Hampton.

Thanking her, he borrowed a Harpers Monthly from the sitting room and went upstairs to his room. He started to notice an odd, remote achiness in his elbows and knees. After an hour or so of reading he went to bed.

The next morning Norman departed early, bound for Hampton, he mused that he soon should get word to Joshua and Edward Markley that he had achieved his goal. He made his way to the Gosport landing and caught the ferry after only a short wait. The morning was rather warm and he noticed that he did not feel very well, attributing it to seasickness and looked out at the warships in anchor on both sides of the Elizabeth River.

A Norfolk Policeman on his morning rounds of the notorious Barry's Row district was summoned by a small boy who, tugging the hem of his frock coat, led him to an alley. He recoiled in disgust at the scene behind a nearly empty rain barrel, in the darkened alley a sailor lay face-down in what appeared to be a dark puddle of blood. With his patent leather boot, the officer rolled the man over. The man's eyes were wide open and glazed, with the stare of the dead that looked out to eternity. Yellowish eyes rimmed in red. The man's face and exposed skin were an un-natural grayish yellow color.

Turning to the boy he sternly ordered, "Stay away from this lad, and let no one come upon this place until I return."

Norman had to walk almost a mile before he realized how to catch a Norfolk City cab, which was to find a fine inn and secure one there. After 2 hours of weaving through the bustling city they arrived at the Barren Spit where a small dock and ferry office sat. The sign indicated that the next ferry would arrive at 1:00 pm. He found a bench outside and sat down to rest. He perceptibly was feeling rather run-down.

He awoke with a start an hour later, having fallen asleep on the bench, looking around he noted that a crowd was gathering and looking around he noticed the wide paddlewheel steamer approaching the landing. She had a bold painted label on her flanks, "Queen of the Roads". Relieved, he picked up his satchel and walked over to pay his fare.

The clerk tending the window stated the price without looking up and Norman paid in coin. As the clerk picked up the coins they were unnaturally moist, looking up he say the man, his face was flushed and red and he was sweating profusely, he was impelled to ask, "Are you alright, Sir?" Norman nodded, feeling too strange for words.

As the day wore on in Portsmouth, sickness seemed to become the order of the day. A mother who ran a boarding house by Gosport busied herself with a sickly son; The Proprietor of the Boars Head announced to his wife that he was too ill to rise out of bed. Mr. Page was alarmed to note 4 men failing to show up to work for the half-day they had scheduled to work that Saturday. A sailor at the hospital North of Town died that morning despite the care of the Ship's doctor who had tended to him for over 3 weeks. Death had come calling in Virginia.

Norman arrived in Hampton, having slept most of the trip on the ferry and felt very disoriented, fortunately hackney cabs awaited in hopes of fares. Climbing in one with another two passengers they rode into town. He chose a boarding house nearest to where the cab had stopped, and washed in the room basin and went to bed, burning of fever. By morning dawn, Norman had joined Elizabeth on the other side.

The Inn-Keeper following the departure of most of her evening fares; knocked on his door and was alarmed that it swung open. Mr. Timmonds had failed to lock it. Looking in, she shrieked and ran back down stairs to notify the authorities.

The policeman and the doctor who looked over the scene, both agreed that an epidemic of Yellow Fever was emerging across the Roads. The policeman reported that 3 deaths had been noted by the Norfolk Argus over the past two days.

Norman had very few papers to identify him as they prepared him for burial, they did find engraved on his watch "To my Love Norman, Elizabeth" The city coroner insisted he be buried as soon as possible and taxed the Charlestonian his last time by employing the coin found on him to provide for his burial at the Ebenezer Church yard with a simple stone marker with a carved epitaph, "Norman, Husband of Elizabeth, died 8 July 1855."

# 2 JOURNEY TO NORFOLK 1855

Abner Cross patiently drove his travel worn freight wagon down the Georgetown Road and turned the corner onto Black Oak Road by old Biggin Church, to get to Macbeth and then beyond to the Main House of the Somerset Plantation. The slave sent to summon him could not explain the hurry of Mr. Markley but dray work from him generally paid well so he did not mind a deadhead trip to meet him. His mules had leads but he rarely relied on them, a simple "Gee" or a "Haw" was all that was needed to get the 4 animals to turn. It was a fine morning following the hellish storm of the previous evening and he happily anticipated a trip someplace with a load.

Edward Markley met him at the porch of the large house and warmly greeted the trusty drayman. Cross had made a good living providing "last mile" hauling from the Santee Canal, and if he did not fall into drinking he was fairly fast and reliable.

Markley approached the wagon and climbing in; he stated "let us ride out to my back barn to pick up this load." Cross smiled and issued a short whistle and the mule team started to pull on their traces.

Once around the house a quick shout of "Haw" turned them right down the dirt road along the uncut forest that led to the Storage Barn.

Cross glanced at Markley and noticing his smile added "they are right smart for mules!"

Markley having a captive audience started his proposal with a question, "Abner, you have pulled lots of loads for me, but can you tell me what the longest distance is that you have taken freight?"

Cross thought a moment and replied, "Once took a load to Wilmington, but it was not at a profit as I lost a mule."

Markley smiled and asked, "Ever gone to Norfolk?"

Cross's eyes widened and he exclaimed "Virginia!"

Markley nodded and added "I have a special load; that I am prepared to pay a delivery fee and reasonable mileage." He then added, "And I would be happy to replace any lost mules as insurance."

Cross ruminated on the proposal; his mind was racing on calculating how far the Virginia harbor lay distant. Following his mental calculation he provided his quote, "Mr. Markley, I would say 15 cents a mile plus 20 dollars delivery fee." Cross then inwardly winced as he awaited the response, he was a poor haggler.

Markley looked up in the sky thoughtfully as the wagon trundled along and responded, "Due to the sentimental nature of this task, Sir, I am happy to provide your price without argument."

Cross grinned, imagining that he might have some free time when he got back.

As the wagon approached the barn the men stopped so Edward Markley could summon two young slaves who were stacking lumber under a timber shed from another wagon that had returned from the sawmill.

Markley in a firm voice commanded, "Jimmy, I need you and Reid here to help me load that indigo the boys were marking for me yesterday, is it still in the barn?"

The older slave smiled and stated "Yessir, we got it in two old wood stave barrels in the barn." He took off his hat and asked, "Sir, you really planning on selling the last of your old indigo?" He was amazed because everyone knew the old man was nostalgic about the old things, and the slave was sure this dye had been made and processed by his father.

Markley nodded and sadly said, "I was thinking maybe I could spur some interest in starting to cultivate it again here on Somerset, but I know that time is past." He inwardly smiled at the irony of telling the truth to a slave when he argued against the truth with his sons. The slaves knew the problems with the crop as it had been their ancestor's labor; that had made the dye possible.

Mr. Cross brought the wagon around to the barn door and expertly commanded the mule team to back against the traces to shorten the distance to the tailgate.

Markley admiringly looked over the team and wagon, surely trail worn but with cleaned and oiled traces and bindings, the mules well shod and groomed. The front quarter of the wagon contained grain feed and a bag of beans and a wooden bucket under the seat was full of rolled up newspapers.

Cross, noting his glance remarked, "entertainment on the drive as well as necessity when nature calls." Both men grinned as the Slaves loaded the barrels in.

Markley climbed up in the wagon and inspected the blocks of burlap wrapped die and noted the painted information on the blocks which read "Somerset Plantation ATTN: Messrs.' E Markley, Charleston District SC" he looked over to the slaves and stated, "Boys fetch me a canvas from the back room of the barn."

He looked over to Cross and admonished, "Abner, you must take great care not to allow the load to get wet. Otherwise you will return with a blue wagon."

Cross laughed and replied, "Not to worry sir, a novelty such as this are sure to excite some trader!"

Markley thanked the slaves and the men climbed back aboard. Markley noticed the old flintlock horse pistol on the floor by the buckboard.

Cross noting the glance commented quickly "highwaymen."

Markley said, "Now for the next item, proceed down to the Smithy shop and turn right."

The wagon passed the Smithy and Old Mose peeked out and seeing Mr. Markley he waved and smiled.

As the wagon pulled up to the Timmonds house, Annabelle opened the back door and waved, she then turned around and shouted inside, "Mister Joshua, come on out, Mister Markley is calling!"

Turning to the men she asked, "Would you gentlemen like some water?"

Markley shook his head indicating no as he climbed out of the wagon but he motioned to Annabelle to follow him as he walked over to the shoeing shed Joshua had established.

Annabelle anxiously asked him, "What do you need, Sir?"

Markley looked her in the eyes and said, "Anna, you will likely be watching over this house alone for some time."

She nodded but still looked fearful. Markley added, "The boy is taking a long trip to try to find Mr. Timmonds; Jacob spends all his time with my boys and I doubt he will return here once Joshua departs. I can take care of Jacob but I need you to watch this house."

She nodded again and started to respond but Markley injected, "you can bring your husband over here if it suits you but I expect this place to be kept as neat as a pin!"

Annabelle nodded and assured him "Sir, I will keep this place as nice as Mrs. Elizabeth did; I just pray Mr. Timmonds is alive!"

Edward Markley nodded but Annabelle noted a look of deep sadness in his eyes.

Joshua stepped out on the porch having gathered together a small satchel. He had decided to wear his best low boots and Sunday shirt, trousers and sack coat.

Doffing his cap he walked over to Mr. Markley and shook his hand, saying "Mr. Markley, I am indebted to you for this help."

Edward seemed moved and patting Annabelle on the shoulder he turned and responded, "Joshua, it is no trouble, I would hope my boys would come looking for me, now let us walk a piece."

The two walked into the woods bounding the Markley place behind the shoeing shop and barn behind the house. The wind swayed through the overhanging live oak boughs above them. "Your father was to visit a ship yard in Portsmouth, Virginia known as the Page and Allen's Ship Yard. I had inquired for him in Charleston among my business associates at the Customs House,"

Markley paused thoughtfully, and added, "I did not want to tell you this but there is news coming into Charleston that Portsmouth has had a terrible epidemic of Yellow Fever!"

Joshua recoiled at the mention of the fever that had taken his mother. He looked at Markley and asked in a pleading voice, "Is my father dead? Is there news of him?"

Edward Markley shook his head and put his hand on Joshua's shoulder and said, "That is what you have to determine, son." He then added, "I have paid Mr. Cross to take you with the team to Norfolk, which is across the bay from

Portsmouth. I have arranged for Jacob to lodge with me and Annabelle and Old Mose will watch this house."

Joshua was very anxious and asked, "How will I find him, Mr. Markley?"

Markley replied, "Joshua, start at the only known place, that shipyard. Your father is a businessman first and foremost; he would lodge close by where his business lay. Feel free to ask Cross to help you in this, he is a man with his ear to the ground most times and he has been instructed to assist you."

Joshua nodded his head and thanked the old man.

Markley patted him on the shoulder as they walked back to Mr. Cross and waiting team and Markley turned to him and said, "I will keep your brother and this place under my direct care, you and Mr. Cross should be on your way!"

As Joshua started for the wagon, Annabelle with tears in her eyes hugged him and said, "God Bless you child, I will pray you find your father and bring him back to us!"

Joshua climbed up onto the seat and greeted Mr. Cross, "Sir, I am Joshua Timmons; I am in your debt for taking me to Virginia."

Cross looked at him with an offered hand and replied, "Abner Cross, son, would not miss this expedition for any price!"

They shook hands and as the wagon began to move, Joshua suddenly cried, "Please stop for a moment!" He jumped out and ran to the shoeing shop and then returned with his tool box, breathlessly explaining, "Just in case the Mules lose a shoe!"

Abner Cross smiled, and exclaimed, "Well, I never! I got my own blacksmith!"

The old drayman and the boy rode in silence down Black Oak Road and admired the cool of the morning and the deep pine forest on either side of the narrow road. The mule team pulled with a deliberate and easy rhythm. Joshua marveled at the fact that the team moved without prodding or reins, obeying the whistles and calls that Cross gave them from time to time.

Cross looked over at Joshua and asked, "Son, do you read well?"

Jacob looked questioningly over to him and Cross stated flatly, "under this here bench is some newspapers, time will pass fast if you was to read something to me."

Jacob leaned over and seeing the wooden pail full of papers extracted a Charleston Courier and Cross noting the choice clenched his eyes as if in pain and exclaimed "Unionists and abolitionists!" He then grinned and stated "Read on Son!"

Joshua glanced at the date 12 May 1854 and added, "Sir, this news you may know."

Cross grunted, "no matter, at my age I have done probably forgot."

As they rode Joshua read articles on the War in Crimea, way off in Russia, to wit Mr. Cross seemed highly knowledgeable and he explained the combatants on both sides. Then Joshua read of something called "Nullification" to wit Mr. Cross gave him an education in South Carolina politics of Unionism versus Nullification. An education of the squabble between President Jackson and Vice President Calhoun, arising from a social spat; that gave birth to repeated calls of secession from the union on multiple occasions. Joshua read to him an article on Governor Adams and the Negro Seaman Act to wit Mr. Cross gave him an education in the controversial law of 1822 that required the imprisonment of Free Negro's arriving on foreign ships if they departed said ships and entered town. Joshua marveled at the simple looking teamster that apparently had a firm grasp on every issue of the age.

"Just read a lot, when I can," said the old man with a wink.

At noontime, Mr. Cross stopped at a wide spot in the road near a small black water river, and announced "Lets water this team and have a bite to eat."

Joshua assisted the teamster with the first two mules, and the animals unfamiliar with him resisted, slightly irritated, Joshua gave them a yank on the reins. Cross had already unhitched the pair closest to the wagon, and he advised, noting the frustration, "Don't never yank a bit on a team mule, boy! Get it in your mind's eye where you are leading them and what you are leading them to and they will follow."

Joshua, heeding this advice, turned and thinking water, got the mules to follow.

As the animals gratefully drank their fill, the old drayman observed, "It don't pay to look them in the eye, neither; scares them." Joshua nodded. After sitting down to cold water and cornbread "johnnycakes" the two men hitched the team back to the wagon and resumed their trip.

Cross after a short while observed, "I imagine we should make the town of Florence by nightfall" adding, "Know a farmer there that will let me camp and build a cook fire."

Joshua never had traveled up the road to North Carolina and he marveled at the vast number of fields under cotton as they emerged from the swampy country. In each he noted large numbers of slaves picking the white bolls from the prickly plants, collecting wagon loads to be carried to the gins for processing.

Cross observed "Takes a huge number of slaves picking from dawn to dusk to harvest a field." He added, "By this time them stalks and bolls are rock hard, picking that stuff will tear your hands plum up! Glad I don't do that."

As the sun, set the two turned the wagon into a small farm tucked into the trees on the north side of the small farming town.

Cross exchanged short pleasantries with the Man on the porch and returned with a small cloth bundle and a jar. He smiled and said, "Lookie here! Biscuits and peach preserves!"

The two ate the minor feast, then fed and watered the mules and turned in by a small smoky fire.

The next morning found them on a plank road heading towards Dillon, the plank roads were smooth and fast but as Mr. Cross noted, "Never can tell how far they will go."

The plank roads were built by municipalities to speed goods to processing or to market. "If the road was important enough, the moneyed interests would make them,"

Cross explained to Joshua. The pair crossed into North Carolina late that afternoon. "Fayetteville will be the next big town a piece down this road. I expect us to reach it by tomorrow afternoon." Cross observed.

Joshua had taken to reading the articles in the copies of the old papers. He noted that the Charleston Mercury expressed opinions regarding the evils of the Northern states and decried the meddling of the federal government in the administration of South Carolina's "Peculiar Institution". He read arguments his father never mentioned and Mr. Markley only hinted at. He had to ask Mr. Cross to explain what an "Abolitionist" was. Subsequently he was educated about Fugitive Slave laws, the Missouri Compromise, the Kansas question, and of the public reaction to the aborted Vesey insurrection. Joshua was amazed to learn that the State of South Carolina, while protecting the institution of slavery with all her might, would hang a man for murdering a slave. Cross regaled him of the court case of just a year ago where the son of a planter and an overseer were hanged by a judge and jury for killing a runaway slave with dogs. Cross explained that the case, known as the "Broxton Bridge Horror" was a prime example of the split between up-state morals and low country practicality. Joshua found himself confused.

Mr. Cross decided to stop for the evening in a sandy pine barren near Aberdeen, North Carolina. Joseph checked the shoes on the mules and noticing a few loose, re-hammered and re-clinched the nails.

Cross marveled at the boy's dexterity with the animals in the shoeing and foot care regard. "Good man to have with on the road," he said under his breath.

Joshua gradually noted the change in the country-side as they proceeded north, the sandy piedmont areas of North Carolina transitions into more pleasant hardwood forests, the late September air started to begin to hint of a coming winter. Despite his worry for his father, he found the adventure fascinating and he began to understand why Mr. Cross loved to travel.

Reading a more recent edition of the Courier to Cross, the two entered into a discussion of the Mexican War.

Mr. Cross patiently explained the controversy of the war. "Some felt we were willing to kill Mexicans to steal their land," he stated. "Most of us that took part hated being there," he proclaimed.

Joshua was amazed and asked "You were in Mexico?"

Cross stated, "Yes, Son, I was, I served as a teamster for the Quartermaster Corps as a South Carolina Militia volunteer."

He looked at the boy and asked him, "I'll bet you never knew that 22 Carolina boys died in the Alamo?"

Joshua remembered hearing of the battle in school but did not know this detail.

"We was itching for a fight back then and everybody wanted a piece of that Santa Anna fellow," observed Cross.

"Once we settled for Texas, Santa Anna went back and angered us some more, so we decided to settle the question once and for all, that's how we got Arizona,

New Mexico territories and California. And, with us finding gold in California in '49 it has made us look like we was greedy,"

Cross grew thoughtful for a while and then added, "It weren't much fun driving a team through an endless desert, but the boys was always glad to see us."

Joshua noted that the road became busier past Fayetteville, North Carolina seemed to be teeming with activity with wagonloads of huge bales of tobacco plied the plank road that led to Wilmington port.

"Now that is a crop!" Cross explained, adding, "Folks in England are interested in two things we make here, Tobacco and Cotton, I should think we will always be well off growing and selling them commodities!"

Joshua returned to reading his papers, Cross sensing the boy was growing interested in things beyond his world patiently waited for the questions to come.

Joshua found a copy of the Courier describing a duel with pistols between a Planter and a Naval Officer that had occurred near Charleston, he was amazed to read that the planter had killed the Naval Officer and the authorities were satisfied that honor had been served.

He asked Mr. Cross about this and he explained that "Duello" was perfectly legal and was often used to settle questions of honor. He had witnessed a duel, himself in Charleston where both men missed their mark, deliberately in his opinion, in order to satisfy the debt to honor.

"So long as they follow the rules of the "Code" there was no issue with the law," he stated.

Joshua started to realize that there was much in regards to his own home that he never knew.

On the third day of travel they had reached the outskirts of Weldon, North Carolina. Mr. Cross announced that they would seek an affordable Inn with a bath and a hot meal. They settled on a place on the approach to town and slept that evening in a real bed after a real wash. Mr. Cross engaged the Innkeeper for advice on the best routes in Virginia. He was on new ground now.

They rose early and noted that the day threatened rain. Mr. Cross industriously cut some saplings and fashioned an awning over the wagon seat and suspended a piece of old canvas to the rickety canopy frame.

As Joshua checked the canvas covering the barrels of Indigo he asked Cross, "Mr. Cross, why ain't Indigo grown anymore?"

Cross, matter of factly replied, "Well, I never been a planter but I understand it took a lot of work to convert the leaves of the plant into a useable dye. From my understanding, they had to grow the crop and then harvest the leaves and then boil them. Once you cooked them down, you had to ferment the whole mess for a spell. Once you did that you poured off the extra water and the stuff left on the bottom was the dye, once you dried it out."

Cross thought a moment and added, "I reckon the market value of it these days may be about 75 cents a pound. Cotton makes a little more without as many steps."

"Now days I hear the English bring it in from the Sub Continent, or what we call India."

He sat in the seat and laying the reins down and spurring his mules with a whistle winked and said, "Old Markley is sentimental about it, I think because it was the art of a simpler time. Things ain't so simple no more."

As they passed by a road sign directing the way to Smithfield, Virginia, Mr. Cross observed, "Best damn hams in the country made here, suspect I will stop on the way back for one."

He noticed that Joshua had become engrossed in another piece of a Charleston Mercury; he asked "how old is that one, boy?"

Joshua without looking up replied, "Pretty new, August 20 of this year. It has a story about Norfolk and the fever."

Joshua read how the event appeared to start with the arrival of the steam ship Franklin. How the city sanitation departments had closed off entire areas of Norfolk and had spread quicklime on the streets of Norfolk and Portsmouth. In another article the text of a sermon described the wrath of god, and the duty of citizens to pray and repent from sin. Another article gave advice that no cure was available, purportedly written by a doctor that advised that nursing a patient was the only way to assure recovery. He read of 30 deaths a day and of city hospitals so full that private residences had been turned over into makeshift hospitals. His mind clouded with dread for his father.

Cross halted his wagon for the evening in the town of Suffolk on their 4<sup>th</sup> full day of travel. He found a small pond that lay a short distance from the plank road and set up an evening camp there.

As the two unhitched the four mule team, they noticed other travelers nearby as well, with wagons full of belongings, "Must be on the move somewheres…" mused Cross.

"Think I will have a chat with them before supper, Joshua take these mules back over and picket them by the wagon, and put together a fire for us, I will be back directly"

Cross made his way over to the other camp and lifted his hat and offered greetings, "Good Evening folks, my name is Abner Cross, you folks going north?"

Cross was hoping to learn of the best bridges or ferries to get to Norfolk.

The man sitting by the small fire looked up and replied, "Jones is the name, we are headed south, we have come from Norfolk."

Cross, brightened at this fortuitous meeting and asked, "Sir what is the best route to get there?"

Mr. Jones looked at him incredulously and asked "Why the hell would you want to go to Norfolk for? Ain't you heard?"

Cross replied, "Got business there, I have heard tell there was Yellow Jack affecting there but not much more."

Jones excitedly spelled it out for him, talking of hordes of people fleeing, of traffic being halted and inspected at ferries, of the boarding off of Barry's Row and then the subsequent burning of parts of town, deliberate burning by the citizenry to stop the scourge.

"It ain't no place to go to these days, Mr. Cross!" exclaimed the man.

Cross thanked the man and poked his way back over to his camp.

Joshua looked up from the fire and asked him when he returned, "What is the news Mr. Cross?"

Cross simply replied, "I expect some delays."

The two awoke early and started out for Norfolk, Cross figured they could get there in a day if the mules cooperated and they did not tarry, Joshua was anxious to start his search but Cross only advised him to be patient, advising, "them folks yesterday were from Norfolk, and they are moving South, I do not expect things to be normal there, we will see. Big eruptions of the fever ain't never good!"

After 5 days of travel, Abner Cross and Joshua Timmonds finally started to be closing in on their goal. As they closed within several miles of the outskirts of Norfolk they suddenly noted what looked like a military camp ahead.

White tentage was on either side of the road and as they drew nearer a Virginia Militiaman in a gray uniform, and bayonet equipped musket, halted them, "Evening Sir, where are you bound?"

Cross replied "Norfolk and then Portsmouth."

The soldier nodded and said, "please wait here sir," and trotted over to a Sergeant inside an open walled tent.

The Sergeant then came out to the Wagon saying, "Sir, we are here to direct all traffic away from the city of Norfolk and Portsmouth, we have a major outbreak of Yellow Fever and my orders at this instant are to allow only relief efforts and supplies related to that effort into the city."

Cross looked over to Joshua and noting his dismay replied, "Sergeant, this boy is seeking news of his father who traveled to Portsmouth in July, how is he supposed to look for the man without getting into town?"

The Sergeant bluntly replied, "At this moment sir, I recommend you proceed to Hampton, Virginia across the Roads, there is a relief center there that may have news of the lad's father, but in any rate you have two choices here, you can go back to Suffolk or proceed around to the Hampton Ferry."

Cross looked to Joshua, who nodded and said, "Hampton."

The old man and Joshua followed the bypass indicated by the Militia and arrived at Willoughby Spit Ferry Station well into the evening, and camped there for the night. The watchman there allowed them to water the mules at the station troughs and he provided Mr. Cross with the news of the epidemic.

Most businesses in Norfolk and Portsmouth were closed. The Gosport Navy Yard operated only as a military station receiving supplies to support the stricken communities. He informed him that his wagon and himself and the boy would be subject to health inspection at the landing in Hampton.

Cross asked about the Page and Allen shipyard specifically and received the reply "Closed, indefinitely, with the Benjamin Franklin still in the slip. It was the source of the fever."

The next morning the Steam Ferry arrived and they clattered aboard with several other freight wagons. Joshua was fascinated by the trip across the wide bay and the size of the steam ferry. He had never traveled by sea and the ocean air, crisp and cool in the early fall morning distracted him from his grim task. Cross was becoming more vocal in his concerns about the limited time he could afford to be away, being near a stricken city made him nervous. Joshua agreed but was already planning to stay regardless of Cross's plans.

He would stay until he found his father. As the crossed the Harbor he noticed the bulwarks of Fortress Monroe and the national colors that flew overhead, the sight amazed him and made him realize the power of the United States, the effort to build such an imposing fortress must be enormous, he mused.

Upon their landing at the wharf at Hampton, they were subjected to a cursory inspection and were questioned about their business. Cross explained that he sought a trader for his load and the location of a center whereby the lad could seek word of this father. The inspector replied that traders would be found at New Port News. There was a relief office there as well.

As they drove through the dusty town of Hampton towards the News, Cross stopped and purchased a paper from a boy hawking newspapers on a street corner, he opened it and looked for advertisements for Commercial Traders, he could not help but notice a death listing for the day under columns from Norfolk, Portsmouth, Gosport and Hampton. Joshua did not speak much but the old man noticed that he studied every face as they transited the town.

The wagon arrived in New Port News late in the afternoon. Mr. Cross, sore of back, suggested they stay at a boarding house in order to get a decent bed and the chance to talk to the locals to find a way to start looking for Norman Timmonds and a place to sell the indigo.

Cross looked at Joshua and said, "Son, I want you to know I can only spend a few days here at the most, you may have to prepare to accept what we find in those few days, but I will have to get back before October starts."

Joshua looked at the man and said, "It is no matter Mr. Cross, if I cannot find my father by the time you have to leave, I will allow you to depart without me."

Cross was flabbergasted by the suggestion, but he remembered Mr. Markley's stern injunction to allow the boy to decide for himself.

He only replied, "Suit yourself, boy, but I do not recommend staying."

Joshua looked at him as they started to detach the team and said, "I know Mr. Cross, but I must know where my father is."

At the breakfast table of the inn the next morning, Cross engaged the lady running the establishment and a businessman who was visiting the town. The news was discouraging, the harbor and freight leaving it was subject to "trade interdict" for at least the next 4 months due to the epidemic. This meant that no outbound cargo would be allowed into ports on the Eastern Coast of the country. The business man suggested a trader in town by the docks across from Fortress Monroe in Chesapeake City as the steamers bringing supplies to the Fortress often took on loads for New York and Boston. He opined that perhaps the trade interdict would not apply to a vessel running goods for the government. The lady of the inn suggested the best point of information for the boy would be the newspaper office in Hampton. There he could check the death lists.

Both parties advised strongly against attempting to cross the harbor to Norfolk or Portsmouth, as the woman said, "There is only death there."

Joshua suggested that Cross drop him at the newspaper office on the way to the trade company and then he return for him once he found a buyer. Cross agreed that this made the best use of time. Dropping the boy at the newspaper office, Cross then proceeded across town to the traders.

He pulled up to an establishment labeled only as "Point Comfort Supply" as he noted a large black steam paddlewheel ship parked against the quay behind it. The presentation of 80 lbs. of American grown Indigo caused some minor curiosity for a few moments with the buyer, and Cross got his hopes up some. In the back of his mind he knew the market price 20 years ago was 75 cents a pound, the trader looked over the barrels and took a parcel out, he unwrapped a corner and licking his fingertip he touched the block.

The fingertip instantly turned a pretty bright blue. "My, that is an effective dye!" the trader exclaimed. He then attempted to clean his finger off with a kerchief to no avail.

Looking up he stated "You have 80 lbs. here in good condition, I will give you 40 cents a pound," He paused a moment and said, "That would be 32 dollars. I do believe."

Abner Cross was slightly disappointed but not really surprised, so he readily accepted without a haggle. The merchant paid him in silver coin and Cross shook his hand and departed. The thought crossed his mind to inquire on items for Charleston that he might take back for sale but then he decided that cargo from an epidemic area might be a risk. Maybe he could pick up a load of hams in Smithfield, instead.

Joshua found the clerk at the newspaper helpful to assist and he provided a large scrapbook with the earlier editions death lists pasted within. The total list was becoming a popular reference for the paper and visiting reporters from other cities. The total count exceeded 2500 deaths officially with more being announced daily. Joshua scanned name after name in the pages. After scanning every page he satisfied himself that a Norman Timmonds was not listed. Deciding to recheck he went back to the start to recheck and noted a disturbing sub listing of "Unknowns" The listings were arranged by "Unknown White Man, Woman or Child and Unknown Black Man Woman or Child" The only helpful information was the cemetery which the deceased was buried. Looking further he noted a disturbing entry after lists published after mid-August that indicated "Mass Grave Norfolk" as an entry.

Joshua asked the clerk for a pencil and scrap paper and started to record the unknown white men and the locations. Joshua had been compiling a careful list for about 2 hours when Mr. Cross returned. He came into the office and Joshua explained what he had found.

Once he heard the story; Abner Cross decided to argue for common sense to the boy positing to him, "Boy you could check every graveyard in this town and you still likely would not find your father if he died unidentified."

He shook his head and stated, "You said yourself it was not like him not to write, and he ain't wrote!" "You know, and I know he is gone!"

Cross inwardly cringed at the look on the boy's face as he yelled those words.

Joshua, felt it deep in his heart that the old teamster was right but he screamed back, "I ain't leaving until I know!"

One of the typesetters came forward from the rear of the shop to see what the shouting concerned.

Cross took the boy outside, excusing himself to the newspaper staff. Outside he set an ultimatum, "I am leaving to go back tomorrow in the morning, this is no place to be! You make your mind up tonight."

Joshua sullenly got into the wagon with Mr. Cross and they silently rode back to the Inn.

That evening back at the Inn, they had dined quietly with the other guest and Mr. Cross announced he was going to bed; he looked at Joshua and admonished, "Remember about tomorrow."

Joshua nodded. After Cross went up the stairs Joshua asked the lady of the Inn if she could spare a sheet of paper and a pen and ink. That evening in his room Joshua wrote,

*"Dear Mr. Markley,*
*Myself and Mr. Cross satisfied your desire to find a buyer for the Indigo as instructed. The situation we have encountered in the Hampton Roads area is dire and confused. There has been such an affliction of death and suffering that free travel to Norfolk and Portsmouth harbors is impossible. Mr. Cross has insisted that we proceed back this Instant, but I am resigned to stay and continue the search for truth as it affects the fate of my father. As his eldest son I must do all in my power to find him and return him home in whatever state he is found.*
*Mr. Cross has ably assisted me and for that I remain in his debt, please accept that I Remain here according to my own will. I am eternally grateful for your assistance in arranging my travel here. I ask you to entrust all current interests in our home and property with my brother, until such time as I return. I will advise you of what I find in a future letter.*

*Sincerely Yours,*
*Joshua Timmonds"*

Joshua folded the paper and wrote "Mr. Edward Markley" on the outside of the folded paper and placed the letter in his sack coat pocket. He reached into his trouser pocket and retrieved the small leather bag he kept there and counted the money he had, it was 25 dollars in assorted coins. Satisfied, he returned them to the bag and returned it to his pants pocket. Turning down and puffing out the kerosene lamp, he went to bed.

As the morning came, he came down the stairs of the inn and spied Mr. Cross eating with the other guests. Cross saw him coming and knew, from the expression on the boy's face that he would return alone.

He said, "Well Joshua, you may as well eat, seeing as how this is the last meal on me for this trip."

Joshua nodded and said "I thank you sir, I appreciate your kindness, I hopefully will see you back in Macbeth before too long."

They ate in resigned silence. When Cross got up to leave Joshua followed him out to help his hitch his team. He gave the mules' one last look at their shoes and announced to Cross that he should have them looked at in North Carolina.

He then handed the folded letter to Cross saying, "Please give this to Mr. Markley for me, it absolves you of abandoning me as I explain in it why I am staying."

Cross nodded and reached in his pocket and produced 5 silver coins, "Here is you pay for your assistance Joshua, I enjoyed your company and I should think you would make a fine teamster."

With that Cross gave a strained laugh and climbed on the wagon, with a whistle the mules moved off.

Joshua lost little time that morning and went to visit Ebenezer Baptist Church which had several listings. The lady at the Inn informed him that it was a short walk from the Inn. The morning started with a light misting rain and arriving at the church he entered and found the sexton inside the back office.

The sexton was a kindly man who explained that the church cemetery was now full and new burials were occurring at other churches but took the time to explain the unknowns to him, "We mark them with wooden markers and paint the name if we got one and also put a number on them. If the dead have personal effects we keep them with the same number on the box." He explained that there are many people doing the same thing as a lot of travelers were caught up in the pestilence and went missing.

Joshua walked the church yard and noted many new disturbances in the yard, most with newly carved stones, each listing individual tragedies that in themselves were heartbreaking, he read "Sophie, beloved Daughter of Dr. Allen and Alicia Bower Born 1 August 1850 Died 20 July 1855" he noted the smallness of the disturbed earth. Walking further in the misting rain he saw the wooden boards near the back reading "No.14 Unknown White Man, Sailor, ship unknown, first name Michael"

Joshua scanned the other unknowns but found nothing that indicated his father. Thanking the sexton he moved on to the next church on his list.

Joshua spent the next week investigating between churches and the newspaper office, and he began to realize he was draining his resources. His daily contact with the newspaper office clerk kept him abreast of the persistent restrictions against travel to either Norfolk or Portsmouth. Since Page and Allen's shipyard remained closed, he was frustratingly denied a start point. He had wanted to find a relief agency to inquire but all efforts flowed directly into Norfolk or Portsmouth and paused only very little in Hampton. There was certainly no desire by the citizens of Hampton to invite the pestilence to visit anyhow.

On his morning visit to the newspaper office in the last week of September Joshua learned from the clerk that the Julappi horse racing grounds had been converted into a large Hospital by the Doctors and Sisters of Mercy that flowed into the Roads. The sick from Norfolk were being transported there as the location was thought to be clear of the swampy low grounds and the miasma that affected the low ground. The clerk had heard that coffins were exhausted to support the Hospital and that a steamer had arrived last night with a load of coffins bound for Julappi Hospital.

The clerk opined that Joshua could offer to assist and thus be able to travel there with relief efforts to check the records for Norfolk. The young clerk sadly added that Portsmouth was going to remain closed for a long time to visiting.

Joshua made his way down to the docks of Hampton; the streets were clogged with wagons making their way to pick up simple pine coffins for transport across the Roads via the ferry. With most of the dockworkers fled, sick or dead, Norfolk's port no longer functioned.

As Joshua scanned the crowd, most wagons had two men in them to handle the loading and driving to the ferry. Soon he noted two odd looking wagons, of an olive green color, being operated by what looked like soldiers, one wagon had a pair of soldiers and the other that followed contained only one soldier.

Joshua, seeing his chance walked up to the waiting wagons and tipped his hat and asked, "Sir would you like help with loading your wagon?"

The Soldier looked him over and growled, "What's yer story lad? If you is looking for a pocket to pick go help a businessman!"

The soldiers in the wagon in front were laughing watching the exchange and the older one shouted over his shoulder, "He likes you Smitty, cause you got that purty uniform!"

Joshua was bewildered by the laughing; he had not heard much humor over the past two weeks.

He decided to be persistent saying, "Look Sir, I need to get across the Ferry to the Julappi Hospital, My father has been missing here for two months and I can find no sign of him, I have no want for money just for cause to go to Norfolk!"

The soldier referred to as Smitty was obstinate and explained, "Look here boy o, this here is an army wagon! And I ain't permitted to haul no civilian in an Army wagon!"

The older soldier in the wagon ahead roared in laughter at this pronouncement, shouting back, "He is probably an English spy! Studyin' our way of team driving it is! Maybe we gotta shoot him Smitty! He knows too much!"

The older man was clearly enjoying the spectacle. Joshua then walked over to the older man and restated his case. He noticed the man wore the same sort of uniform as "Smitty" but he had red stripes on his sleeve.

After hearing the story from the boy the older man leaned over to his companion and said, "Newby, go sit with Smitty on his wagon, I will take the boy with me."

Turning to Joshua he winked, and added "don't mind us boy, we've been pulling all sorts of loads into Norfolk, it is pure shit there! That's why we laugh, to forget the shit."

He looked at the wagons ahead of them taking on loads of coffins, and said, "This cargo tells you the state of affairs there, boy, I will help you but you must do everything I say!"

Joshua nodded quietly, and stared dully at the coffins stacked on the dock.

After a short wait, the two olive drab wagons pulled up and were able to load 6 coffins each within the beds, being empty the were easy to lift and Joshua quickly assisted the Sergeant with tying down the load. The wagons then were driven over to the Ferryboat landing to await the ferry. As they waited the Sergeant asked Joshua where he was from. Joshua retold his entire story and the story of his father's travels here. The old Sergeant listened without interrupting him.

He told Joshua matter of factly, "Son, if your father came here in July, and you ain't heard from him, then he is in the ground."

He solemnly added, "Anybody who went to Page and Allen's that month is either dead or flown away like the birds! I will take you to Julappi and then bring you back but both them towns across the way are struck down by this pestilence! They got so many dead that they have lost count. We have sent Engineers over to dig another mass grave now, and nobody will even get a get a stone for a marker."

The rain came back, and a strong wind was blowing that made Joshua feel chilled and depressed, the old sergeant reached behind him and produced a rubberized canvas poncho and told the boy to put it on to stay dry. Joshua needed assistance in getting the poncho on over his head but with it on, he felt warmer.

Soon the ferry arrived and the two wagons and several others loaded with coffins clattered onto the bay of the steamer. As they stopped the soldiers dismounted to calm the horses that were uncomfortable with the closed in bay of the ferry.

Joshua admired the fine quality of the horses, all big, sleek and well fed Morgans of equal stature. The harnesses and collars were high quality leather with beautiful brass fittings and bridles. He instinctively checked the feet of the 4 horse teams and noted the expert job of shoeing. He was unaware of the 3 soldiers who stood and stared at his actions.

When he stood up to walk back to the wagon, the old Sergeant laughed and exclaimed "We hope you are satisfied with our trim, Captain!"

The other two snickered. Joshua smiled and went to sit back in the riding seat.

The Sergeant walked back over to Joshua and extended his hand, "Since we are now on the job it's time for introductions boy, I am Sergeant O'Brien, 2nd US Artillery."

He turned and motioned his thumb to the two other men, "Them two pieces of work are Privates Smitty and Newby, they are caisson drivers for the regiment."

"Welcome to our detail, boy, we was short one man today anyhow, so we feel fortunate to have you join us."

As the ferry progressed the weather was definitely worsening, Sergeant O'Brien observed, "Nor'easter blowing in, it's about time the fall came in."

With the mention of fall, Joshua pondered what his next steps would be; he was down to 7 dollars now and was long since being able to afford ocean passage back.

Once docked, the teamsters snapped the reins and moved quickly onto Willoughby Spit and then south to the Julappi race track. The Army teams moved far faster than the civilian wagons, and Joshua was alarmed at the seemingly reckless rate of speed.

Sergeant O'Brien smiled as he watched the boy grip the hand rail with both hands and remarked, "Boy, the U.S. Army pays us to be the fastest mounted artillery on earth, first man to the good ground wins the battle!"

They arrived at the makeshift hospital in about half an hour, Joshua was shocked at the vast expanse of tentage and buildings full of the sick.

He started to assist with the coffins but Sergeant O'Brien took him aside and said, "look boy, here is the deal, I will give you an hour to investigate for your Pa, you be back here by 4 pm."

He looked him in the eye, "Look for Sister Andrews in them sheds over yonder. If anyone knows what's here it will be her!"

Joshua nodded and trotted to the sheds.

Entering one shed he saw row upon row of beds and cots full of human forms, some sat up and some moaned and thrashed about. He heard a droning voice and saw a militarily dressed man with 4 others gathered around him as he looked at a prostrate man on a cot by the wall.

The man talked in huge words that Joshua could not understand, speaking of "Cathartics" and "Prognosis" Joshua listened more closely, and watched as the man suddenly pinched the patient's nose and pushed down forcefully on his chest, a dark black fluid erupted from the patient's mouth. The man talking observed "this bloody effluent is the clear indicator of yellow fever and it's onset is your clear sign of morbidity." The men watching solemnly nodded.

Joshua quickly left and entered another stable, again full of cots with prostrate forms. He saw a woman on a ladder pushing a piece of canvas through a hole in the roof.

She saw Joshua and said "May I help you young man?"

Joshua replied, "I am looking for Sister Andrews."

Sister Andrews smiled and said, "You have found her! I apologize for my distraction but the water leaks in this weather onto my patients; I simply must get this roof fixed."

Sister Andrews climbed down and wiped her hands on her apron the walked over. She asked him, "What can I do for you, young man."

Joshua replied, "I came here with some soldiers who told me that you might have information on my father."

Sister Andrews became very animated when he mentioned soldiers and blurted out, "Coffins! Have they brought them?"

Joshua nodded. She quickly grabbed his arm and dashed out of the shed towards the wagons. The soldiers paused from their labor and took their forage caps off as she approached.

Sister Andrews called out as she approached "Sergeant O'Brien, you are indeed heaven sent, I have over 20 poor souls that have awaited this delivery!"

O'Brien shyly replied, "My apologies sister for taking so long, we've managed 12 but there are 10 more wagons behind us."

Joshua was disappointed that she was more interested in coffins than the living.

Turning to Joshua Sister Andrews said in a soft and soothing tone, "I apologize, my child for being so short with you, please understand that I have the dead in deplorable conditions and the coffins are essential to remove them from here and to provide them with a Christian burial."

Joshua nodded as she asked, "Tell me of your father."

She nodded quietly as he described his tale and of his fruitless search so far. She looked to Sergeant O'Brien as he talked and the Sergeant sadly shook his head.

Sister Andrews was moved by the young man's earnestness and she promised "Joshua, I am afraid I know nothing now, as all of the sick I tend to now are from Norfolk city alone. If you will provide me your father's description and full name I can inquire at our next Howard Association meeting. We are in contact with Portsmouth City representatives during our meetings."

She then looked around and frowned at O'Brien and remarked, "You gentlemen must insure you get this young man gets back through the inspection at the

Hampton Ferry Landing! In his attire he will be accused of fleeing Norfolk and will be returned! Did you consider that when bringing him here?"

Sergeant O'Brien looked guiltily over to Smitty and muttered under his breath, "shit!"

Smitty, noticing the look smiled viciously, and exclaimed "Shit is right dear Sergeant, Now you gots us spreading pestilence!"

Sister Andrews smiled and said, "Joshua, try to stay in contact with Sergeant O'Brien if I receive news I will provide it to him. It is far too dangerous for you to come here, only recognized aid agency volunteers and the Army may enter this place!"

She sternly looked at O'Brien and directed, "Please promise me to get him back to Hampton." O'Brien nodded.

As the men finished the unloading and prepared to depart, Private Newby asked O'Brien if they could, "ride normally?"

O'Brien thought and replied "why not? Would be faster, after all."

The men did not want to miss the Ferry, camping was for campaigns not details. Sergeant O'Brien looked at Joshua and asked, "Can you ride, boy?"

Joshua looked at Newby and Smitty and was amazed to see them move over and mount onto the first and second horse of the team on the left hand side of the team. He had not noticed in the rain earlier that the team all were wearing minimal saddles.

O'Brien took Joshua over to the rearward horse of the wagon and said" climb up", and checked the stirrups for length. He grunted in approval and asked again, "You said you could ride, right?"

Joshua nodded and asked, "Sergeant, what are we doing?"

O'Brien smiled and said, "*Postilion*, boy'o in the style of Ringgold! fastest way on this man's earth to move a wagon, or a gun."

He moved to the lead horse and mounting he nodded to Newby and Smitty and they spurred the team.

At first Joshua was frightened, the team of horses was moving faster than he had ever rode. He was amazed at the sheer power of the 4 horse teams as the two wagons raced towards the ferry landing. After the first couple of miles he settled into the rhythm of the horses and looking behind him he notice that the wagon was literally leaping into the air at points. He then realized that at these speeds a rider in the wagon would be hard pressed to remain on board.

Sergeant O'Brien looked back from time to time and was relieved to see Joshua still on the horse, he smiled.

The two wagons dramatically drew up and came to a halt at the ferry landing. Off in the lowering light of the evening they could make out the ferry boat approaching the landing, it looked like the other wagons would not make this last ferry back to Hampton.

Upon arrival of the ferry, they quickly brought the teams aboard over the ramp of the steamer and again soothed the high spirited teams. As they returned across the Roads, Sergeant O'Brien snatched the forage cap off of Private Newby's head and set it on Joshua's.

Newby protested but O'Brien explained the ruse, "We will ride the same way through town once off the ferry, all riding in the rain fast like soldiers." He looked Joshua over, the oversized oilcloth poncho and forage cap made him a passable soldier.

Approaching the Hampton side the ferry boat sounded its' steam whistle, alerting the health commission inspectors to the landing. O'Brien had all mount the teams as before and when the ramp came down he moved quickly off the boat.

The inspector dreading a wet inspection saw only two army wagons and soldiers come off, so he simply waved, Sergeant O'Brien waved back with a broad grin on his face.

As they neared the outskirts of town on the approach to Fortress Monroe they pulled up and parked across the road in front of a public house that was brightly lit.

Joshua looked up and noticed the sign of the public house, "The Columbiad", O'Brien took the hat off of Joshua's head and handed it back to Newby, who quickly snatched it and beat it on his leg before returning it to his head.

O'Brien then signaled for Joshua to return the raincoat.

Once Joshua had it off and returned, O'Brien announced, "Who wants to pause for supper and a pint?"

No sooner had he uttered the words and Newby and Smitty had vaulted through the door.

Joshua hesitated and looked at Sergeant O'Brien and said, "Sir, I thank you for your help, can I meet you at the docks tomorrow?"

He wanted to get back to the Inn to try to find a room.

O'Brien looked at him and asked "What is the hurry boy? Come inside and I will buy you a supper!"

Joshua smiled and followed him inside the Columbiad.

As the men entered the public house there was a fair crowd surrounding the bar and loud discussions were underway. As Joshua's eyes adjusted to the light he noticed almost half the room was filled with soldiers as well, all wearing the same red trimmed blue uniforms.

Sergeant O'Brien scanned the room after lifting two fingers at the bartender, and said to Joshua, "follow me, I have found an important table!"

He proceeded through the crowd towards a table where a portly older soldier sat. Joshua noted that he had 3 red stripes like O'Brien but this one had a flat stripe topping the uppermost of the 3 red ones on his coat. The man had an entire roasted chicken sitting partially eaten on a pewter plate on the table before him.

"A good evening to you, you old Bastard! How's yer quota?" O'Brien shouted to the other sergeant, who replied just as loudly, "That's Quartermaster Sergeant Johnson to you, you mick!"

When Sergeant Johnson spied Joshua, he smiled and quickly returned his bored gaze to O'Brien.

Sergeant O'Brien pulled out a chair and motioned Joshua to sit and Sergeant Johnson reached over to shake his hand remarking "welcome boy, don't mind O'Brien, he is Irish and cannot help himself."

Joshua returned the handshake and replied "Please to meet you sir, I am Joshua Timmonds." The older man nodded.

Quartermaster Sergeant George Johnson had spent the past 20 years in the regular army. His specialty had been the manning and operation of the heavy 24 and 32 pounder guns in the Casemates of Fortress McHenry and Fortress

Monroe. The duty had been nice and boring but as he aged and his girth increased, he found himself detailed to occasional recruiting. The Columbiad was his lair; young lads like this one were his prey. He smiled at Joshua and awaited O'Brien's recommend.

Sergeant O'Brien had wandered over to the bar, clearly upset and arguing with the bartender.

"I am recently from the state of Maine, and I find these southerners of Virginia rather tedious!" Johnson exclaimed.

He then looked again at Joshua and asked, "Are you from here lad?"

Joshua replied, "South Carolina, sir."

Johnson raised his eyebrows and exclaimed, "Ah hah! A cavalier!"

He then leaned over his chicken and asked conspiratorially, "Tell me boy, how many slaves do you own?"

Joshua quickly replied, "None sir, I am the son of a small farmer!"

Johnson looked away in disappointment remarking, "Ah a pity it is, I was hoping you could buy me supper."

The two continued the banter and Sergeant Johnson carefully and cleverly extracted a set of information from Joshua that he assessed. When Sergeant O'Brien returned the two engaged in good natured banter.

Joshua studied the familiarity of all the men in the public house, there seemed to be no man in uniform that was not at one point talking to each other either individually or in shouted conversations across the bar. He admired what appeared to be a gathering of family.

The innkeeper brought two quarters of roast chicken to the table and set a pint of beer before Joshua, he instinctively pulled his leather purse out to pay, but O'Brien snatched it from him and stated, "No worries boy, I got this!"

He then flipped a coin to the innkeeper who walked back to the bar.

Sergeant Johnson quickly snatched the purse from O'Brien's hand and looked inside.

He then let out a low whistle and observed, "Running low aren't we, my cavalier?"

O'Brien leaned towards Joshua and snatching the purse from Johnson's hands returned it to Joshua and asked him, "What are your plans, son?"

Joshua shook his head and said, "I don't know."

Sergeant Johnson suddenly loudly stated, "Do you love your Republic!" looking off into space.

Joshua looked quizzically at Sergeant O'Brien who winked and pushed his finger to his mouth to silence a response.

Johnson slowly swiveled his eyes to Joshua and asked, "Why is a fine specimen like you, young cavalier, not here with us defending the republic?"

Joshua simply shrugged his shoulders and replied, "I am just a farmer's son!"

Sergeant Johnson smiled as he repeated the statement "just a farmer" and launched into a 15 minute oratory into the history of the minute men from Maine, the Continental Army, the revolution, the war of 1812, the Mexican war, and the vital nature of the Army.

When he was complete the soldiers in the bar erupted in raucous cheers and clapping.

Johnson noting the approval slowly heaved his portly frame up and shouted, "A Toast!" The soldiers roared approval and raised their mugs.

Sergeant O'Brien pushed the mug into Joshua's hand and then stood. Sergeant Johnson shouted "To the Army!"

The soldiers roared back, "To the Army!" Then all, Joshua included, drank deeply.

Sergeant Johnson then decided to close the deal; he leaned closely to Joshua and laid it all out,

"Look boy, you can be like us. O'Brien has told me your troubles, I can see now that you are an orphan, without a future, come join us and get a family, get a purpose."

Sergeant Johnson grabbed his sleeve and asked, "Would you like to join us? We will give you fine clothes, feed you and pay you 12 dollars a month!"

Joshua despite a woozy feeling, nodded yes, and slowly he uttered, "Why not?"

Quartermaster Sergeant Johnson then smiled and leaned back.

He produced a piece of foolscap with an ink signature on it and tucked it into Joshua's coat pocket and said, "You go to Fortress Monroe gate tomorrow, you show this chit to the guard, and he will grant you an interview with a nice man known as O'Keefe. If he finds you fit, you can be like us."

Johnson shook O'Brien's hand and winked. The two men then arranged for the thoroughly drunken youth to be provided a room upstairs, given a decent breakfast and then to be directed to the gate of Fortress Monroe in the morning. The innkeeper smiled and pocketed his gratuity, helping the army was a nice living.

# 3  THE ARMY 1855

Joshua awoke with a start.  He got up and looked around and realized he did not know where he was, looking out the window of the tiny room he saw the massive granite walls of Fortress Monroe in the near distance and remembered last night.  He quickly got dressed and digging into his trouser pockets, he found his coin purse; he opened it and glanced inside.  To his relief he still had his last seven dollars.  As he put on his coat he checked the pockets and found a wrinkled scrap of paper with a signature on it.  Remembering Sergeant Johnson, he sat down on the rickety bed and thought.

After weighing his options; he finally said to himself, "why not!"

He realized that at this moment that he had spent most of his life laboring to achieve his father's dreams.  He had never asked himself what he wished to do.  He had only sought to please his father; to be that good son.

The innkeeper wished him a good morning and explained due to the lateness of the hour that he only had corn cakes and some side meat remaining of breakfast.  Joshua thanked him and ate the cold breakfast in the tavern on a table with some lukewarm coffee.  When he finished he brought the plate and cup to the bar and asked the innkeeper about the way to enter the fort.

The innkeeper gave him simple directions, "You just cross the bridge out front and from the road you will see a plank walk that leads to the main sally port, over the moat.  There is a guard there and he will show you where to go."

Joshua attempted to pay the innkeeper but he waved the money away.

The rain had stopped and it was warming up outside he put his hand in his coat pocket to insure the paper was still there.  When he reached the gate he noted a soldier in a blue frock coat, cartridge box and musket with a tall hat with a brass plate on the front and a fuzzy wool ornament on the top that reminded him of a cat tail seed pod.

The soldier watched him approach and as he drew near the entrance he brought up his bayoneted musket and challenged, "Halt! What is your business?"

Joshua produced the scrap of paper and showed it to the guard, announcing, "Sergeant Johnson gave me this and told me to get an interview with Mr. O'Keefe."

He was surprised as the sentry gave him a wicked broad smile and countered, "Mr. O'Keefe is it?"

He turned and pointed with his free hand to a 2 story brick building with a neat side walk leading to it and with a flourish of his gloved hand said, "First room on the left on the first floor, good sir, Mr. O'Keefe is awaiting."

Joshua thanked him and walked in; he thought he heard the sound of someone laughing.

He was amazed at the neatness of the inside of the Fortress, it looked very much like a park with Soldiers moving about in singles and in small groups. On the parade grounds he saw at least 3 kinds of cannon with men gathered about them under instruction.

When he reached the two story building he strode purposely through the door and turned into the first office on the left. Inside he saw first a soldier sitting at a wooden desk facing the door and the man looked up at him.

Joshua asked him, "Are you Mr. O'Keefe?"

The soldier's eyes widened and he smiled and said "Why no good sir, but you have a seat here and I will get him."

As he got up he turned and asked, "Did you meet Sergeant Johnson?"

Joshua nodding his head produced the scrap of paper.

The soldier took the paper from him and walked out of the small office and trotted up the wooden staircase. Joshua sat on a hard bench and looked at the clouds outside the windows of the office.

Shortly he heard footsteps enter the adjacent office and he heard a door slam.

The soldier returned and pointing to the door beside his desk he said, "Knock once and wait for his command."

Joshua gave the door a rap and waited. A loud "Enter" was heard through the door.

Joshua entered and saw another soldier, a much older man in a neat frock coat with red trim; He had 3 red stripes pointing downward and a diamond shape in red trim in the middle. The man had a very large mustache and penetrating eyes set in an extremely leathery face.

The man stared balefully at Joshua and muttered "Jesus, Mary and Joseph! Who in the fook are you?"

Joshua was startled as this Sergeant sprayed spit as he shouted.

Joshua stammered out "Joshua Timmonds, sir!"

The Sergeant roared, "Sir? don't you see I work for a fooking living boy! I ain't no goddamed sir, you shit! I am a fookin First Sergeant!"

He had approached Joshua from around his desk, and was uncomfortably close to his face now.

He looked Joshua up and down and asked, "Who found you? Was it that fook, Johnson?"

Joshua frozen in fear could only nod his head.

The First Sergeant shaking his head returned to his seat and asked, "What the fook have you done to make you want to join the Army?"

Not waiting for an answer he fired out again, "Are you runnin from the law?"

Joshua stammered No S…, No First Sergeant!"

O'Keefe was slightly disappointed in him stopping the second "Sir", but he quickly followed up with, "So! What is it then?"

Joshua finally found his equilibrium and shouted "I am an Orphan, First Sergeant!"

First Sergeant O'Keefe, growled, "Touching, boy'o."

He turned and called the other soldier in and ordered, "Corporal Mills, take this bag o' shit over to the surgeon and see if he clears, if he does, send him over to Sergeant Rourke."

The clerk nodded and grabbed Joshua by the arm, as they left O'Keefe shouted, "And send that arsehole Johnson over to see me! If, he is awake yet!"

Corporal Mills shouted back as the hurried out the building, "Right away, First Sergeant"

Joshua quickly walked down the sidewalk with the Corporal Mills, who had little to say, except to stop a passing soldier and direct, "Go find Quartermaster Sergeant Johnson and have him go to see the First Sergeant, post haste!"

The soldier nodded quickly and trotted off. Joshua had an odd feeling that the small man beside him was also somewhat powerful.

They approached a building marked "INFIRMARY" and Corporal Mills directed, "Go inside and report at the desk, do what they tell you, when you are done stay here, just inside, on the bench, I will return for you."

Joshua nodded and went into the door and stood at the reception counter.

Another Soldier working inside, looked up and asked, "You a recruit?"

Joshua nodded despite not knowing what a "recruit" was.

The soldier came over to the counter with a pencil and paper and asked, "Can you read and write?" Joshua nodded.

The soldier then pushed a piece of paper that had preprinted lines and boxes and a drawing of a human form on it.

Pointing to the top of the form the soldier directed, "Fill your full name in here and your birthdate if you know it. Write it out last name first, first name last."

Joshua was confused and asked, "First name last?"

The soldier smiled and pointed with his finger to the first space, "Last name here," moving his finger to the next space he said, "First name here, Got it?"

Joshua thanked him and filled out the form; he decided to lie about his birthday and made himself 18, just in case.

The soldier took the paper and directed Joshua to sit on the waiting bench on along the wall of the reception. He then went down a hall behind the reception desk.

After a few moments the soldier returned and said, "The Surgeon will see you now, follow me."

Joshua walked behind the soldier as he led him into a room with a long wooden table in it.

He turned to Joshua and said, "Take all your clothes off and sit on the table."

Joshua did as instructed and waited for what seemed to be an hour, suddenly a much older man wearing a white coat and smoking an evil smelling cigar strode in. He looked at Joshua and instructed him to stand. He walked around Joshua and after puffing out some smoke instructed him to lay down, the doctor pushed on his belly and then higher up on his stomach and then asked him, "Have you stayed in Norfolk or Portsmouth?"

Joshua shook his head.

The doctor asked him to open his mouth; the doctor peered in and asked, "Teeth hurt?" Joshua shook his head and said "no."

The Doctor directed, "Good lad, get dressed and go back out front and wait." Joshua quickly dressed and returned to his bench on the front.

Corporal Mills returned and briskly instructed Joshua, "Follow me."

He took the sheet of paper from the medical clerk and walked with Joshua over towards the fortress wall facing the town of Hampton and Joshua noted that the windows that faced the town were actually rooms.

The Corporal led Joshua to a door marked "QUARTERMASTER" and went in with him. Joshua noticed a long bench with men stocking shelves along the wall behind the counter.

Corporal Mills had Joshua back up against the wall that had marks on it.

The Corporal called out, after noting the marks, "five foot eight tall!" Looking down at marks on the floor he called out, "Foot, nine and a half!"

He then turned to Joshua and said, "This is your issue recruit; stop at each station marked by the line on the floor and get your kit."

Joshua was simply amazed at the fine quantity and quality of things he was being given, two woolen blue sack coats, a woolen frock coat, 4 pairs of sky blue trousers, 2 pairs of boots "for parade and fatigue", a forage cap, a "shako with pompom", leather neck collar, cartridge box, waist belt, bayonet, scabbard, bulls eye canteen, 4 shirts, 4 drawers, knapsack, rubber blanket, haversack, folding knife, tin cup, pound of beeswax, foot artillery short sword and scabbard, and a woolen blanket.

Seeing him fumble with the rapidly accumulating pile of issue, the corporal demonstrated to him how to gather the pile in a blanket to make a transportable bundle. At the end of the line, a clerk made Joshua sign his name on a ledger indicating his receipt of the issue.

The corporal quickly led him to another section of the wall facing the city of Hampton and there, Joshua noted a wooden sign painted with golden crossed cannon and the annotation "M Company, 2nd US Artillery Regt."

The corporal turned and said as he opened a door, "Timmonds, meet your messmates."

As he opened the door, Joshua to his surprise saw, Private Newby, who upon seeing Joshua, said only, "Well I'll be goddamned!"

Corporal Mills instructed the men to leave the new recruit's gear alone, and instructed Joshua to continue following him as they returned to the headquarters again.

Following the corporal into the company headquarters, Joshua was told to stand by the desk and the corporal pulled a small book out of a drawer, and dipping a pen he wrote Joshua's name and date of birth from the medical record onto a facing leaf of the small book and then handed it to him saying, " This is your pay book, Timmonds, do not lose it, do not write in it, keep it on your person at all times, everything about you will be in this book."

He then looked him in the eye and asked, "Do you understand?"

Joshua nodded.

The corporal then directed, "Wait here." He then rose from his desk and went out the door and trotted back up the stairs.

Joshua awaited, his mind reeled at the sheer control he had been subjected to thus far. He reflected that in the course of this day he had heard more cursing than he had heard his entire life and had accumulated more worldly goods than he had ever seen in his whole life.

Suddenly a much more fancily dressed soldier with a great side burns strode in the room with the fearsome First Sergeant O'Keefe and the Corporal.

 Joshua seeing O'Keefe swiftly rose to his feet.

O'Keefe looked towards the corporal who nodded, and announced. "Captain Hunt, I am pleased to display to you the newest recruit to M Company, Private Timmonds!"

Joshua looked at the man; he was a handsome man with ruddy features and the same leathery features as O'Keefe.

Captain Hunt looked him over quickly and asked, "Where are you from son?"

Joshua answered, "Charleston District, South Carolina, Sir!"

The Captain remarked, "Ah yes, Charleston, wonderful place, served there in 1852."

Hunt smiled briefly and asked, "Do you want this, son?"

Joshua nodded and replied, "Absolutely sir!"

Captain Hunt then took a piece of paper and looked Joshua in the eye and commanded, "Raise your right hand!"

"Repeat after me."

*"I Joshua Timmonds, swear to be trued to the United States of America and to serve them honestly and faithfully against all their enemies, opposers, whatsoever; And to observe and obey, the orders of the Continental Congress, and the orders of the Generals and Officers set over me by them."*

Captain Hunt looked over Joshua one more time and said, "Son, listen to these men and they will teach you to succeed in this business. Forget what you knew before and pay close attention!"

The officer then turned and walked back up the stairs.

First Sergeant O'Keefe then turned to Joshua and said, "Hear this boy'o; you've seen me and the Captain now, here in this place. You will learn this is the last place now, on this earth you will want to be! That Captain is God to you and I am Jesus! Do you understand?"

Joshua nodded.

First Sergeant O'Keefe then turned to Corporal Mills and directed, "Get his sorry ass over to the armory to draw a musket and deliver him into the hands of Section Sergeant Rourke."

As Joshua and the Corporal departed, O'Keefe shouted through the door, "Put him in the school of the soldier in the morning! And get him in a uniform, NOW!"

The Corporal shouted back, "Right away First Sergeant!"

Corporal Mills walked Joshua over to the armory and he drew a rather heavy Model 1842 Musket, signed for same and was taken to Sergeant Rourke.

Section Sergeant Rourke, upon seeing the bewildered youth, simply said, "Welcome to the Caisson Section son."

He turned to the assembled men inside the vast Casemate and directed, "Teach him to dress and get him in uniform. After supper I want to talk to him. Show him the ropes boys, I hear he has potential according to Sergeant O'Brien."

He then turned to Joshua and looked him in the eye and said, "Welcome to the Army son, no worries, we all been where you are right now."

Back at M Company headquarters, First Sergeant O'Keefe completed his morning report to provide to Captain Hunt. Gathering up his notes and his company ledger he walked up the steps to the officer's office.

Captain Hunt looked up from his reading and greeted his old friend. They had served together in the war with Mexico. O'Keefe had served on a gun crew that then Lieutenant Hunt had pushed with the crew by hand down the causeway at Tacuba. Every man had been wounded. They had driven Mexican skirmishers out of the town with point blank charges of canister and had been reduced to 3 men on the gun. Those three were Hunt, O'Keefe and Sergeant O'Brien.

O'Keefe deeply respected the plain spoken officer who had been raised in Detroit when it was but a frontier town.

The two men talked of their current fight.

"First Sergeant, we have to fill our company roles quickly!"

O'Keefe nodded and replied, "Sir, with the new one today we are only 4 short from a complete fill. Johnson is doing a hell of a job."

Captain Hunt nodded and observed, "First Sergeant, I am receiving word that the Company may receive orders relieving us of duties here with the School of Artillery Practice, and transferring us to the Kansas Territory within a year."

He studied the morning report provided by the First Sergeant and continued, "The people of this country have gone mad. They are calling it "Bloody Kansas" it is the whole slave state, Free State thing."

First Sergeant O'Keefe nodded his head and remarked, "Well Sir, Kansas, Texas, California or The Oregon Territory all works for me, just don't accept a posting to Florida and I will be happy."

Captain Hunt smiled, of the units of the 2<sup>nd</sup> US Artillery Regiment; the First Sergeant had just run through the current locations of half the Regiment's Companies.

He handed the report back to O'Keefe and said, "Thanks First Sergeant, get me those other 4 soldiers."

Captain Hunt returned to his paperwork, he had been involved in a lengthy rewriting of the Field Artillery manual with Major French and the two had corresponded frequently on upgrading the Mexican War vintage document.

He had heard that a commission had been sent to Europe and that Mordecai was on it. He hoped the ordnance officer would bring some modernization back to America.

Pausing from his editing he pondered on going to Kansas. This would be a chance perhaps to actively campaign with the Company, inwardly he was anxious to go. Garrison duty while pleasant, did not answer the gnawing need to get out and do things. He craved that. If he was in command then he would have the best Artillery Company in the Army.

He resolved to finish his labors early today, as Elizabeth was ill again in their tiny quarters, she had been ill more and more often and Henry Hunt worried over her much.

The small cluster of junior officers and young enlisted men were gathered outside the walls of Fortress Monroe on the sandy plain that overlooked the tidal inlet of Mill Creek West of the Fortress.

First Sergeants O'Keefe and Swanson were providing oversight for School of the Piece today. The companies of the 2<sup>nd</sup> Regiment came to Fortress Monroe for periods between campaigns in the South or West but the easy duty at Monroe meant serving as the training cadre for the School of Artillery Practice. O'Keefe enjoyed the duty as the hours were regular and he had a chance in this capacity to train the young officers coming out of West Point.

He thoroughly enjoyed the chance to marvel at the ignorance of Subalterns and to teach them in the school of "Hard Knocks".

The class had taken a while to arrive at the appointed location since the enlisted men had been duly marched to the location being the new recruits for Companies M and H.

The junior Lieutenants had sauntered over following a "Gentlemen's" breakfast at the Hotel Hygea.

O'Keefe had huffed and sworn under his breath at the Subalterns showing up late. First Sergeant Swanson was enjoying the sight of the primary instructor getting worked up.

Following a wave of his arm, First Sergeant O'Keefe had two complete Gun and Caisson teams approach unlimber and establish a position with a 6 pound field gun and a 12 pound Howitzer.

The soldiers and officers watched in amazement as the well drilled artillerymen quickly unlimbered the guns, established positions, detached and separated caisson sections from the gun positions and established a field firing position.

The two gun crews quickly assumed positions under the commands of the section chief, advanced and loaded a blank charge for each gun and then quickly fired a thunderous salute.

Joshua stood with 6 other recruits and they all jumped with the loud roar of the field pieces. He had spent the past two weeks in the "School of the Soldier" learning facing movements, how to march in step, the manual of arms with the 1842 musket, and above all how to listen to commands and execute as expected.

The experienced soldiers had patiently coached him and insured that the new recruits fit in. He had been anxious for this next phase to come. He found the new world that he was in to be constantly exciting and challenging.

Joshua realized that he was forgetting from time to time his concern for his father, but he remained determined to learn the answer. He was resigned; however that the time to look would have to be later.

The relief wagon crews returned each evening with the same bleak news from Portsmouth and Norfolk. September had proved to be just as bad for the deaths as August had been, and both cities were ghost towns.

The enlisted recruits and the Subalterns stood in two distinct groups, hesitant to mingle.

First Sergeant O'Keefe approached the group and announced, "Now Gentlemen! Let me have your attention! Today begins the School of the Piece! For the next week you will learn each position and will drill on that position 3 times a day under the direct supervision of each corporal who is the Chief of the Piece."

He quickly noted his gentlemen, the Subalterns were commenting amongst themselves and added, "That is regardless of the rank you hold!, Each of you will learn the drill required to keep a field gun in operation and you will learn it until you can accomplish it correctly and without error, in your sleep!"

O'Keefe and Swanson quickly arranged the enlisted recruits and the Subalterns into initial positions tending the guns and limber chests, assigning each to the 7 supporting positions of a gun crew for the light 6 pound gun and the rest on the 12 pound howitzer.

Joshua found himself at position number 1 by the muzzle of the 6 pounder, with a new Lieutenant occupying position number 2 across the muzzle from him. Another two Lieutenants assumed positions 3 and 4 by the breech and another Lieutenant and 2 enlisted recruits became number 5, 6 and 7 by the limber chest.

The experienced crew members handed each the tools of the position and backed away a few steps and the corporal then announced, "Listen closely as we explain the job of each of these positions. The crewman you have taken the place of will explain your steps and movements as I give each command. You need to learn how each step feels, and do exactly what your assisting crewman tells you to do."

The corporal clearly knew his job and went to each man at his new position and explained the role and expected movements that his oral command would require. Joshua was surprised at the exactness of location and posture he was expected to assume and execute at the number 1 position and he noticed as he watched the explanations to the Lieutenants that the same exactness of motion was expected at each position around the gun.

The corporal then announced, "Gentlemen, we have just fired a shot in the demonstration so now for the next step, Attention!"

Each man in position stood upright, the corporal looked the crew over and loudly announced, "Sponge!"

Joshua tried to remember the step off to the right, the turn the raising of the sponge end of the rammer, inserting the sponge into the bore and then turning it 3 times with the head fully bottomed in the gun.

The experienced number 1 came up and corrected his stance and had him correct the action by actually dipping the sponge head into the bucket to wet it, explaining "This step boy is to insure there ain't no embers in there before you put a live charge in. Now see number three back there on the vent? You make sure he has his thumb on that vent the whole time. It must remain closed from this step to the seating of the next load!"

Once the crew was finished the corporal looked over the crew and Announced, "Range 1000 yards, Shell! Advance the Charge!"

Joshua noticed a lengthy amount of discussion with the corporal and the two Lieutenants around the limber chest. Finally the recruit acting as number 5 moved first to Corporal Sheppard who inspected his pouch and then to the Lieutenant standing at number 2 position and handed him an imaginary round. The Lieutenant under coaching from the real number 2 then inserted the fantasy round into the 6 pounder muzzle taking care to insert it seam side down.

The corporal again loudly announced, "Ram!"

Joshua found himself repeating the awkward sidestep and manipulating the staff to bring the wooden rammer end about and into the muzzle he rammed the imaginary shell home.

The real number 1 came back and removed his thumb from the top of the ramming staff and said, "Just imagine boy that the load you just loaded gets ignited by a ember down in there....you never grip this staff that way, if the charge fires it will take yer arm off with it!"

He then paused to show him the correct grip. Joshua was enjoying this process immensely.

First Sergeant O'Keefe kept a stern eye on his enlisted recruits, as that was what he cared about in the drill.

At one point he noticed the young Timmonds looking all around at the activity that was going on in the battery so he approached him from behind and menacingly whispered to him, "As you learn about this fooking duty boy o, don't be fooking lookin around! You keep your fooking eyes on the duty you do, look to that water bucket! Is it empty? Look at that fooker on number 3 is he closin' that fooking vent tight? You do not worry over shit except your fookin job! Is that clear?"

Joshua quickly stood to attention and shouted, "Yes First Sergeant!"

O'Keefe then interrupted the drill and observed, "I do not want to see no damn gun crew lookin' at nuthin' but the tending to the gun, The Gunner looks at the fight and the enemy before you, You each must focus only on your duty to the piece!"

He looked to the corporal and said, "You may resume!"

Joshua noticed now that the charge was rammed that the corporal approached the breech and removed a brass pendulum sight from a leather pouch and hung it from cast hooks on the back of the gun, he remembered that he had announced a target at 1000 yards, the corporal adjusted the sight and directed number 3 and 4 to assist in moving the trail of the gun to imaginary directions as he elevated and sighted the piece. Joshua then noticed that the spike on the swell of the muzzle was a front sight.

Once complete, the corporal stepped back from the breech and announced, "Prick and Prime!"

Joshua watched as number 3 produced a gimlet from his pouch and pricked a hole in the imaginary charge with the tool, with his actual number 3 coaching his actions. He then retrieved an actual friction primer from his pouch and inserted it into the vent. Number 4 then approached hooked his lanyard to the small ring on the friction primer and stepped back keeping a good degree of slack in the cord as explained by his actual number 4 coach.

First Sergeant O'Keefe was back after haranguing the Howitzer Crew, loudly announcing, "Here is another place where the stupid shit kills men!"

He looked the acting number 4, a Lieutenant in the eye, saying venomously, "When you is commanding a section, SIR!, mind that you keep a keen eye on the number 4, he gets anxious you see, particularly when the Mexican infantry is 20 yards off raising a rank o' loaded muskets, He wants to yank that cord real bad, and if he thinks he runs the gun, he will!"

O'Keefe then pointed to the positions of the various crewmen of the piece, and added, "If this dumb shit yanks this lanyard, you are dead and you are too!"

O'Keefe pointed to number 3, 4 and 2 who were respectively in line with the wheels of the gun and just adjacent to the muzzle. "It is absolutely necessary that you understand that the Gunner will call the shot!" he growled.

O'Keefe looked to the corporal and shouted, "You may resume!"

The corporal nodded and shouted, "Make Ready!"

With this command each of the experienced crewmen showed the trainees the appropriate positions. Joshua's coach taught him to step back and away from the muzzle. The Soldiers coaching number 3 and 4 showed them to stand clear of the cannon wheels and showed number 4 how to take up the slack on the lanyard attached to the friction primer.

When the corporal in charge of the piece was satisfied he shouted, "Fire!"

After he shouted the command he instinctively craned his neck watching the imaginary shot as number 4 yanked the lanyard out and away firing the friction primer that burned instantly with a loud "Pop."

First Sergeant O'Keefe returned when the firing drill was complete in its first iteration and had the officers and men gather around him.

He then commenced his lecture, "Men what is important here is to think through each of the duties of your position on the piece, a well drilled crew can fire once every 40 seconds indefinitely. When you have ranks of Infantry or Cavalry closing on you they want nothin' more than to bayonet you! Remember you have been punishing them for thousands of yards! Your weapon is this piece! You must learn to act as a crew and think of nothin' else. Your Company Commander will place you, Your Chief of Section will tell you what to shoot at, and your Gunner will tell you when!"

O'Keefe paused and gave an evil stare to the nearest Lieutenant, and continued, "And your Gunner will command your actions to the letter! So forget about them foolish muskets and the stupid short swords! Your only hope in battle is this piece firing as fast as practicable! Am I understood?"

The trainees to include the Lieutenants all answered in unison, "Yes First Sergeant!"

First Sergeant O'Keefe then strode over to Joshua and directed, "Timmonds, you have just had your head taken off by a Mexican shot! You go now to replace number 7 on the limber chest."

He then turned to the others and announced, "Number 2 replaces number 1, number 3 replaces number 2, Number 4 replaces number 3, and so on and such and fookin such! When you need a new number 7 go to the Caisson section and get a driver off the ground!"

He then turned to the corporal with a grin and directed, "Repeat the drill!"

The trainees repeated the drills over and over each time changing the positions in the order of replacement established by the First Sergeant. Joshua was fascinated by the charge table glued onto the lid of the limber chest and the steps required to cut the fuse based on the Gunner's commands.

During the course of the day's drill he attracted the First Sergeant's attention again by leaving the Limber Chest lid open during an iteration of fire. That infraction led to another round of profanity in regards to blowing up an entire chest full of fixed ammunition with descriptive language about how many arms and legs he would lose.

Upon conclusion of the day the First Sergeant promised the trainees that by the end of the week they might have the chance to fire live shot and shell.

The trainees, officers and enlisted alike had become almost crews and started to banter among themselves through the course of training.

Joshua was frightened slightly in talking to the officers but at least one was friendly enough to introduce himself, "Private Timmonds it has been a pleasure, I am Lieutenant Henry Benson and I hope to serve again with you some day!"

Joshua realized that he was the same young officer that served as number 2 when they started the drill that morning.

O'Keefe watched them reattach the guns to the limbers that evening and remarked to First Sergeant Swanson, "Shame most of them Lieutenants will get detailed to the Engineers or the Ordnance Corps. Some of them are learning to be first class Section Leaders."

Later that evening after evening Roll Call, Captain Hunt sat down with O'Keefe and reviewed the daily reports in the Company office. He advised O'Keefe to focus on the crew duties and to start horse team training and carriage and caisson maintenance as soon as possible.

He looked at his old gun crewman from Mexico and explained, "Word from Regiment is likely to be a campaign to Kansas in the spring."

O'Keefe snorted and dug into his frock coat pocket for his pipe, and replied, "Sir, You know sure as hell that once we go west for one reason, the damned Army will send us somewheres else and then somewheres else! It never ends!"

Hunt simply laughed and observed, "First Sergeant, you know we have a Manifest Destiny to defend!"

The First Sergeant lit his pipe and got to some business questions, "Sir, Do you know what our campaign order will be yet?"

Captain Hunt thought a moment and mused, "I would assume a battery of four 6 pounders and two 12 pound howitzers with caissons and a basic load of ammunition for all."

He then added, "And we will likely get our own allotment of horses again."

The First Sergeant added, "I would recommend the entire company go if possible, don't want to rely on some fort blacksmith for our repairs."

Captain Hunt nodded his head in agreement. After a moment he added, "First Sergeant plan for a movement overland, I expect we will move by rail with some marching when we get orders, I expect Fort Leavenworth will be our initial destination. Our reason for going is the upcoming national election next year from what I have been told. It appears that Kansas is tearing itself apart over the Free State Slave State question."

First Sergeant O'Keefe nodded, he could not fathom what it must be like to buy and own another human being. Ireland had been bad enough when he was young, but at least a soul was free to leave.

After a hard week of constant drilling the detachment of trainees on the guns had become teams.

First Sergeant O'Keefe focused on the 6 pounder crew and First Sergeant Swanson attended to the howitzer crew based upon their extensive experience in each respective piece.

Today they would allow the crews to fire one round of shot, one round of canister, one spherical case shot and one shell. To facilitate the training the First Sergeants had soldiers in rowboats tow buoys out to 300 yards, 1000 yards and 1200 yards from the knoll where the cannon were placed.

First Sergeant O'Keefe had instructed Corporal Shepperd to place Privates Timmonds, O'Leary, and Brannon on positions 5, 6 and 7 as they were going to be drivers or caisson team members for the Company and he wanted them to get accustomed to their actual places.

He decided to put the trainee Lieutenants on the gun crew proper since he already had crews assigned in M Company.

The First Sergeant then assembled the trainees off to the flank of the two guns. Off in the distance the buoys could be seen in the Mill Creek inlet rocking in the choppy water, a brisk wind was blowing in from the East.

Once the men were assembled he began, "Alright Gentlemen, the day you have awaited has come to fire live ammunition, I want you to remember the steps of your drill, the new factor you will learn is the recoil and behavior of the piece, I will be watching you closely so if you hear me call Cease Fire, you will stop everything and stand stock still, Is that clear?"

The trainees replied, "Yes First Sergeant!" in unison.

The first round designated by Corporal Sheppard was shot at 1200 yards, Joshua as number 5 approached the limber and opened his leather pouch to receive the fixed round of shot from Harry O'Leary acting as number 7, Sean Brannon as number 6 had no task as there was no fusing to be set on the solid projectile. Joshua received the round and briskly strode first to Corporal Shepperd who inspected the round in his pouch and then to Lieutenant Benson who served as number 2 and he passed off the round and quickly returned as drilled to the limber.

Joshua prepared his pouch to receive the next round and he heard Corporal Sheppard command, "Make ready... Fire!"

The 6 pounder discharged with a loud roar and he watched as the Corporal side stepped the smoke to view the target. The piece recoiled back on its carriage a good 6 feet in a fairly violent fashion. Joshua suddenly realized why the positions in drill were important. Down in Mill Creek inlet a large splash emerged in the water about 30 feet in front of the buoy and it then the shot ripped through the plank target, skipping once more on the water before impacting and striking the water, sinking below the waves.

First Sergeant O'Keefe then strode between the limber and the gun and loudly announced, "The point of solid shot gentlemen is to skip the round into infantry or cavalry in order to break their formations at extreme range. This round is your long range option in all cases!"

Corporal Shepperd then commanded, "Sponge!"

After a short pause he commanded, "Spherical Case, 1000 yards!"

Private O'Leary quickly lifted the lid and handed the red painted fixed round to Private Brannon who screwed in a tin Bormann time-fuse with a fuse tool, then he returned the tool to his pouch and produced the fuse cutter, which was a brass handled gouge, he then glanced at the firing table and looked at the range and time setting indicated by Private O'Leary, he found the corresponding timing mark on the flat surface of the fuse and dug a hole through the thin tin cover at the 4 second mark.

Corporal Sheppard then shouted, "Advance the Charge!"

Joshua quickly strode to Corporal Sheppard who checked the cut fuse and then to the piece where Lieutenant Benson took it from his leather pouch and carefully inserted the round into the bore. Joshua quickly returned to his post by the limber, and after preparing his bag, he eagerly watched for the shot.

As the gun discharged and recoiled, he noticed a faint smoky trail as the fuse was ignited by the muzzle blast and it sailed towards the distant buoy. The round burst in the air in a puff of white smoke, the crack of the explosion heard slightly later due to the distance. He could then see a spray of water kicked up by the shrapnel balls that were released by the airburst all around the target; it was again a nearly perfect shot.

First Sergeant O'Keefe paused until the shell thrown by the adjacent howitzer burst overhead the 1000 yard buoy before resuming the instruction, "The object of Spherical Case is to air burst your shot at least 50 yards in front of and before massed troops or cavalry, for the 6 pounder you can expect effects approximately 30 feet wide at that distance. Your spherical case has 27 iron balls as well as the fragments of the case itself that strike the formation killing in multiples. Make sure you keep a sharp ear for the range called out by your gunner, you gents on the limber insure you double check the firing table before cutting your fuse!"

Corporal Sheppard returned the crew to attention with the command, "Sponge!"

Joshua and his two companions watched the Lieutenants prep the gun.

Sheppard then commanded, "Canister, 300 yards!"

As Joshua received the tin can shaped fixed round in his pouch noticed Corporal Sheppard elevating the gun while peering through the Pendulum Hause and directing on of the Lieutenants to adjust the trail slightly to the right as he sighted on the nearest buoy at 300 yards. Upon firing, the plank target was clearly shredded by the hail of iron balls impacting on it.

O'Keefe was clearly pleased by the performance of his trainees in this exercise as he continued his instruction, "When the battery is reduced to firing canister the fight has come to the decisive point! When you hear the gunner command you will stand ready and focus on nothin' but your task. Infantry can begin to range you with volley fire in about 2 minutes from your first maximum range engagement with canister. They will be focusing on you on the crew with that fire. Do not watch the enemy! Mind your tasks and your drill at this time. You only got 15 rounds of canister in your limber and the caisson chests so each shot has got to count, If you are ordered to fire double shotted canister you must cut away the powder bag from the second can before you load it, do that away from the limber. Once you are more experienced I will instruct you on other shortcuts but for now good job men! Now prepare the pieces for returning to the Fort."

Later that evening as Joshua sat and talked excitedly with his messmates about their day; Sergeant O'Brien from the caisson section came by and seeing Joshua, directed "Timmonds, tomorrow you and O'Leary report to me at 8:00 o'clock for school of the team. You two have been picked to be limber drivers for Corporal Sheppard.

# 4 A NEW GUN FOR AN ARMY

## Liege, Belgium
## September 1855

Major Alfred Mordecai was anxious on this day. After exhaustive negotiations with the French Army Ordnance Officer assigned to them for this portion of their visits, the Lieutenant Colonel had finally relented to seeking them clearance to visit the Arsenal at Liege.

The Officers were assembled in the lobby of their Hotel in Saint Laurent waiting the cab that would take them to the Armory in Herstal.

It was a wet and rainy day and the wet cobblestones in the ancient streets glistened. Captain McClelland had been late coming down for Breakfast and Major Delafield was anxious to be done with the arsenal visit in order to visit the works near the outskirts of town.

Mordecai had been exasperated by the endless tours of fortifications with his Engineer colleague but patiently and professionally had endured.

Each member of the commission had an agenda and Major Delafield being the senior officer tended to focus each visit on his particular area of interest at the expense of what Mordecai and McClelland had come to see.

The tour of Europe was so far an exhausting affair. Their ultimate goal was to visit the front of the Crimean War but diplomatic requirements were delaying their objective.

The three officers had made up that time by visiting the armies and fortifications of England, France and now Wallonia.

Mordecai had come far, for a tobacco farmer's son from North Carolina. He had accepted the command of the Watervliet Arsenal shortly before departing for Europe. He remembered their meeting with Secretary of War Davis as he charged them with their objectives. He remembered how Davis had emphasized that they were to seek out the modern and cutting edge developments being employed in Europe and to bring them home. It became clear to him that Davis was a man who would obtain support from Congress to update America's arsenal and he had felt particularly honored to have been chosen to make this trip.

Rumors had already abounded that Davis had received a promise from Congress, to increase the army by at least one regiment of Cavalry and one of Infantry prior to 1856. Hopefully this would occur as the expansion West was draining the Army of men and material.

Lieutenant Colonel Fontaigne had arrived late as usual and he insisted on coffee before proceeding further, so the officers paused a little more before proceeding from the lobby.

Mordecai did not totally trust the French Officer and he had come to the conclusion that the feeling was reciprocal. Captain McClellan and him had hit it off, but that had been more socially than professionally. Major Delafield just seemed distracted.

Alfred Mordecai did enjoy this trip nonetheless; Europe was an exciting and exotic place with extremely good quality food, lodgings and beverages. He appreciated the fine things he had seen here and wished he could come to visit outside of his labors to visit.

Finally after a short and rainy cab ride through town the industrial district of Herstal hove into view.

Mordecai was astonished to see the scope of the works that made up the Royal Armory of Liege. Due to the nature of the tiny principalities proximity to two constantly warring European nations, the industrious Walloons had decided exploit the mineral rich Ardennes and proceeded to arm everyone, and in the process had become too skilled and precious to destroy. Liege had become the center of Europe for the design of arms. And on this day, Europe would share with America, some of her secrets.

By late afternoon the delegation was taken to the Royal Foundry. Mordecai had noticed a clear degree of boredom on Delafield's demeanor; McClellan had been constantly bantering with his French friend, but he had been fixated by what he had observed thus far. So far within the development of infantry rifles he had received the privilege to see the entire developmental history of Minie' and his bullet designs.

Mordecai was secretly relieved to see that the musket design that the U.S. Army ordnance board had approved was just as good, if not better, with some anticipation he realized that now they would see the artillery works up close.

Mr. Davis had been emphatic in his letter of appointment that they focus on the developments of France and this day had come. He had not realized that France had relied on the Walloons to be that agent of development.

As they entered the main foundry floor a singular gun caught his eye.

Lieutenant Colonel Fontaigne had noticed and in his broken English had described it, "This is our Canon obusier de 12!" he proclaimed proudly.

Mordecai was quite taken by what he was looking at and asked "how much does it weigh?"

Fontaigne seemed confused so Captain McClellan translated the question.

The French officer replied, "600 Kilograms." Mordecai quickly took out his sketch pad and began to record the overall dimensions of the piece.

He peered into the muzzle and noted no chamber recess at the end of the breech, he turned to Fontaigne and asked, "Is this a Howitzer?"

Fontaigne, looking somewhat bored replied, "Non, this is what we refer to as a Gun-Howitzer, it can fulfill the objective of both a gun and a howitzer with greater range than a howitzer."

Mordecai had begun to see enormous potential for this concept. Up to now the American army had to configure artillery for either campaign or siege but could rarely move equipped for both.

He remembered the frustratingly limited effect the 6 pound guns delivered in Mexico. Now he was seeing a 12 pound gun that could serve every purpose in a size that suited the mobility of campaigning. He rapidly began to sketch the concept and recorded the dimensions of the gun in every regard.

Fontaigne seeing his charge's fascination motioned to one of the Belgian Foremen to come over to provide more technical details to the American. Mordecai and the Foreman spend the rest of the afternoon talking. Fontaigne decided to take McClellan and Delafield on the remainder of the tour at Mordecai's insistence, and when he was done Alfred Mordecai found he had a notebook full.

The Belgian foreman had broken Mordecai away from the piece to show him factory samples of the ordnance that it fired. He demonstrated to the Major fixed shot, fixed shell, fixed spherical case-shot, and canister rounds. He explained the specifications that the French army had insisted on and indicated that the piece had an effective range of over 1400 meters. He allowed the officer to copy the range and charge tables but was mildly surprised when the American seemed to have already seen the Bormann time fuse he produced. Mordecai attempted to explain in his broken French that the U.S. Army had been buying them from France since 1852.

Mordecai decided later that evening that this design would not wait on his official report. After dinner that evening he eschewed the normal night cap with McClellan and retired to his room to draft a letter to his friend Major Huger who currently served on the ordnance board. His letter contained teasing details of a new gun that offered to replace at least 4 types in the current inventory. He asked his fellow expert to build expectations among the board. He would formally present the design upon his return.

Mordecai trusted Huger to keep the secret tantalizing to the board. Both men were Southerners, one a Huguenot and the other a Jew; they had worked their way through an Army that looked mildly askance at their "different background" but tolerated them in their midst so long as they served and fought well.

Mordecai remember the sneers as a young lad, only 16, when he had reported to West Point. He had been the first Jewish cadet at the academy.

He persevered; however and when his classmates began to realize his grasp of mathematics, calculus and algebra exceeded theirs, they had accepted him. He had been frequently solicited to tutor his classmates and by graduation in 1836 he had become an enormously popular young man.

The Army had been quick to recognize his talents and had assigned him to the coveted field of ordnance upon his commissioning.

Despite the slowness of promotion Alfred Mordecai had decided that his love of science was satisfied in the labors at the arsenals of the fledgling republic. He remained frustrated at the slowness of development. The nation had little funds to dedicate to the Army.

Experiments were tolerated but the Ordnance Board required exhaustive proofing and examination prior to approving and funding new innovations. Mordecai had learned to be persistent in arguing merits.

He reviewed his notes from England and the technology that they had observed there, admiring the Blakely gun and the James rifling system, he pondered on how the existing stocks of 6 pounder cannon could be converted to the rifled system but he found his mind wracked with doubt about whether bronze guns could handle the system. Iron after all, was the ideal method provided it was properly wrought.

After finishing his letter, he considered going to bed. Tomorrow they would board a train to Prussian and then Poland. From the Polish frontier they would then transition to Russia to see a front from the perspective of the "enemy" of their friends, newly made, in England and France.

He pondered on the uniqueness of being able to observe a bitter war from both sides. Thinking of Mexico, he recalled the deaths and the suffering that both sides must be enduring. The sad reality of his calling sometimes made him regret what he did.

He instead decided to expand and refine his sketches, focusing not on what he had seen on this day, but rather on what the American version of this piece would look like. Mordecai decided that it should be a more businesslike refinement of what he had witnessed. He imagined that the weight of the gun tube, nearly 1200 lbs., would require a carriage similar to that which supported the current Model 1841 howitzer. Such an adaptation would not require new design, only modification.

Limber chests for the Model 1841 would suffice to service ammunition to the piece so the only work that American armories would have to provide would be to cast the bronze tubes for the gun.

He tried to imagine which foundry would be best to approach for prototypes.

He would write Huger again when they had arrived in Prussian to see if he could find a foundry that would work on a design that would be cast and then bored from the bronze to make the strongest tube that could be devised. In theory if done properly, a higher charge than the French 1 kilogram could be tolerated and perhaps greater range could be obtained.

Mordecai's mind raced as it did whenever he discovered something that needed to be adapted for American use. He agreed with the Secretary of War's assessment that the United States needed to keep a close eye on the developments in Europe.

The Continent seemed to be always at war with one another, and war bred development. America needed to keep her ear to the ground in this regard. The War of 1812 had provided a bitter lesson in the foolishness of assuming that the world would leave America alone.

Finally as he finished his estimations and sketches, he checked his watch. To his horror he realized he had been at it until past 1:00 am in the morning. He quickly undressed and tried to go to sleep, but his mind continued to race about the piece. He knew he would not rest until he had gotten the approval for a design. The Army might thank him someday.

In the morning as the officers dined over espresso and croissants in the Hotel in Sainte Laurente, Mordecai noted that George McClelland was in a gay mood.

McClellan had observed "We missed you Albert in the tour of the musket works! We saw some amazing breechloaders!"

Mordecai, dourly remarked "George, you know they are fine for sporting but are only a liability for us. They are mere toys. And you know the ordnance board will only consider those weapons that range far and are reliable."

Feeling jovial as it was a nice morning, Mordecai returned the jest with a tantalizing offer, "I just suppose you have found a design you will wish to introduce to the board for the cavalry!"

McClellan only grinned and said, "No Albert, what the French have is no better than the work of Christian Sharps at the moment, but I have found myself fascinated by their horse accoutrements, they have recommended I review the Prussian Cavalry for their saddlery and tack."

The three officers finally checked out and arranged the shipment of their considerable baggage to the rail station in Herstal and secured a hackney to the station for the journey to Prussian.

They highly anticipated the visit to Prussia and each recalled the influence Von Steuben had provided to the Continental Army, perhaps they would learn much.

As they traveled Alfred Mordecai marveled at the notion that such an advanced society and civilization such as the Monarchies of Europe could continually engage in costly and destructive wars.

Although he bemoaned the rough edged crudeness of much of America, he was glad to know that Americans valued peace.

## Chicopee, Massachusetts
## January, 1856

Major Benjamin Huger gratefully accepted the cup of coffee from the foundry foreman as they sat in a tiny office above the foundry floor of the large brick casting hall.

He had come to deliver a set of specifications that the Ordnance Board had approved funds to create a prototype cannon. The Board nominated Huger to deliver the order as he routinely came to Chicopee to proof and stamp guns cast here during the infrequent runs of government orders. The Ames Company had made nearly every sword carried by the U.S. Army since the revolution and would; for the right price, cast bronze guns when requested.

The foundry foreman had summoned his best form maker to come up to the office, and the two men chatted amiably while they enjoyed their coffee. Huger had to perform acceptance inspections on four 24 pounder howitzer tubes later that morning but he wanted to review the prototype with the foundry first.

When the form maker arrived, Major Huger produced a rolled up set of plans that the men spread upon the wooden table in the office.

"We have funding available in this instance for one test gun to be cast in Bronze employing the Gribeauval method, that will be bored to a 12 pound howitzer diameter," Major Huger explained running his hand over the drawing.

Mr. Norwalk, the form maker, nodded and asked, "Do we bore it as a howitzer?"

He was confused by the specifications indicated on the blueprint as it had a straight tube like the government 6 pounder with no recessed chamber like most howitzers; that accommodated the reduced charge of powder.

Huger shook his head, explaining, "This prototype is to be a copy of a French Gun-Howitzer and will have no chamber."

He ran his finger along the sketch of the cannon and continued, "you will note the extra thickness of the reinforce around the breech, we will require a thicker and unadorned barrel as the cannon will need to be cast to support gun strength charges."

The form maker nodded, it struck him that this was a minor yet significant departure from what the Army had ordered before. Norwalk mentally calculated the amount of bronze that would be required for the design.

He observed, "You will have to accept a weight of around 1200 pounds for the tube with these specifications," he wanted Major Huger to realize the cost of the prototype as it would come out to nearly 400 dollars.

Huger emphatically restated the need for plainness of profile, wanting the foundry foreman to focus on the strength of the tube. He wondered of the extra cost borne by the government in bronze that the stylistic astragal rings cast onto the inventory of 6 pound guns that all demonstrated decorativeness more characteristic of church bells, than of weapons.

Norwalk nodded and asked for the specific bore diameter and asked, "You understand that we will have to make a new boring head for this profile?"

Major Huger replied, "Yes, I can assure you that we are likely to order at least 6 guns of this design for our testing. However; we only wish to produce this first single prototype to test. I will correspond with you on the progress of this initial gun, and once it is complete I will return to proof test it and then give you directions for delivery."

The men all shook hands and Major Huger delivered over the plans to the foreman. He knew the Ames Company would do good work.

Major Huger picked up his heavy bag of stamps and gauges and announced to the foreman, "Let us see to the 24 pounders."

The two men walked down the wooden steps from the shop office onto the hot and dirty foundry floor and weaved through the hub of activity on the shop. The workers were busy casting small brass parts for the sword production orders that the government had placed to equip the new cavalry regiment.

The foreman, proud of his laborers, showed Major Huger a few of the still warm rough castings of the hilts of model 1840 heavy dragoon sabers. Major Huger nodded approvingly noting the fine quality of the castings and the nice color indicating a high degree of purity.

The foreman and Major Huger exited the factory through the large doors at the end of the building to a small detail of Soldiers standing by 4 new bronze guns laying horizontally on two Iron topped wooden beams. The detail had preceded the Major on his visit by two days.

Their task had been to proof test each tube with 3 ½ pounds of powder and solid shot, followed by cleaning and water testing the barrels. The process required the proof fired tube to be set upright with the muzzle in the air, the vent plugged and filled with water under pressure, obtained by driving a wooden plug into the bore and the vent. The next day the Soldiers and foundry men had removed the water and laid the guns out for Major Huger's inspection.

The Major initially conducted a painstakingly slow external inspection of the tubes looking for pits and imperfections on the surfaces. He dug into his tool bag for his trunnion gauge and wooden rule and measured the dimensions of the trunnions and their distance from the cascabel of the tube. He noted that Ames Company had stamped their Manufactory data and date of manufacture on the face of the right side trunnion of each cannon.

The sergeant in charge of the detail stood by with an inspection staff as Major Huger pulled out and adjusted his star gauge to measure the interior dimensions of the barrel. Slowly and carefully he checked the interior dimensions.

He then removed the star gauge from the staff and inspected the barrels again with a sheet iron cylinder gauge. Satisfied with the boring and reaming he replaced the cylinder gauge with a wire "Searcher" and moved the feeler slowly and carefully down the bore to detect any cracks or pits that would indicate a void.

He then produced a tiny wire feeler gauge and tested each vent for the same. Finally satisfied with each of the four tubes he attached a mirror to the staff and gave the interior of the tubes a visible inspection.

He was looking for water dripping from cracks or making wet spots in the bore. The water proof was designed to fill invisible voids and indicate their presence by persistent release of water during the inspection.

Huger was a stickler for details in his inspections having witnessed the result of burst gun tubes. No cannon would have his acceptance without scrupulous inspection.

Upon completion of his inspection Major Huger compared his inspection notes with a small leather bound table of variations in his ordnance manual. Huger was quite familiar with this manual as he was one of the original co-authors of in in 1847. Satisfied with the acceptability he asked the relieved foreman to bring him a hammer.

Huger removed a small box from his bag containing his personal acceptance stamps. On the face of each cannon muzzle on the bottom he carefully stamped the letters "B" and "H", for Benjamin Huger on each howitzer. On the top of the gun he stamped the numbers "11" through "14" on each, to indicate the order of acceptance to match the recorded inspection in his ledger.

Major Huger thanked the Sergeant and his detail and gathered up his inspection tools. He bid farewell to the foreman, again promising to correspond with him on the prototype and departed.

Later that day the foreman and the form maker again looked at the sketches and specifications provided. With the large amount of bronze being produced they decided to accelerate the manufacture of this prototype as the material was available. The form maker decided that the gun howitzer, like all other howitzers should have handles cast above the trunnions.

This aspect was considered utilitarian and he would insure no excess of adornment was added to the mold blank. With the roll of design specifications in hand he proceeded down to the shop floor to get his work crew busy making a mold.

Two weeks from the date of their initial arrangement the Ames Company had a completed prototype of Gun Howitzer number 1 cast and bored. The foreman had directed a rather careful final machining of the exterior of the gun bringing the piece to a nice polish. He regretted the decision of allowing the form maker to cast dolphins onto the top as it made a lengthier job of the exterior finish.

Following final factory gauging the foreman directed the Ames Manufactory stamps to be applied to the face of the right trunnion. He returned upstairs to draft out a telegram to notify Major Huger that his prototype was complete.

Major Huger was surprised to receive the telegram when his orderly provided it to him at his office at Harper's Ferry Arsenal near the end of January.

While he had no other inspections to conduct in Chicopee yet, he decided that this project would be a priority. Mordecai had repeatedly asked about the gun in his correspondence from Watervliet and soon the board was scheduled to meet and discuss projects spurred by the European Commission's findings.

Huger summoned his Ordnance Sergeant and instructed him to assemble a detail to visit Chicopee as soon as possible. He would follow the next day to witness the proof firing.

Three days later, Benjamin Huger greeted the Ames Foundry foreman and the two men went out to meet the Soldiers at the proof firing site.

As Huger saw the prototype and noted the cast dolphins, he frowned, the foreman was taken aback somewhat and asked, "What is wrong Major Huger?"

Huger motioned to the handles cast on top and stated, "I specifically asked you to focus on making this cannon as a gun, simple and unadorned! What assurances can your firm provide to me that these handles have not introduced weaknesses into the overall integrity of the tube?"

The foreman replied, "You have accepted our 24 pounders with dolphins!"

Major Huger nodded, deciding to let the issue rest.

He stepped back to look at the rest of the work. Huger liked the overall bulk of the design, the clean lines and obvious strength of the thickened reinforce would likely handle the heavier charges he had in mind. His earlier calculations led him to believe as Alfred Mordecai also theorized, that charges over 2 pounds, perhaps to 2 ½ pounds would be feasible. If this concept worked the gun could likely achieve ranges one full third beyond that of the 6 pound gun, as well as throwing a much more accurate 12 pound shot.

The handles disturbed him nonetheless and he directed the foreman that the next 5 prototypes would possibly not be cast without the unnecessary appendages.

The factory workmen and the Soldiers prepared the gun with a 3 pound proof charge and a 12 pound howitzer shot and conducted the proof fire while the foreman and Major Huger watched.

Following the first discharge, Major Huger visually inspected the gun, then satisfied he directed another identical proof charge with two 12 pound shot loaded. He agreed with the ordnance sergeant to allow the gunner to triple the length of his lanyard for the proof test.

The gun again roared, this time louder than the first. Again Major Huger inspected the smoking gun tube, satisfied he directed the soldiers to clean the gun and conduct the pressurized water test and announced that he would return tomorrow to inspect the piece. He turned to the foreman and emphatically repeated his opinion of the dolphins on the prototype.

The foreman nodded and determined himself to have a discussion with the form maker.

The next morning, that proved to be a rather foggy day, Major Huger returned to the foundry. Again he greeted the foreman and the ordnance sergeant and producing his heavy bag of gauges proceeded directly to the now dismounted cannon barrel. Following the identical inspection of the exterior and interior he marked the tube with a large " BH" on the bottom and a numeral "1" on the top of the muzzle.

Huger turned to the foreman and said, "Good sir, It must have been some time since your firm made a new design. I will ask you to produce 5 more copies of this design to equip a standard Company set of gun-howitzers. Can you accomplish that prior to final payment?"

The foreman nodded yes, as the factory characteristically made the guns in runs of several.

Huger smiled and asked, "The Ordnance Board is anxious to test this prototype, would your firm be troubled if we shipped gun number one back east immediately for testing?"

The foreman assured him it would be no problem. The two men shook hands to seal their agreement. Major Huger then turned to the Ordnance Sergeant and directed him to arrange delivery of the tube to Fort McHenry for testing

Huger walked with the Ordnance Sergeant back to his horse and told him to include a note that the recipients at Fort McHenry were to mount the new tube on the standard number 2 carriage. The Major wanted to get back to Harpers Ferry as soon as possible to establish a testing protocol with Major Mordecai on the new gun.

Gunners Pendulum Hause

# 5 BLOODY KANSAS

Joshua and Harry O'Leary attended to the team on the late October morning; the trees surrounding the Fort had turned full color.

As the two Soldiers curried and brushed the horses they talked of home. Harry had been fascinated by Joshua's stories of the plantations particularly of the keeping of slaves. While Joshua had perpetually explained to Harry that the slaves always had belonged to others the Irishman, who had only known a fatherless and impoverished city life, called him "the gentryman." Harry admired Joshua's ability to read the complex technical manuals and instructions and he had often assisted his friend in sorting out the complex written instructions issued by the Company Command.

The two soldiers inspected their teams, each man responsible for two of the limber horses, and checked them for the tell-tale white spots of hair around their necks that indicated the harness collars were ill fitting or chafing.

They wore the more comfortable fatigue uniforms of sack coats and the shako hat without stiffener, crest or pom pom, which caused the crown to droop down over the brim in the "Western Campaigner" fashion.

After grooming they would exercise them for an hour by riding one and leading its companion, they took special care to alternate each to insure each horse would be comfortable functioning as either an "off" or "near" side horse.

Joshua asked Harry, "So how do you like the Wild West?"

Harry had gone into the growing Leavenworth City yesterday with the battery wagon on a detail and he remarked, "It's damned crazy, I'll say. Red Indians and bushwhackers, Teamsters, boatmen and Jayhawkers all drinking and fighting all the live long day!"

He grinned broadly as he slung the minimal artillery saddle on his gelding's back and fastened the girth, "I like it, beats the streets of Boston with all them Constables keeping an eye on ya!"

Harry seemed to like everywhere he was posted, the Army was the best life he had known, regular meals, clothes and pay. The adventure of different postings was a definite bonus.

Joshua had grinned remembering a supply trip the previous week to Weston, Missouri across the river. He had noticed that everyone had a large knife, due to fights from time to time the Captain had instructed details to wear the foot artillery swords which the locals greatly admired due to their resemblance of a huge Bowie knife. The result was that most soldiers were left alone.

As the men rode the mounts to exercise them in a crowded drill field with the other drivers and mounts, Joshua thought about home. He remembered the last letter he had received from Mr. Markley that contained the legal documents that he had to sign and have notarized by the Cavalry Regimental Adjutant that declared his father dead.

The document had split the land and the house, and remaining accounts between Joshua and Jacob. Markley's observations in his letter in regards to Joshua had been terse and businesslike, but he had sounded optimistic in regards to Jacob, who now was E.J. Markley's primary assistant in the surveying trade.

Joshua had replied once the Company had arrived at Fort Leavenworth in order that Jacob would have a new address, but Jacob never wrote.

The artillery horses were in a playful mood, clearly enjoying the crisp October air; it was a rare windless morning with a bright sun overhead. Joshua marveled at the great distances you could see from the knolls of the fort.

He realized why people wanted to leave the East for the adventure of the West. Everything was new or under construction and most of the land was owned yet by anyone, save God.

The two soldiers returned the horses to the Artillery Paddock and again groomed the animals and picked clean their feet, tomorrow was a fully rigged maneuvering drill for the Company so the guns and limbers as well as the caissons would maneuver as a battery under Captain Hunt's direct supervision.

Joshua enjoyed the complexity of maneuvering the teams of six horses through the paces of moving from column to line to unlimbering and forming the guns in battery. Because of the Captain's insistence on frequent drills, even the horses seemed to remember each task and uncannily anticipated commands by the drivers.

Joshua was fascinated by the intricacies of the drill as Captain Hunt's directives started to make sense of the confusing diagrams in the Artillery Manual.

As they released the horses back into the paddock with the others, Harry described what he had heard in Leavenworth City yesterday, "I watched this Free-Stater get in an argument with a Missouri bushwhacker outside the Planters Hotel. Four other Missouri fellows appeared like out of nowhere and they tried to push him in front of a freight wagon on the street!"

Joshua nodded, when he could get a copy of the Kansas papers there were terrible stories from all over Eastern Kansas of people being shot and homes being burned down, as the two sides tried to sway the formation of the new State into either a slave state or a free state.

Joshua asked Harry, "Were they arguing politics or were they just drunk?"

Harry smiled and replied, "This Free Stater, he was drunk and orating to a couple of gentlemen. The minute he mentioned somethin' about "Squatter Sovereignty" is when the five friends tried to waylay him."

Joshua nodded; he had heard from the Corporal that slavery supporters were crossing the river to Kansas to vote in the election next month. To him it made little sense to fight over the issue and he had asked Corporal Shepperd if that was why the Company had come west.

Corporal Shepperd had replied, "Yes and No." He had explained that two separate campaigns were to be getting underway to suppress Indian trouble in Nebraska Territory and possibly due west through Kansas.

He smiled and said, "We are just staging here for a while in case somebody needs artillery. We also will be available to do anything else the Army thinks we need to do."

The following day Captain Hunt watched his Company execute company maneuver from Order in Column to Order in Line to Order in Battery in the open terrain west of Fort Leavenworth.

He wanted to be prepared for campaign in the rare event that the Cavalry commanders' dominant here in the Department of the West would tolerate the slower rate of travel that the standard 6 pounder companies usually traveled.

Since M Company, 2<sup>nd</sup> Artillery was a "Mounted" artillery company; it was more configured to match the pace of Infantry as there were no mounts for his gunners.

Henry Hunt was glad for the distraction in being posted to Fort Leavenworth, the death of Elizabeth at Fortress Monroe had gutted his spirit. He had to leave his son and daughter with his brother in law in Washington. Campaigning in Kansas kept his mind off his sorrow and he immersed himself in the work.

What had transpired in the past 5 months at Leavenworth had been highly political missions to "keep the peace" between two increasingly violent political movements within the new state of Kansas.

Captain Hunt had become thoroughly disgusted with the job of placing the Army between civilians.

General Smith had also repeatedly voiced his distaste for the missions that the Army was being asked to do.

Earlier in the summer they had received orders to disband an attempt by Free Staters to establish an alternative legislature in Topeka. The assignment had been passed to Colonel Sumner of the 1<sup>st</sup> Cavalry Regiment, and he returned from the mission a disgusted victor.

In just about every case of violence, there appeared to be always something beyond the political beliefs of the opponents. Usually there was a feud, dispute, or act of retribution that the Free State or Slave state belief was laid over like a veneer to cover the lawless act.

As the day's maneuvers were entering into the late afternoon, Captain Hunt turned to First Sergeant O'Keefe and remarked, "pass my compliments to the Sergeants, First Sergeant, the intervals are excellent and the sections are moving well!"

First Sergeant O'Keefe nodded and answered "Yes Sir."

The First Sergeant was inwardly fuming, he was noting a good degree of missing equipment where the men of the company were taking shortcuts.

O'Keefe turned to the Captain and suggested, "Sir, I would recommend we bivouac here on the maneuver ground for a few days, I would like to practice establishing camp and check the sections for the accuracy of their load plans for the guns and the caissons."

Captain Hunt smiled and asked, "Tentage?"

First Sergeant O'Keefe smiled back and replied, "I have 6 wagons coming out this evening with tents and rations."

Within the 1$^{st}$ Section of guns, Joshua had received direction to ride the near "Leader" which was the first two horse team of the 6 total horses that pulled the limber chest and attached 6 pound gun and carriage.

Corporal Sheppard had wished to see how he could handle on leader and maintain interval. The young private was clearly a quick study, although he was the quiet type. He tended to avoid discussions with the Sergeants, but he did everything he was asked and could always be found.

As the Gunner of the number 1 gun of the number 1 section, Corporal Sheppard was the most highly respected corporal in the company aside from Mills who bore the company guidon on this day. There might be a day where he could sew on the stripes of a Sergeant; of course Mills would get it first.

Since he had a new Lieutenant, the same Lieutenant Benson that they had trained last fall, he figured he could convince him to put in a good word with the Captain from time to time.

He watched as Timmonds guided the team to break off from the line of column into the right direction of travel for a transition to "on Line" before he had to be given command and grinned.

He remembered Sergeant O'Brien's amazement at the request by Timmonds to borrow a copy of the Drill Instructions for Field Artillery after he had finished the school of the piece at Fort Monroe.

O'Brien had secured a copy from O'Keefe after much asking and had presented to Timmonds with the stern enjoinder, "Lose it and you die, Boy'o!"

Sheppard had witnessed the transaction there and remembered O'Brien exclaiming, "Shit, I couldn't read at all until I was a corporal!"

Late in the Afternoon as the sun was getting low and the sections had relimbered the guns from their positions from battery on the plains, First Sergeant O'Keefe loudly announced, "We will resume column formation and proceed west gentlemen, we will stop when I direct it!"

A low moan came up from the ranks.

O'Keefe met the moan with, "Some of you didn't think on a bivouac now did ye! Hell I will bet I can find missing blankets, empty canteens, no rations and missing lamps in the battery wagons!"

He paced the line of men, horses and guns and shouted, "When this company leaves any camp at any time with any size element, you will proceed configured and loaded as if you expected to meet Armageddon! Is that understood?"

The men and the officers all nodded. Captain Hunt had notified them that he intended to stay as well, which effectively trapped them in place with their men. There would be no brandy and cigars at the club tonight.

Soon the small train of 6 baggage wagons appeared from Fort Leavenworth below the prairie training ground and the Company proceeded in column into the setting sun to the West. The First Sergeant directed a halt near a flat spot of ground about 4 miles from the training ground beside a small copse of trees.

He shouted out to the column, "Bring the guns and limbers on line on me!"

First Sergeant O'Keefe spread out his arms to indicate the line of guns and instructed the Sergeants to gather on him.

Once the Section Sergeants and Corporals had assembled around him he ordered, "Here we will establish a camp according to the 1st plan of Encampment, place the guard tent behind me facing the trees and get me 4 men for the first guard mount, with their muskets and bayonets if you please!"

Corporal Sheppard instructed Privates Decker and Brannon to go to the supply wagons at the trail of the column to draw 2 tents and poles and a picket stake as they would have to set the left stake of the Horse Picket line on the left side of the Guard tent. He turned to Timmonds and instructed him to report with his musket to the Sergeant of the Guard for the first watch.

As he secured his musket from the pile strapped to the limber he trotted over to the Guard Tent as it was being erected and reported to the Sergeant of the Guard, who immediately put him to work helping erect the tent. He then turned to Timmonds once the tent was up and instructed him to watch the southern corner and approaches to the camp, his relief would occur in 3 hours.

As Joshua stood in the dark, with his stomach rumbling in hunger, he watched as the encampment quickly took on order. The encampment had a row of tents being erected on the South and North axis of the 6 guns and limbers pointed to the West. The six caissons were neatly lined up behind the guns and limbers.

The horse picket lines were long ropes lined up along the tent rows between the tents and the guns, limbers and caissons and the harnesses and collars were laid neatly on the ground between the picket lines and the tents. Joshua was amazed that it only took the company about an hour to get everything in place but he did hear load grumbling and shouts about missing blankets and solicitations for water from amongst the gun crews. This side trip was a definite surprise.

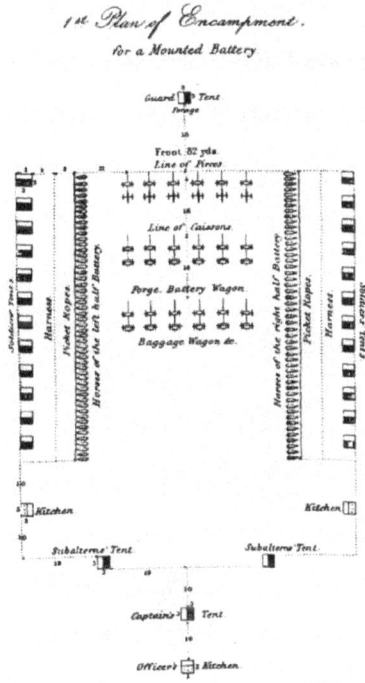

1st Plan of Encampment.
for a Mounted Battery

Joshua was relieved after 3 hours by Private Newby from the caisson section after it was completely dark outside, returning to his tent he saw his messmates, Corporal Sheppard, Private Brannon and Harry around a small smoky fire, they handed him some hard army crackers and asked him if he wanted some coffee.

Joshua gladly accepted and after stowing his musket in the tent he produced his tin cup and took a cupful from the small boiler perched precariously on the wood of the fire.

"We had to start it with Buffalo shit." Remarked Brannon, "Corporal Sheppard found us the wood in the trees."

Sean Brannon was yet another Irishman who came out of New York nearly fresh off the boats of immigrants escaping the great depression that swept the British Isles.

He looked at Joshua and with a wink he said, "If you give me your share of the pork I can cook it up for us, then we can soften this Army bread in the grease."

Brannon liked the job of Mess Cook, having done it all through the journey to Fort Leavenworth by both rail and riverboat down the Missouri River.

Joshua remarked that he never drew a ration in the morning because he was hooking the teams.

Brannon smiled and said, "Not to worry lad, we've stolen an extra for you!"

Soon he had produced a small iron skillet and was frying the salt pork. Joshua loved the smell of the cooking meat and the freshly ground coffee combined with the brisk fresh air of the October evening.

If only the wind did not blow so much.

The men talked into the evening, Corporal Shepperd had begun to loosen up towards Private Timmonds as he had clearly proven to be a natural for the regulars.

Shepperd simply wondered why a native would elect to join the Army coming from such a life of privilege. He shared with Joshua his origins as the son of a Nitrate miner in Western Virginia, Joshua politely asked him many questions concerning the why and how of the trade, and Shepperd explained that it was the raw material for gun powder, like what they were using on the guns.

He concluded his answers with, "I decided not to have the life of my father, working in the dark all the live long day, with mother never knowing if he would come back."

Captain Hunt had gathered the Company officers in his tent for an evening meeting. He was pleased overall and wanted to keep them isolated in the field so they could bond and rely upon one another.

Hunt worried that the Company would be split up to do odd details like other companies had witnessed, He remembered one Officer telling him how they had used artillery horses and gun crews to assist in hunting a slave that had run away last summer.

Hunt was determined to make M Company 2$^{nd}$ Artillery the best in the Army. He had spent too much of his time being a development and tactics staff officer for the Ordnance Department and he genuinely feared the affect his intellect would have on his career.

He had sworn to himself that so long as he commanded this Company it would be the most effective and professional Artillery Company in the U.S. Army. The command of a line company was essential to remain competitive in the small branch of Artillery.

He started out his meeting by introducing Lieutenant Benson to the rest of the Officers, adding "If you recall, we trained this young lad last year at Fortress Monroe! I was so impressed with his performance that I twisted his arm to request M Company and he was foolish enough to accept!"

The other officers laughed. Crowded in the tent was Captain Hunt, Lieutenant Benson commanding the 1st section, Lieutenant Platt, commanding the 2$^{nd}$ Section, Lieutenant Thompson, commanding the 3$^{rd}$ Section, and Lieutenant Pender who as the executive officer commanded the caissons and trains.

Captain Hunt loved Archie Pender the most, as his devious initiative usually resulted in the Company enjoying excesses that a Captain normally could not procure. Pender sometimes was of the habit of "eliminating the middleman" and coordinated many a direct deal off post for items as the situation warranted.

His unplanned bivouac was possible because the enterprising executive officer had intercepted rations at the landing at Leavenworth city yesterday direct from a Russell, Majors and Waddell freight wagon before it had made the turn into the Fort.

Hunt was direct with his officers, "I want you to use this time to visit your men, go and visit the crews of your section tonight, see that they have been fed, listen to gripes if you have to, and instill in them that they have to practice readiness."

The younger officers nodded in unison as Captain Hunt was considered at West Point to be a demi-god of artillery.

The rumors had been thick; according to Lieutenant Benson, that this was a leader to follow as, "his coat tails were likely to go far."

First Sergeant O'Keefe had quietly sat in the background puffing on his pipe. The Captain never barred his presence from the meetings of the officers as he desired to lead with an "open book" and wanted his senior enlisted leader to know what he had said and directed.

Hunt knew O'Keefe would beat the Lieutenants out of the tent and prepare the way for them.

The rising sun was only reddening the Eastern horizon when the Company bugler sounded *The Reveille* and the men of M Company groggily rolled out of blankets, stretching and yawning and the morning chill encouraged a sudden rush to find their woolen shell jackets and get dressed.

Corporal Mills, strolled among the men and said, "Once you are dressed get your gear picked up and stowed where it belongs, if you want to keep it. I expect to move this morning."

Moments later the Bugler sounded Water Call, and Joshua and Harry went out to collect their teams, the companies drivers after releasing their horses from the picket rope all to a man were looking about in confusion, the common question arising, "where is the water?"

No one had thought to reconnoiter the location when they established camp.

First Sergeant O'Keefe who had mounted himself on a limber parked at the head of the camp shouted out to the confused drivers, "There is a small brook behind the Guard tent; behind me. In the future make damn sure you know where to water the animals before you gets under your blankets!"

He shook his head disgustedly, newly determined to have a Sergeants meeting tonight, a meeting out of earshot of the Captain.

A collection of stupid errors could cause a unit to be lost, the Company had enjoyed far too much garrison duty, a few days in the prairie would make them see. In his walk about last night he noted a distinct weakness in his Sergeants taking the responsibility to see that the men did not make their own decisions about what gear they needed to bring when they departed the post.

He decided to reinforce his "Hook and Strap" principal once again as the Sergeants who had heard the rant before, knew it was O'Keefe's personal philosophy; that directly quoted was, "If the Army made a fookin' hook or a fookin' strap for the fookin' shit then it best be there hangin' on its fookin' hook or fookin' strapped down!"

O'Keefe held these beliefs not because he was small minded, rather combat in Mexico had amply illustrated to him, how small things become large when they are needed badly.

After the horses and men had been fed, Captain Hunt ordered the company to move several miles East until he came upon a piece of terrain that had a low ridge that made an ideal location for Artillery.

Hunt directed his bugler to sound "By the Right Flank" to break the column to the right and into line for establishing in Battery on the ridge. The Captain then spurred his horse and quickly rode to the position forward of the crest of the ridge where he wanted the guns to position.

As the limbers and the guns came up he insured that the men were spurred by the Lieutenants to move quickly. The Company needed to be able to action left or right instinctively and also the Lieutenants needed to understand the ground.

Hunt directed them to place the guns on the forward slope of the ridge to provide full freedom of fire and not silhouette the piece on the skyline. He then directed the horse teams to be led onto the reverse slope where they would be protected from counter battery fire, which was most effective when targeted against the horses.

Hunt walked the line and watched as the crews unlimbered the pieces and moved them by hand into the proper positions. He made it a point to pause with each Lieutenant and indicate to them the folds in the ground before the positions and to quiz them on the ranges to those distinct areas.

Joshua led his team to the crest of the ridge and noting the Captain motioning him on, continued past it and quickly halted. With a tug on his reins he expertly backed the team to take the tension off the pin tail hitch that linked the lunette of the 6 pounder to the limber, the gun crew who had been trotting alongside quickly pulled the link pin and unhooked the gun.

Joshua then led the limber around behind the gun as the crew rotated the piece to face forward into the small valley below the ridge. Then he dismounted along with Harry and Corporal Shepperd and readied the limber chest as Harry held the team. The caisson teams followed the limbers up the ridge but stopped short of the crest on the other side as ordered by Lieutenant Pender.

Joshua watched as Corporal Shepperd announced, "Prepare to Fire" and the crewmen secured their implements from the mounting points on the gun. The crews once in battery conducted gun drill for the rest of the morning. At the conclusion of the session Captain Hunt assembled the Officers and ran through his observations with them. He then directed them to do the same with each section, so that every Soldier would also understand the reason for the drill.

The Company paused for lunch at the battery location, then remounted the guns and repeated the drill on the same ridge. Captain Hunt directed the sections to rig the prolongue ropes to the lunettes of the guns and had the crews' practice manually displacing the pieces back over the ridge, without horses it was sometimes necessary for the cannoneers to move the pieces to safety employing only man power.

Company M returned to the previous night's bivouac location and quickly reestablished camp, Due to the heavy maneuvering the Company forge was lit and the blacksmith went to work replacing several lost shoes on the horses from the day's exercises. While the crews and gunners checked and stowed equipment, the drivers checked and oiled their harnesses, First Sergeant O'Keefe conducted a lengthy Sergeants call.

Later that evening a rider from Fort Leavenworth arrived with urgent orders for Captain Hunt at the Guard Tent of the Bivouac. The Sergeant of the guard directed him to the Captain's tent at the far end of the Bivouac and he rode there and delivered the folded dispatch to the curious officer, who was concluding his evening officer's call.

Captain Hunt read the message and loudly exclaimed, "Well I'll be damned! I have orders to go to Harper's Ferry, and to be there no later than the 10th of November."

Lieutenant Pender quickly asked, "Sir, are you losing your command?" with a certain look of worry on his face.

Hunt, waving his hand dismissively, answered, "No, no it's the damn manual again. We are being assembled to rewrite the Instruction for Field Artillery, again!"

He shook his head and looked at the assembled officers, "I expect this will last through the winter, I will likely have to depart tomorrow. Lieutenant Pender will act as commander in my absence. You are dismissed to your men, I expect you to take the lessons of today and apply them, get these soldiers out in the field often to practice what we have done. And work with the damned quartermasters to allow them to live fire!"

He turned and looked at Archie Pender as he made his last comment.

Captain Hunt left the tent to find and talk to First Sergeant O'Keefe, he would have to rely on him to keep things running during his absence.

In the months that followed, the absence of Captain Hunt became painfully apparent, General Smith assigned every manner of political assignments to M Company. While the cavalry and infantry units were sent on campaigns into Nebraska and the Platte River valley the artillery troops were detailed to support the National Elections. The typical duty on that day was for a section to defend a polling place with empty gun and limber chest.

Lieutenant Pender was only to hold two more bivouac field training sessions with no ammunition. With Captain Hunt gone, the quartermasters starting to become tight with every aspect of supply and Lieutenant Pender began to realize that his Captain had been in a constant fight to protect the interests of M Company, he wished he would conclude his business at Harper's Ferry and return.

In Mid-November Joshua heard his name when Corporal Mills conducted Mail Call, He was dumbfounded to receive an envelope written in a feminine hand, tearing it open he read,

*"My Dearest Joshua,*
*Having found your letter to Father and having ascertained your most recent*
*address, I deign to correspond with you from time to time if you will permit.*
*It is odd to see your brother Jacob almost daily and never a word is heard*
*in regards to your health or daily business. Father has said that you have*
*gone for good like the men who left for California after gold. I sincerely*
*pray against this being the case as many, to include the slaves, discuss the*
*pain of your absence from our lives. If you find the time, between fights*
*with wild Indians, to write, I would be most grateful for news. Jacob has*
*been discussing joining the militia with E. J. as it is all the fashion in the*
*Charleston District now. There is word that the Governor will form a*
*regiment of cavalry to defend South Carolina if Nullification occurs.*
*With your military experience you could likely return and find high favor in*
*such company as our brothers.*
*Please give me the courtesy of a response when you are able.*
*Earnestly*
*Lottie"*

The letter left Joshua dumbfounded he exclaimed to himself, "damn! I never noticed!"

Harry quickly snatched the letter from Joshua and quickly reading it he laughed, "Boy'o! You never told us you had a Maureen!"

Joshua just shook his head stammering, "It ain't like that!"

Word of Lottie's letter spread throughout the mess. Most of the soldiers received no mail except from worried mothers.

The fame surrounding it made Joshua a minor celebrity in the Company.

Joshua wondered about the additional mention of Nullification, remembering his discussions with Mr. Cross on the trip to Norfolk. It disturbed him to think that the fools that were constantly fighting in Kansas were discussing similar notions, and forming similar types of militias. He wondered what was happening to the country he had sworn to protect.

Nevertheless he decided to write a reply, it would help to maintain contact with what remained of his family, indirect contact with Jacob was better than none at all. And if he could finally determine his father's fate, he would at least be able to get word to his brother

# Macbeth, South Carolina
# October 1857

Jacob Timmonds was sweating profusely as he drug the heavy surveyor's chains through the swampy creek to lay out the distance of a new boundary that E.J. had been hired to mark. E.J. had promised they would have the line marked by noon so he hurried to finish the task.

Jacob was in a hurry because Tom and Louis Markley had suggested they ride to Bonneau that afternoon for a Hog Barbecue that the militia company was putting on that evening. Tom and Louis had joined the Wassamassaw Cavalry last spring for the pure hell of it and tonight had marked the end of 1$^{st}$ annual encampment for the company.

In part the boys had been motivating by the grumbling of their grandfather. Tom was to be 18 soon and he had been pressing his father to support him enrolling at the Arsenal in Columbia.

If Tom got his way, then Jacob could fill his spot in the militia company. Key to joining the Wassamassaw Cavalry was the introduction from a respected member. The organization contained far more social than military content.

E. J. understood Jacob's haste, he knew the boy had lost his entire family and he needed to genuinely belong to something. He sometimes wondered what Joshua was up to, but Kansas sounded like it was keeping him fairly busy. He laughed to himself to watch Lottie read the Mercury feverishly every time a story about Kansas was printed.

"Stop about there!" E.J. cried out to Jacob, "Read out the mark!"

Jacob looked down at the last pull and replied back through the deep woods, "37 and a quarter!"

E.J. had him hold the staff up and he sighted as well as he could through the thick woods.

Taking the sighting he moved him several feet to the left and rechecked the azimuth on the transit, then shouted out, "Drive a stake where the staff sits!"

He leaned back and watched Jacob hammer in a wooden stake deep in the woods.

E.J. wiped his brow and called out, "Alright Jacob, that's our last corner! Bring back the chain!"

Jacob trotted back, hastily retrieving the surveying chain in coils. Once back he carefully loaded the equipment into the mule drawn wagon and waited as E.J. carefully packed the transit back into its protective box. He then made some notes on the land plat map of the property and then rolled them carefully and returned them into a round leather carrier.

Looking at Jacob, he said, "I would advise you to clean up once we get back to Somerset, and put on some decent clothes. The boys in the Wassamassaw Militia don't accept no ragamuffins, you know!"

Once they had returned Jacob thanked E.J. for the short day and dashed into the main house. Edward Markley had given the boy a bedroom upstairs and the family had basically become foster parents to him. Edward had consented to allow him to take up Tom on the invite to Bonneau. The elder Markley was somewhat concerned that the Militia would corrupt him. He knew that they loved their whiskey and most of the musters degenerated into drinking festivals, he felt responsible for the boy.

Edward and E.J. sat on the front porch and discussed the day. Edward had just finished reading the latest Mercury and he told him about a story he had read about a certain Senator Sumner who had insulted South Carolina's Senator Brooks on the floor of the U.S. Congress. He then read parts of the story that detailed how the South Carolina Senator had physically beaten the man with his cane.

"Damn near killed him!" exclaimed Edward.

The recently released news of the Dredd Scott case from the Supreme Court seemed to reinforce the Democratic Party stance on the slavery issue, but the radical Republicans and Abolitionists never seemed to quit their fervor. Edward expressed his concerns to his eldest son.

He was concerned that the loss of his labor force would make the cultivation and sale of cotton impossible to conduct in a profitable fashion.

E.J. mentioned to his father that he had heard that nearly 400 South Carolinians had traveled to Kansas to vote in the '56 election. Edward nodded, he had heard the same. Edward remembered then the last letter he had received from Joshua.

"That older Timmonds boy sounds like he likes soldiering," Edward mused.

E.J. countered, "Yep, he is free as a bird while we watch his family for him."

Edward just waved his hand; he secretly admired Joshua's adventurous nature and said, "Boy's just like his Pa was. He strikes out and don't look back."

E.J. wiped his brow and asked, "You going to let Tom go the Arsenal in Columbia this fall?"

Edward rocked some and replied, "Can't see why not, might do him good. They might kick some of the wild out of him."

The older man then added, "Word is the Governor may be increasing the size of the Militia, Tom could get an education and a commission in the State Troops."

E.J. nodded.

After a pause E.J. blurted out, "You know I caught Lottie writing him a letter the other day."

Edward grunted and said, "Nothin' like a hopeless romance between my youngest daughter and a wanderer."

As the two men sat and talked they saw Jacob come around from the back mounted on one of the hunting horses wearing his best clothes and boots.

E.J. called out to him, "Mind your manners in Bonneau boy!"

Jacob laughed and Edward commented, "Make sure you come back with Tom and Louis! And tell Captain Winters that I said hello!"

He turned to his oldest son and said, "I wish his father was alive to see how the boy has grown up."

Jacob rode fast down Black Oak Road, he wanted to get the 15 miles to Bonneau behind him as fast as he could. He had admired the fine uniforms Tom and Louis wore for the infrequent Musters and craved to wear one as well.

If Joshua could join something he could too, he thought.

The Marsh Tacky pony was starting to lather with the exertion of the trip but Jacob would not let up, he felt uniquely qualified to be a Cavalryman, and he knew the horse had a lot of endurance left in her, they were a tough breed.

Tom was talking to Louis as the Commissary Sergeant was checking the progress on the pig that had been roasting since before dawn. The Sunday morning drill had dissolved by noon by disinterest of the irregular Cavalrymen.

The Sunday night party was eagerly anticipated and Captain Winter did not begrudge them their relaxation. The previous day had been spent in morning riding drills in the small open field east of Bonneau and had concluded with a target shooting session with the old Hall breech loading carbines that the State had issued them.

Captain Winter had not been able to get sabers yet but was pestering the State when he got a chance between his job as a lock keeper on the Santee Canal. He resolved they would just train as mounted riflemen until he got the rest of the weapons. In the interim he kept the militiamen coming to drills by the sheer fun of the assemblies.

There was a clear desire among the members to associate and recreate over practicing the military arts. The men were becoming anxious to engage in festivities following a hard day of drilling.

The State had actively encouraged the formation of the Militias partly in response to the constant threat of insurrection among slaves and partly to insure South Carolina could defend her borders if threatened.

The people of the state were proud of the thrashing they had given the British in the revolution and remained resolved to thrash anyone who dared threaten them again.

Tom saw Jacob approaching the encampment at a gallop, he nudged Louis and said, "Betcha' he galloped that poor ass pony the whole damned way!"

With a whoop Jacob pulled up to his "half-brothers" as he called Tom and Louis.

Tom observed, "Well Jacob you are just in time, the Captain is about to hold the final muster roll call and plans on giving an oration, will be a good chance after to have your introduction!"

Jacob nodded and took the pony over and tied him off with the others on the picket rope.

Captain Winters had his bugler sound "Assembly" and the sharply dressed militiamen assembled in a quick formation.

Jacob greatly admired their smart looking shell jackets with buff facings and black trim and 3 rows of brass buttons. Most of the men wore fine English riding boots with kid leather tops.

He imagined they looked just as Francis Marion's swamp cavalry had looked during the revolution. He was also fixated on the businesslike hall carbines each bore on the hip hung upon a broad leather shoulder strap. He resolved to ask Tom and Louis if he could examine one once the muster was finished.

Once the men were assembled Captain Winters ordered the First Sergeant to call out roll. Once the calling of names was complete he had the men fall out around him in a semi-circle and invited them to sit if they chose. He then removed his feather plumed slouch hat and addressed his company;

*"Men, it has been an honor to share in your company this week! On behalf of the Commander of Coastal Cavalry I thank you for your dedication to South Carolina by making the time to assemble as part of this newest force protecting our State and our way of life! Our Governor has called upon the citizens of the State to remain aware that South Carolina must always be prepared to stand alone, if need be; to protect her peoples. Your participation here demonstrates that you have answered that call. Most of you are aware of the strange clamor that dominates the news today, radical elements call for the destruction of us and our way of life, as well as demanding the release, without recompense, of our private property by demanding manumission of our slaves. In some quarters, within our supposedly holy union of States, there are those who are actively planning servile insurrection against the good people of our State. We must collectively endeavor to stand ready to protect the interests of the people and to defend the sovereignty of South Carolina from these radical and extreme elements. The Governor and the legislature have placed their faith in you to stand proudly in defense of your homes and families against any foe, be he from afar or from within! So long as there is a Wassamassaw Cavalry there will be no "Turner Revolts" in the Charleston District. Remember your proud heritage as South Carolinians. When the British attempted to subdue us, your forefathers rode with Marion. When the Country called, your Fathers and some among us went as volunteers to fight Santa Anna in Mexico, more from the South than any other place! I ask you to remain resolved to take a stand for South Carolina if we are called. Our honor will be defended, remember that! Our next muster will*

*be in March. I expect to procure an issue of sabers and have made plans that we will train the platoons in both saber and carbine at that next assembly. Tonight after you collect your pay I will be happy to share in our feast and you will be released to home in the morning. If any man has issues with his employment or needs me to discuss your calling with overseers or supervisors I am happy to assist you in that. First Sergeant, have the Troop Fall out!"*

First Sergeant Dennis quickly issued minor administrative instructions to the distracted assembly, who were becoming increasingly interested in Barbecue and spirits, and directed them that the pay table would be ready to begin issuance of drill pay in an hour.

Tom and Louis grabbed Jacob and made their way to the Captain who was discussing with First Sergeant Dennis when he expected the carbines to be cleaned and returned that evening.

Turning from his business he looked at the trio asking, "Is this the Timmonds boy?"

Jacob without hesitation replied, "Yes Sir! Jacob Timmonds!" and extended his hand.

Captain Winters looked him over quickly and asked, "So are you determined to join our company? I will have an opening if Tom is accepted to attend the Arsenal this fall."

Jacob quickly nodded.

Tom added, "Sir, he is an excellent rider and Father has basically adopted him since the death of his own father. He is from an old Charleston family that has sadly been beset with tragedy so the Markley family is willing to vouch for his character."

Captain Winters nodded and said, "Well then provide me a written application at the March assembly, you may attend the entire assembly as a recruit, there will be no pay sadly, but you will be fed. I would like to see how you get on with the others."

Jacob again shook the Captain's hand and thanked him for his consideration and was towed away back to the platoon area so they could clean their carbines for turn in to the Supply Sergeant's wagon.

As they sat around a large fire and cleaned the weapons, Jacob got the chance to handle the strange breech loading carbine. He was fascinated by the assembly that opened from the top allowing loading into the tip up breech that also contained the hammer and lock works.

Louis exploited his curiosity by allowing him to clean his carbine for him. He would occasionally inspect and reject his work. Tom chuckled at the exploitation and joked with Bill Carson, a neighbor of the Markley family.

Jacob asked Tom when and how recruits got their uniforms. Tom patiently explained that members got a paper pattern and it was the responsibility of the recruit to have one made.

He then offered, "I will give you mine anyhow, Momma can tailor it to you, I will not be needing it anymore as once I am at the Arsenal they will issue me State Militia uniforms."

Tom explained to Jacob how the system worked. He described how the cadets there were enlisted into the South Carolina State Militia and performed guard duties at the Arsenal in Columbia while studying various higher education degrees for two years. Those who excelled were then sent to the Citadel in Charleston to man the Armory there and complete their respective degrees. He gave the boy a short history of the system that was founded following the Turner Revolt and formed the basis of the standing State Militia system.

Jacob noticed that the cavalrymen were closing onto the fire pit where the rather large pig was being prepared.

Nudging Louis who had started to share drinks with their platoon mates, he asked, "Is the barbecue ready?"

Louis laughed and assured him, "Be patient Jacob, the First Sergeant will have the bugler call us when they are ready."

The men sat, drank and talked as the sun set. Jacob envied the ready friendships they all shared, as most of them were neighbors since childhood, he realized that he was fortunate to receive an offer to join. As Tom introduced more and more of the men to him he realized upon hearing the names, that these were the sons of the richest families in Saint James, Santee, and Saint John's Berkeley parishes.

To his delight they all welcomed him and warmly accepted him in their company.

The evening repast was some of the best eating he had experienced. The outdoor air, alcohol, and good company made the Barbecued pork, steamed oysters, cornbread and stewed vegetables taste even better than he could imagine.

As he grabbed his plate to secure a third helping, Tom reminded him, "remember too, Jacob they do this at the end of every muster!"

The Company turned in to sleep very late that evening. Captain Winters used the Barbecue as a valuable recruiting and retention tool for his fledgling organization. By releasing them in the morning also no one would go home drunk and stain the honor of the Wassamassaw Cavalry.

That next morning as the boys saddled their horses to return to Macbeth, a rider approached the Markley house at Somerset with a letter addressed to Norman Timmonds. The servant summoned Edward Markley from his breakfast with the letter.

Edward considered waiting on Jacob to return but decided to open the letter anyway since the return address was from a shipping company in Charleston and had been postmarked from the week prior.

He quickly opened the envelope and exclaimed out loud, "Well I'll be damned!"

Elizabeth asked him what was wrong, Edward looked up, holding the letter, "Seems that Norman did find and purchase a marine steam engine when he went to Norfolk!

That self-same engine is currently warehoused in Charleston, having come in by ship last month. They want to arrange shipment of it here to Macbeth and someone has to pay the bill!"

He pondered a moment and decided; he went to the hall and pulled on his boots.

Elizabeth was puzzled, "You haven't finished your breakfast!"

Markley replied, "No matter dearest, I have to go into Moncks Corner and find Mr. Ebaugh, he is the only man in the parish that understands steam engines!"

Elizabeth stared at the unfinished meal and exclaimed to herself, "Oh, my! Another project."

# 6 THE MODEL 1857 LIGHT GUN

## Fort McHenry, Maryland
## May, 1857

A warm ocean breeze blew by the cluster of officers on the tidal flat; that had assembled to test a new gun for the Army.

Major Alfred Mordecai had overseen the creation of the prototype and was determined to see the Army accept the light 12 pound cannon as a standard piece for the artillery in the 4 artillery regiments that made up the U.S. Army's artillery structure.

He had been frequently frustrated but felt the Secretary of War Davis had brought to the efforts of the Ordnance Corps; a veteran's perspective to what soldiers and armies needed in terms of practical and modern arms.

In charge of the weeks' proceedings was Colonel Horace Brooks of the 2nd Regiment of Artillery, he had the unfortunate task of assuming command following the death of Colonel Bankhead that same month.

He had assembled a board of note, consisting of Major Reynolds of the 4th Regiment of Artillery, Major French of the 1st Artillery, author of the current manual of instruction for artillery, and Captains Phelps of the 4th Regiment and

Barry of the 2<sup>nd</sup> Regiment. All were keen to see if the concept of the light gun-howitzer would prove practical.

In their collective experience, all thought the aged 6 pounder fell far short of what the modern artillerist required to prevail on the battlefield. All were eager to see the new light 12 pounder Field Gun.

Journals from the war in Crimea had detailed the superiority of the French design and now America would have the same, perhaps; if Congress would assent to purchasing enough to make a difference.

Alfred Mordecai wanted to see the piece, and had shown up early in the morning at the training ground as Captain Phelps and Barry had, well before Colonel Brooks. It had been a rainy week and the drill grounds chosen to host the mobility test were definitely soggy.

The artillery company providing the testing teams and gun crews had two standard 6 horse teams and limbers with a 6 pounder field gun and the new prototype tube, mounted on a No#2 24 pounder carriage.

Mordecai strolled over and wished the men a good morning while returning their salutes. The gun gleamed with the appealing crispness that new bronze guns displayed.

While most had assumed the gun would easily be accommodated by the No#2 carriage; Mordecai quickly noticed that the elevating screw on the carriage stock was offset too far to the rear; he made a mental note to have the carriage modified to correct the misalignment.

Walking around and peering into the shining bore, he noted no chamber, simply a straight tube with a rounded bottom. He remembering the French Canon-obusier at Liege and was pleased. He glanced at the muzzle and smiled again to see the "BH" stamped there, Huger had wasted no time getting this prototype produced.

While they waited on Colonel Brooks to arrive Mordecai chatted with the Soldiers on the detail, asking "Well gentlemen what are your thoughts on this new piece?"

The corporal who would be the gunner replied, "Not sure yet sir, we have not been able to fire her yet, but she is trim and if she throws a 12 pound shot well, we will certainly have a better gun."

After a pause he added, "Her weight is funny though, she is too heavy at the breech, you really have to yank on the screw to elevate the tube."

Mordecai nodded and returned to the gun and putting his hands on the knob of the cascabel, he lifted. Clearly a balance problem, the trunnions had been cast in too far forward a position. He produced a pad and pencil from his pocket and made a few feverish notes.

He then returned to the corporal, "I am grateful for your observations as we do this test, I would like to interview you from time to time as we conduct each test to gather your impressions of this gun."

The corporal astonished by being solicited by such a high ranking officer happily assented.

Colonel Brooks and Major French arrived at the small testing grounds and warmly greeted Mordecai. Major Mordecai walked him over to the prototype and explained some of the initial problems noted in the compatibility between the cannon and the carriage and suggested that the blacksmiths and ordnance men at Fort McHenry correct the elevation screw mismatch prior to firing tests, Colonel Brooks had Major French consult with Captain Barry to arrange for the modifications.

The officers watched as the artillerymen pulled both a 6 pounder and the new light 12 pounder along identical terrain attached to limbers behind a 6 horse team. Mordecai watched the men carefully to see if there was significant difficulty with the larger caliber gun as the cannoneers assisted the team in moving the gun through a boggy spot.

To his satisfaction both appeared to neither trouble the teams of horses or the men on foot assisting the carriage when needed.

After an hour of various demonstrations, Colonel Brooks turned to Mordecai and observed, "It appears the mobility test is a success, Major Mordecai, I propose we assemble with the Ordnance department this afternoon to look to the 12 pound ammunition to be assembled for the live fire testing the day after tomorrow."

Mordecai agreed.

After lunch at the Officers Mess at Fort McHenry, the delegation visited with the Ordnance Sergeant preparing the rounds for the test at the central magazine casemate at the fort. The Sergeant showed them the collection of solid shot, shell, spherical case shot, and canister he was preparing for the test.

The Sergeant asked Major Mordecai, "Sir, just to confirm before we make up powder bags for the fixed rounds that your desire is for charges of 2 and 1/4 pounds?

Mordecai nodded but added in response, "My intent is to ultimately attempt to determine ballistics of a 2 and ½ pound charge, but for now I intend to use the French load."

Mordecai also asked the Sergeant to insure that there were at least 12 blank charges for both the 6 and 12 pound guns. He wanted to test the friction primers, and vents of the pieces. The men examined the fuses that would be employed and decided to use only the Bormann fuse for the firing.

Major French emphatically agreed hoping that Mordecai might consider discontinuing the wooden fuses altogether as they proved frustratingly unreliable.

That evening the officers assembled after dinner back at the club and over brandy and cigars, discussed the on-going rewrite of the manual for Instruction for Artillery.

Mordecai had already updated the Ordnance Manual but he reminded Colonel Brooks that this new gun would have to be proofed and accepted before a full update could be realized.

The Officers were fascinated as Mordecai described future developments underway. He described at length some of the concepts being worked at present, sharing early findings of Captain Parrot at West Point and of some ideas for wrought iron rifles under consideration that might prove far safer than the current generation of cast iron.

Major French quizzed him on the English guns and the rifle designs that he had heard about. Mordecai explained that he had seen them but was far from convinced that bronze cannon would last very long firing the English iron lugged Blakely projectiles. French had spent the past 3 months with his friend, Henry Hunt laboring over the rewrite of the manual of instruction at Harper's Ferry.

Henry had been anxious to complete his work in order to return to his Company at Fort Leavenworth. French admired his desire to return to his soldiers and had heard from Colonel Brooks that he was receiving high praise in the Regiment.

French resolved to volunteer Hunt's Company to test the new guns, as no one understood artillery as well as Henry Hunt.

The next morning Mordecai had eschewed an invitation to visit Baltimore with Colonel Brooks and the Majors of the testing party.

He elected instead to observe the artificers at the Ordnance shop as they modified the 24 pounder carriage to fit the new gun.

The men quickly removed the elevating screw mechanism and chiseled out a new channel further up the stock to fit the shorter tube. Mordecai had always been fascinated by the talent of the artillery mechanics, his visit had also permitted him time to compare his large schematics against the actual gun.

As the men labored to complete the modification, Mordecai planned a few more on his schematic using a red pencil. It occurred to him that he must communicate with Benjamin Huger at Harper's Ferry very soon in order to introduce these changes to the next 4 versions before the foundry started work on the next set of guns.

After a few hours labor he decided to visit the Headquarters to get a telegram drafted and sent to Huger.

Later that afternoon at Harper's Ferry, Benjamin Huger was preparing to leave the office when a clerk brought him the telegram, it read,

*"Huger, wish to advise dimension changes to light 12 pound gun. Advise foundry to cease production on next 4 guns until plans delivered to you. Mordecai"*

Huger after reading the message, quickly scribbled a note for the clerk and said, "Get this sent to Ames in Chicopee as soon as possible."

On the 18th of May the Officers assembled again on another part of the tiny peninsula that Fort McHenry dominated to see the firing test. Mordecai inspected the final work on the carriage and was satisfied that at least the contact between the elevating screw and the breech of the light 12 pound gun was adequate, only a dimensional change would change the weight problem.

The firing trials would be into the water as there was no sufficient amount of land to fire across without placing hazard to activities around the fort. An old salt pork barrel had been placed on a raft to serve as a target roughly 500 yards distant.

Mordecai was amazed to see several civilian onlookers who had come to observe the test. Cannon tests were highly entertaining to the citizens of Baltimore, it seemed.

The crews upon the direction of Colonel Brooks loaded both guns with blank charges, deliberately omitting pricking the charge bags,

Mordecai looked at Major French quizzically and he explained, "We have had considerable discussion in regards to the efficacy of the new copper friction primers. We are deliberately loading blank charges, seam up, to see if we can induce a misfire."

Each gun fired six blank charges in every possible configuration without a misfire. The thunderous discharges were attracting more civilian spectators.

Colonel Brooks then instructed the gunners to try live fire with shot. Major Mordecai produced his notebook and moved closer to the guns, he wanted to note recoil on the light 12 pounder. The gun crew expertly executed the loading drill and on command discharged the gun, the discharge was clearly louder than the 6 pounder and Mordecai noted that the gun had recoiled nearly 15 feet back. Major French noted that the shot had been fired at zero elevation and had impacted the water, with a skip at around 600 yards; he realized a clear point blank range advantage to the 12 pound gun.

The crews then fired shell with maximum elevation. Mordecai noted lesser recoil distance and was pleased, as were the spectators with the distant boom of the projectile over the water. Spherical Case Shot was fired next with nearly identical results.

Major French noted a much larger impact splash when the shrapnel balls impacted in the water in comparison to the 6 pound case and pointed out the difference to Mordecai.

Canister was fired last, Colonel Brooks commanded the 6 pounder to fire first at the barrel and the observers noted the large splash around the barrel. He then directed the 12 pound gun to engage the same target. Following the much louder discharge, Mordecai was astonished by the difference in impacts, the Barrel was shredded and the beaten zone of the canister balls looked to be almost 50 feet wide.

Major French simply observed, "It is a hell of a gun!"

The following days testing was cancelled due to the torrential downpour.

Mordecai and the board spent the day at Colonel Brook's quarters discussing the impacts of what they had seen. Brooks and Mordecai agreed that the Army must have the gun but it should be tested first to build proper firing tables either with a unit or at Fortress Monroe.

Major French voiced his opinion that a unit would be best in order to put the pieces through a thorough troop test.

Mordecai interrupted his observation with, "You understand we can only afford to make 4 more prototypes at this time?"

French nodded but added, "Yes Alfred, I understand you would be short 2 guns of a complete battery, but you could equip the test unit with 2 1841 12 pound howitzers and you would at least have commonality of projectiles."

Brooks was clearly thinking about French's idea.

Mordecai simply shrugged and said, "It will be up the 2$^{nd}$ Regiment as the overall testing unit, how and who you have test the next 4. Just advise me on where to ship them."

Mordecai then showed the officers his amended dimensional sketches so they could understand the effect of the changes to the carriage. His objective was to redesign the tube to properly mate with a number 2 carriage without modification to the carriage. He also explained that he had seen some shoddy issues with the carriage pointed out to him by the artillerymen on the demonstration crews.

He concluded with, "It is our job as Ordnance to fix these flaws in manufacture to aid the soldiers on the piece. Just do not grumble if you get a lot of small modifications to make on those carriages."

On the last day of the test, Colonel Brooks did more mobility tests with full limber chests and only 4 horse teams. No notable difference in mobility was noted and both guns managed to become considerably mired in the muddy ground. Mordecai was satisfied that the light 12 pound gun was no more a hindrance to the men and horses than the standard 6 pound gun.

He conducted one final interview with the gun crews and was amused when one of the men asked him, "Can we keep her sir?"

Mordecai bid Colonel Brooks and Major French farewell, anxious to get back to work.

Lieutenant Colonel Brooks asked him as he was leaving, "What are we going to name it?"

Mordecai shrugged, "Not sure at all sir, will have to discuss it with the Ordnance Board. I suggest we refer to it as the "light 12 pound gun" for now."

Mordecai thought about the question and concluded; a gun this good would have to get a distinctive name.

## Fort Leavenworth, Kansas
## January 1858

Captain Hunt was glad to be returning to his company. And he had interesting news to share with his command. As he departed the gangway of the riverboat at the Leavenworth City landing he first wanted to meet with the newly established Ordnance officer at Fort Leavenworth to discuss the development he had worked out with Major Mordecai who had visited Harper's Ferry as he had labored over the still unfinished manual of artillery. Once he had learned why it could not be finished he was delighted to be the reason.

His battery had been selected to be the testing unit for an entirely new type cannon. Once Mordecai had described to him the concept he was anxious to develop a firing table for its unique set of capabilities.

In his baggage he had carefully secured a letter of authorization to have the newly forming Ordnance Depot at Fort Leavenworth to provide support to mount and equip the four gun tubes that were being shipped to Kansas within the month. Once refitted he was to conduct intensive gunnery; in order to build the firing tables that would be included in the updated manual of instruction.

He decided first to visit with his First Sergeant to catch up with M Company and determine how Lieutenant Pender had fared in his absence.

When he entered the Company offices, First Sergeant O'Keefe jumped up from his desk, knocking the chair over and shouted, "Jesus, Mary and Joseph the Captain has returned!"

He had a broad and happy smile on his face as he smartly stood to attention and saluted, "Welcome back Sir, you are a sight for sore eyes, by God!"

Corporal Mills was amazed; he had never seen O'Keefe smile like that. But he too was glad the Captain had returned. M Company had become an orphan without the presence of their notable Captain.

The men of M Company had become a constant source of unwanted details and found themselves constantly being parceled out to augment Cavalry and Infantry units that were vainly attempting to stem the violence between Militias of the Free-Staters and the Slavery advocates. He ruefully remembered that they always got there too late to change outcomes or to protect anything.

Lieutenant Pender returned to the Orderly Room as word got out that the Captain had returned and together the officers closed the door and he debriefed Captain Hunt on the past 4 months. He discussed the deployment to Lecompton under Lieutenant Colonel Cooke and the repeated expeditions to separate the confusing number of legal and illegal militias roaming the new State.

Shaking his head, Henry Hunt produced the orders and authorizations produced by the War Department and the Ordnance Department and showed them to Pender. "Things are going to change today."

Hunt stated grimly. "If you will excuse me now, I am going to visit General Smith," he said as he donned his hat and coat.

Major General Persifor Smith was just completing a dispatch to the War Department detailing the expeditions that had departed last summer, in response to War Department orders to the Department of the West to stage and initiate an expedition of Troops to the Utah Territory in response to threats posed by the followers of the Mormon Religion and their leader Brigham Young,

Smith was busy assisting Colonel Joseph Johnston with massive supply trains to support the expedition at the newly established Fort Douglas. He sincerely hoped that it would not come to an actual fight as the Department of the West would be hard pressed to reinforce or support Johnston in any meaningful way outside of contract resupply. Johnston's correspondence was indicating that the locals were none to helpful in provisioning his garrison. General Smith had originally been designated as the commander for this expedition but he was beginning to have longer and longer bouts of sickness, and Colonel Johnston had been selected to assume the command.

As he finished his report, his adjutant knocked on his door, "Excuse me sir, but Captain Henry Hunt from the artillery company has returned with specific instructions from the War Department."

Smith paused from his writing and replied, "By all means Major, send him in."

Smith knew of Hunt and liked him; his actions in Mexico were something that had made him a household name in the small community of the Army. Also the reports from Lieutenant Colonel Philip Saint George Cooke after the Lecompton affair proved the training and discipline of his company of artillery had been first rate.

As Hunt entered Smith said "Welcome back Major Hunt, we have missed you." Henry Hunt appreciated the use of his brevet rank as it was an indicator of respect by the senior officer and smiled.

"A good day to you as well sir, I hear you run an Ordnance Depot now."

Smith smiled and replied, "And damned little I know about it, to qualify me to run one Henry!" He added, "Please, by all means sit."

Hunt noticed the General looked very weak and frail.

Captain Hunt took a chair by the generals desk and produced the orders and letter of authorization, "Sir perhaps I can help, I have here letters of authorization to task the Ordnance Depot for direct support in the establishment of an experimental 12 pound light gun battery for research with orders to correspond directly with Major Mordecai of the Ordnance Department."

Smith looked over the letter and the orders and nodded. He was glad he had not attached M Company to the Utah expedition.

Hunt added, "Sir, this project promises to change Army artillery in perhaps a significant way; and the way I see it you are likely to be mentioned as an author of this change as it is your depot that will sponsor it."

Smith liked this and smiled. He reflected on the prospect of doing something that was interesting for a change. He was convinced that the entire Kansas affair had ruined his health.

He looked up at Captain Hunt and replied, "Henry, I will instruct our Ordnance officer, Captain Jenkins that he is to cooperate with this in every way. May I borrow the letter of authorization to make a copy?"

Hunt smiled and replied, "Please sir, keep the original as your record." Hunt kept it to himself that he already had asked for a duplicate of each order from Major Mordecai before he had left Harpers Ferry.

Smith looked Hunt with a certain sad expression and asked, "Henry, I heard the news of your wife last week. Please accept my condolences."

Hunt nodded, and mumbled, "Thank you sir, it has been hard but at least my children are in a nice home."

Smith countered, "Some evening I should like you to come to supper, Ann would be delighted to see you again."

General Smith directed his adjutant to show Captain Hunt the Ordnance offices and provide the introduction to Captain Jenkins so that the two could initiate the collaboration the endeavor would require. He was happy finally to be doing something good for the future of the Army, Kansas and the problems emerging in the Department of the West, while exciting was becoming depressing to him.

Captain Hunt wasted no time in getting the introduction to Captain Jenkins, there was much to be accomplished before the arrival of the guns and he wanted to get M Company into the field as soon as possible.

As Alfred Mordecai had expressed as they departed, "Get all you can accomplished before Mr. Davis leaves office because he has proven to be the best friend of the Army. If you can prove this gun perhaps he can influence Congress to equip the whole of the Army with them!"

Keeping this in mind Henry Hunt decided that he would have a firing table within weeks of receiving the guns. The creation of this data would enable him to have his company all to himself and they would be free of the mess that was Kansas.

To his surprise Henry Hunt found that David Jenkins was already aware of the project. Jenkins had warmly welcomed him into his office and revealed that he had been in recent correspondence with Major Mordecai and Huger in regards to the light guns. He indicated to Hunt to follow him and he took him on a tour of the Ordnance shops established in the Cavalry Stables recently built for the expedition to Utah.

"These are the 24 pounder carriages we are modifying for your guns, Henry," Jenkins said as he walked Hunt through the shops.

"We are simply adapting these limber chests from 12 pound Howitzers to facilitate the charges for the light gun," as he led him through another stable dedicated to the caissons and limbers.

"I expect to have an entire battery rolling stock available for you by the 1st of February if that is acceptable."

Hunt nodded amazed at the efficiency of the Ordnance Department artificers.

Jenkins motioned to Hunt, "Follow me to the magazines for a moment."

Hunt nodded and followed him as they crossed over a field to a complex of brick storehouses, inside an Ordnance Sergeant and soldiers were assembling fixed cartridges for artillery. They were working to load charges of large grained black powder into the woolen charge bags and affixing them to the wooden saboted projectiles.

Jenkins picked one up and handed it to Hunt, explaining, "Mordecai wanted you to know that we have decided to increase the standard charge to 2 and ½ pounds instead of the French load. He wanted to assure you that the tubes would safely accommodate the increase."

Hunt nodded, surprised by the larger size and weight of the fixed shot. He was familiar with the speculation and liked the boldness of the decision understanding that the charge increase would significantly increase the range of the piece.

Joshua warmed himself by the wood stove in the wooden troop barracks; he was chilled to the bone by the sharp Kansas winds that made a mockery of their issue overcoats. The drivers had been conducting the morning exercises of the horses. Harry brought him a tin cup from their bunks and the two shared what remained of an old pot of coffee from breakfast.

Corporal Shepperd and Sergeant O'Brien came in and muttered, "Make some space boys for us old men! Christ I hate these Kansas winters!"

As the soldiers stood warming themselves, O'Brien informed Sheppard that Captain Hunt was back. He was going to meet with O'Keefe this afternoon.

O'Brien then added, "I hear there is news that we may be doing something different."

Joshua asked, "Are we going on campaign Sergeant?"

O'Brien simply shrugged, "Not real sure Timmonds, guess we will have to wait to find out."

The Sergeant turned to Corporal Sheppard and directed him to assemble a wood cutting detail for the afternoon. They would be sent to the Northeastern edge of the post to cut more firewood for the barracks.

Harry nudged Joshua and winked, "We can volunteer Josh! We can look at them fine ladies on the fancy part of post on the way over!"

O'Brien laughed and countered, "We seen you ogling that damned ugly wash woman O'Leary!"

Members of the fairer sex were rare at Fort Leavenworth, the officer's wives made it a practice to hire the most homely and plain servants as possible, in futile hope of discouraging the enlisted men from being distracted. Most were quickly romanced by the troops.

The winters were the worst part of being in the West, there was no respite from the bitter winds scouring the plains, Drills on the guns had been reduced to once a day by Lieutenant Pender, who having been rejected by both expeditions for being "too much trouble and too slow" spent the majority of the available time cutting wood to provide heat for the quarters.

That evening First Sergeant O'Keefe summoned all the Sergeants and Corporals to assemble at his quarters for a meeting. Sergeant O'Brien and Corporal Shepperd were amazed as were all the others to hear the news that they had been selected to test the newest cannon in the Army inventory.

"It is going to be called the light 12 pounder, and it can throw a 12 pound shot close to 1600 yards at 6 pounder velocities," announced O'Keefe. "You can expect gunnery followed by gunnery for the rest of the winter so's the Captain can build himself a firing table for use by the rest of the Army."

He paused and then added, "Gents this is the Army telling us we are the best! Make sure you tell the men that. Remember that the drill will be important. It is a much bigger piece than you are used to. If you don't believe it, then go take a look at the carriages being prepared in the Ordnance shops!"

O'Keefe fielded questions from his sergeants and then dismissed them to their troops.

Near the end of February, 4 Russell, Majors and Waddell heavy freight wagons arrived on the Ordnance Grounds workshops. The teamsters advised the artificers there that the wooden crates were extremely heavy, close to 1300 pounds each and the unloading of each crate proved to be a large undertaking.

The Ordnance Sergeant sent a runner to notify Captain Jenkins that an important delivery had arrived.

Jenkins upon hearing the news saddled a horse and rode over to M Company to notify Hunt. The two expectantly rode over to the Ordnance yards to inspect the guns. By the time they had arrived the crews were tipping the first carriage with its trail straight up in the air, in order to load the tube into the cap squares on the cheeks. Hunt noticed that it took three men to steady the heavy gun tube during the mating process. Once the ordnance men had the alignment correct the cap squares were fastened to secure the trunnions and the men then pulled the trail down using a prolongue and the officers were allowed to view the piece. Hunt marveled in the much greater size of the gun, as it gleamed in the morning sun.

"Mordecai has nicknamed her "The Napoleon" since the idea is a gift from France," observed Captain Jenkins.

Hunt approvingly nodded as he ran his hand along the smooth lines of the great barrel and admired the businesslike lines of the gun. The newly cast bronze easily allowed inspection of the barrel inside. Hunt moved to the breech end and tested the elevation screw; he was pleased to see the balance issue had been resolved.

"Mordecai wrote to me and explained that these 4 are 3 inches longer than the first prototype and the trunnions have been moved to the rear as well. She can be mounted on a number two carriage without modification now," observed Jenkins.

The Ordnance Sergeant approached and saluted the officers, "Sirs, we will have all four guns mounted in another hour or so, I will suggest Captain Hunt send a detail with teams to pull the four guns and four caissons this afternoon. I will have arrangements ready for you to sign for them then sir."

Captain Hunt nodded. The Sergeant then interjected, "Sir, I will also suggest you send over a battery wagon as we have boxes of special tools and appurtenances to accompany the guns."

Hunt nodded again and asked, "Six horse teams?"

The Ordnance Sergeant nodded, "Yes Sir, believe it or not she will handle just like the 6 pounder."

First Sergeant O'Keefe had the bugler call assembly immediately following lunch and once the battery had assembled he directed the drivers to collect together 8 teams and the battery wagon to ride over to the Ordnance shops with Captain Hunt to pick up the guns. The crews were anxious to see them but would have to wait until the drivers returned.

As they approached the Ordnance shops on the Eastern Grounds of the sprawling Fort, Joshua was astonished at the size of the 4 new guns. They looked to be a full third larger than the 6 pounders they had become so accustomed to.

The drivers with their older 6 pounder limbers had to wait for the ordnance men to change out the old chests for the larger 12 pounder chests on the limbers and the caissons were simply swapped out for new ones fabricated at the shops. Lacking gun crews to assist, the ordnance artificers lifted the guns lunettes and hooked them to the pin tails of the limbers and readied the battery to return with their new guns.

Captain Hunt having finished signing for an entire replacement battery stuffed the sheaf of papers into his saddle valise and signaled for the drivers to follow him.

Joshua and Harry commented on how easily the teams appeared to pull the new load despite how much larger the guns looked. When the teams arrived back at the M Company barracks the cannoneers rushed out in various stages of dress to look over the new guns.

After much low whistling and great rubbing of hands upon the shiny bronze tubes, First Sergeant O'Keefe growled, "Alright dammit!, get ready to assemble in an hour, in the proper fookin' uniform of the day to unpack and stow appurtenances and prepare the guns for drill!"

He looked around and added, "Your new bride will age quickly once we drill 3 times a day on her!"

Captain Hunt was anxious to start training and he had received assurances that M Company would be shielded as much as possible from troop requests from Governor Geary by General Smith. Smith had also revealed that he would likely be replaced in the summer so he asked for a personal salute from the new 12 pound battery at his change of command.

Despite the bitter cold and howling prairie winds, First Sergeant O'Keefe demanded three drills a day for the gun crews, twice a week he conducted short maneuvering drills with the teams attached so the men would grow accustomed to the handling of the guns with their increased weight. He began to realize watching the drill that perhaps a minimum height requirement might be necessary for a number 3 in order to insure he could reach the vent.

The crews dutifully drilled and groused afterwards for the chance to live fire but O'Keefe stubbornly insisted on two weeks of drill first, as he put it "I want you to be able to touch her in the right places in the dark, boys!"

M Company performed crew drill and mounted drill through the month of March and April, Hunt wanted the crews, drivers and the horse teams to perfect the handling and movement of the heavier guns.

He had read Mordecai's report of the Fort McHenry test but felt that there had not been a sufficient test of the carriages and limbers to the newer and heavier gun. He noticed after all his effort that while heavier, the Napoleons, once the men were used to them were quite handy and did not change the rate of march or difficulty in handling presented by the 6 pounders.

As the weather started to hint of spring he arranged for Captain Jenkins to create a battery of wooden "Quaker Guns" for him to shoot at. Hunt arranged to have them established on a range area west of the post. When the lingering snow was gone he would direct the survey of the firing range so that total yards could be captured upon firing of the projectiles. This way he could conduct his live fire testing against targets more representative of an actual battlefield.

First Sergeant O'Keefe announced to the men during evening roll call in late April 1858, that they should prepare to depart the next day for an intensive two weeks of maneuver and live fire exercises. The gunners were so bored with the constant drill that they cheered the news. Shortly after his announcement Corporal Mills stepped forward with a mail bag and started to call out names of the recipients of its lean contents.

Joshua was surprised to hear his name called, as he stepped forward, he immediately noted the envelope with distinctly feminine handwriting and knew that Lottie had written yet again. He ignored the catcalls of Harry and Sean and returned to his quarters to read the letter.

He started to open the letter and was interrupted by Corporal Sheppard, "Josh, you and me have been summoned to talk to First Sergeant O'Keefe tonight right after the Sergeants meeting, follow me over and you will wait outside till we are done. Be ready to follow me in an hour!"

Joshua nodded, wondering what he had done wrong. He shook his head and read the letter;

*"Dear Joshua,*

*Thank for being so gracious to reply to my silly letters, I truly miss the chance to tease you like we used to do at the school all those years ago. E.J. wishes that I might express his regards to you and he wanted you to know that Father received word that the steam engine that your father had purchased during that terrible trip to Norfolk was delivered to Charleston last summer. Father is storing it on the property until you return. If you desire him to dispose of it through a sale he would be happy to do so, but wished for you to express an opinion.*

*Your brother Jacob was accepted into the Wassamassaw Calvary this fall, he was given brother Tom's place in the company as Tom was enrolled at the Arsenal in Columbia. He looks so dashing in his militia uniform, I would love to see you in yours! Jacob sends his regards and says he stays too busy to write so I am happy to serve as his liaison to you.*

*I hope you are in good health, perhaps if you are stationed nearer you could take leave and return home, Anna is keeping the house in beautiful conditions and she always asks how you are faring. Each time I receive a letter, I try to visit and read her the news of your adventures. Mother has mentioned to me a fine finishing school in Charleston that I might attend next year. If that proves to be my future I will inform you of the news.*

*God Bless*

*Lottie"*

As Joshua finished the letter he was flabbergasted that his father had actually succeeded in his dream. He decided to see if Mr. Markley had an addressee from the delivery that might be able to shed more light on what had transpired. He realized he missed home and seeing Lottie despite having paid little attention to her. He would try to write her tonight but he would have to assemble his equipment first.

Joshua followed Corporal Shepperd to the Sergeants meeting at the First Sergeants quarters, he had to wait outside but noted that he could hear most of the conversation and it concerned insuring all essentials were packed and that all basic kit was to accompany the Company when they departed. Only post property and non-essential luxury items would remain in the barracks.

When the meeting had broken up, Corporal Sheppard came out and motioned Joshua to come in. As he entered he noticed that Captain Hunt was also present. Joshua became greatly nervous.

O'Keefe told him "Private Timmonds we are about to ask you some questions, consider it an evaluation."

Joshua nodded and sat down at the small table when Corporal Shepperd indicated for him to sit.

O'Keefe then placed a short pencil and a piece of paper on the table before him and stepped back.

As Joshua looked at them quizzically, Captain Hunt asked, "Private Timmonds, imagine you are on the far bank of a river and you see a man on the other side. How would you determine the distance to that man from your position?"

Joshua vaguely remembered the question as being one in the Manual he had read at Fortress Monroe. Joshua then remembered E.J. instructions from his youth more clearly.

He immediately roughly sketched the river, the man, and his position and began to sketch a triangle and began the basis for the equations to base the law of sines. He then explained the information that he would have to obtain to complete the equation by the degrees to the man and the degrees to a known object adjacent to him.

Captain Hunt broadly smiled and asked, "What work experience did you have before the Army, son?"

Joshua explained the surveying he assisted with and his horseshoeing piece work.

Hunt nodded and turned to O'Keefe and said, "Draw up the paperwork and I will sign it."

O'Keefe noting Joshua's quizzical look said, "Congratulations Private Timmonds, you are to be made a Corporal, and will be a special assistant to the Captain for the gunnery, following that, you will be trained as a gunner. I have been watching you closely these past few years and I think you have earned this. Let us just see if you can keep it!"

Sheppard beamed and clapped him hard on the back as they left the First Sergeant's quarters, "Congratulations Joshua! I have asked to assist you in your training. We have been discussing what a waste it was for you to be a driver."

Joshua did not know what to say and only managed to say, "Corporal Shepperd, I cannot thank you enough, I do not know what I have done that has gotten me this!"

Shepperd stopped and said, "My name is Jon, Josh. Now let's get back to the barracks and I will give you some stripes to sew on. Now you are making a dollar more a month!"

When M Company moved as a complete company to the firing range established the next day they would spend the next two weeks in the field learning to fire the pieces.

Captain Hunt had arranged for Engineer topographical specialists to accompany the unit to the range and they had set up intricate surveying equipment, some of which Joshua recognized.

Joshua's duties were to act as the final down range surveyor as the battery fired initial long range shots. He was positioned astride the targets down range with a party that measured extreme range of shots fired by measuring with surveying chains beyond the 1000 yard marker line in the target area.

He missed being on the guns for the firing drills even though at the extreme distance he was from the guns he could tell they were much more powerful than the old 6 pounders. It was thrilling to hear the rushing approach of the solid shot as they impacted in the target area.

After the end of each 4 gun iteration of firing he would ride back with his data to Captain Hunt who dutifully recorded the distances in the ledger, he was amazed at the extreme range of the Napoleons to be 1,680 yards at 5 degrees of elevation. It was almost a thousand yards further than maximum range of the 6 pounder.

His next task was to note and mark the functional distance of the Case Shot detonations by providing a range estimate of the burst of the shot down range and measure the distances in yards from the known distances that the case shot functioned over. As he watched from the safe offset he was impressed by the size of the beaten zone as the small shot within the case impacted around the target area.

He would adjust his position 100 yards off from the line of fire until all 4 guns had fired. He would then proceed to measure from the yardage markers to his stakes that he placed at each approximate bursting distance. His measurements were compared to the estimates of the topographical engineers estimates made from the transits.

For the first week every possible combination of firing was performed and Joshua saw each test from the enemies eye view. He reflected each night how he would not like to be on the wrong side of a Napoleon battery.

The second week ended Joshua's amateur surveyor role.

O'Keefe had summoned him after morning roll call. "Corporal Timmonds, you are to become the number 2 section gunner, Section Sergeant Schwartz will be your direct supervisor! Report to him right away!"

Joshua found Schwartz over at the 2$^{nd}$ section caissons as he checked the drivers. The German Sergeant was familiar to him as everyone remarked you had to listen to his heavily accented speech carefully to understand him. But he clearly knew his work. Word was that he had been an artillerist in the Prussian army before he immigrated to America shortly before the war with Mexico.

As Schwartz saw Joshua approach he heartily greeted him, "Corporal, is good thing to see you!"

He looked him up and down and asked, "What work you do on the gun?"

Joshua simply responded, "Number 1, Number 5 and Number 6, Sergeant."

Schwartz grinned broadly, "Good thing, I will show you gunner!"

Schwartz presented him with a leather pouch from the caisson. It contained the finely made Pendulum Hause, the elemental tool of the gunner.

When the crews hauled the guns up to the windswept Kansas range, the First Sergeant had a surprise in store for the Company.

He shouted over the wind, "Today, all day, we will practice the repair of battle damage that you will encounter in a fight! I will come to you on your gun and designate what is broken or shot through and you will practice the repair on line of your pieces and the practices by which you will maintain the mobility of the firing battery!"

The First Sergeant ran the crews through dry gun drill and walked along the 4 sections of gun, limber and caisson and periodically would stop and inform the crew to cease firing and point to crewmembers that were now dead or wounded and what damage had been done to the gun.

He came to Joshua's gun crew and announced, "Corporal Timmonds, your right wheel on this howitzer is shot to pieces and your number 2 is dead! What do you do?"

Joshua paused and then ordered number 5 forward to replace number 4 and for number 4 to replace number 2. He then ordered number 7 to move to the caisson to remove the spare wheel. He then directed number 1, 2, 3, and 4 to secure the handspike from the trail and had 2 men prepare to lift on the axle as number 1 unpinned the hub of the damaged wheel. As the crewmembers rolled the heavy spare wheel to the side of the gun he then directed numbers 3 and 4 to lift using the handspike as a lifting bar, and number 1 and 2 removed the damaged wheel, number 7 and one of the caisson drivers then put the replacement wheel on the axle and repinned it in place.

O'Keefe was pleased, "Good speedy work 2$^{nd}$ Section! Each time you have to do this don't forget to have someone regrease that axle from the tar bucket before sliding that replacement back on."

He was pleased with Corporal Timmonds quick grasp of what needed to be done. He admired how the boy worked through a threat as opposed to cowering from one.

O'Keefe drilled the crews on horse replacement as well, showing the men how to strip and recover harnesses from downed horses and in what order horses were to be sacrificed from caisson teams to keep the guns mobile.

He resolved himself to ask the captain for permission for allowing them to fire using battlefield expedients once the firing table data collection was complete. He wanted his gunners to have ideas in case they were ever needed.

By the end of the second week, Captain Hunt was greatly pleased with the work of the Company. He had a firing table roughed out to send to Major Mordecai, and he would dedicate one more final day to First Sergeant O'Keefe to train the men. While it made him nervous he allowed the Senior Sergeant to train the crews in practical battlefield realities. These shortcuts came in handy in Mexico and could be necessary the next time war came to visit.

"Today gentlemen I am going to teach you some shortcuts on these new guns!"

O'Keefe again walked along the open ground between the limbers and the cannon. "You may find yourself becoming the focus of enemy infantry and cavalry with little or no space between you and your gun and them!"

He looked the eager crews in the eyes as he paced, "I will tell you now that once you have seen the way your enemies look at you when they are that close, it is a look you will never forget!"

He then shouted, "Action Right, Double Canister, Point Blank!"

O'Keefe then walked the limber line showing the crews how to secure one canister fixed round in the pouch and demonstrated how to cut away the charge bag of the second canister and add the canister alone to the pouch. Once the crews had loaded and driven home first the fixed canister followed by the second canister, he returned to a position center of the battery.

"Fire by Battery!" the Section Chiefs echoed the command "Battery, Fire!"

The Battery fired in unison with a tremendous roar of orange flame and white smoke; each gun recoiled back nearly to the limbers. The crews could not help but cheer and shout.

O'Keefe again paced the line in the blinding smoke, "Congratulations gentlemen, you have just poured 916 balls into the faces of your enemy. An artillery battery of six guns firing this load is the equal to the volley fire of an entire infantry regiment! Never forget that, particularly when you are getting scared!"

"The next is a desperate trick we worked out in Mexico. We will only do this one gun at a time. We call this "Rotten Shot" this is when your number 5 comes up lookin' pale and such and he tells you there's no more canister in the limbers or the caissons."

He then described how number 5 and 6 would remove the Bormann fuse from a spherical case shot and bring it to the gun with only the iron fuse base plug in place. This exposed the main bursting charge exposed to the muzzle flame of the gun. The result of firing Spherical Shot in this manner caused the shot to detonate at the muzzle.

"Gun Number 1 will demonstrate for you, I want all other crews to step back from their pieces. In combat if you resort to this by battery; wounding of your own crews is nearly guaranteed so this is a method of last resort."

As gun number 1 fired the initial roar followed by the burst of the shell at the muzzle caused the men to jump, but Joshua noted that the effect forward of the gun, while not as impressive as double canister, was still impressive.

Each crew was allowed to practice one round of "Rotten Shot" and Captain Hunt winced with each report, fearing damage to the guns or injury to the men. He realized though that he had the best trainer in the Army with O'Keefe.

The old Irishman consistently would refuse promotion or reassignment to Ordnance, rebuffing each offer with a gruff, "Ain't nuthin' but a field soldier, Sir!"

He then ordered the Company back to Camp to break down for return to Fort Leavenworth.

The men of M Company following their training finally received their chance to fire the salute that had been requested by General Smith, but not in the manner they had anticipated.

In the early spring the old warrior clutched his chest in leaving his office one evening and died. As they loaded the coffin of their commander onto a caisson provided for the occasion to be transported to a waiting steamer, M Company fired a perfectly timed 21 gun salute.

# 7 THE UNION IS DISSOLVED!

## Fort Brown, Texas
## February 1861

Joshua had begun to hate Texas, first with the oppressive heat and now the confusing blend of winter weather extremes that blew in across the Gulf Coast.

No one was quite sure why M Company was posted to Brownsville but it was quite apparent that things had come completely apart for the Union. With the news of the election of Mr. Lincoln it seemed to Joshua that the situation he had witnessed in Kansas now was happening across the entire country.

M Company had traveled to Texas, after receiving orders, in the summer of 1859 and now on their second year here, the situation had greatly changed.

First Sergeant O'Keefe had begun to brief the noncommissioned Officers at his evening Sergeant's meetings of the political situation in the country. In last night's meeting he had discussed the looming secession of the State of Texas. The decision had been made to depart the Union that was confirmed by a legislative vote on the previous Friday whereby Texas would secede effectively on the 2$^{nd}$ of March.

Captain Hunt and the Infantry and Cavalry Commanders had received word from Major General Twiggs that all units may be required to depart Texas and steamers to provide evacuation had been ordered to Galveston and Brownsville.

M Company was to begin preparations to depart and instructions had been provided that weapons may have to be left behind.

O'Keefe had sternly emphasized that Captain Hunt had replied in writing to the General that he had no intention of leaving the Napoleons behind as they were articles of specific interest to the Ordnance Department and he still awaited a reply back to his correspondence. In the interim the orders were that; "where the troops went, these guns were to go with."

Joshua departed the evening meeting after receiving guidance and encouragement from the First Sergeant. He purloined the latest copy of the Harper's weekly from the First Sergeant's office as it contained excerpts from the latest Dickens' novel that would be of great demand among the boys of the 2nd Section, plus it contained news of A Company 1nd U.S. Artillery in their interesting dilemma at Charleston Harbor in Fort Sumter. While he knew none of the men there, it was their sister Regiment and everyone wondered what the outcome would be.

It seemed that South Carolina had demanded they surrender and the Commander, Major Robert Anderson had refused. News from home both fascinated and horrified Joshua. He had always felt proud to represent his State to the Army and now he wondered how the Army felt about him now.

Joshua returned to his mess and his gun crew that he had finally gotten to know as their functional leader, Sergeant Schwartz was technically the overall leader. He attended the meetings and came by often but his language; frustratingly unimproved over all these years only allowed him to provide the most basic of orders and guidance and effectively blocked any further bonding with the section.

As it was, Schwartz spent most of his time with Mueller, the Blacksmith, who was the only other "Dutchman" in the Company.

Joshua entered the low stucco barracks building, built in the hasty Texas adobe style and handed the Harper's to Private Lyttle, who eagerly took it over to the light.

Privates Mulcahy, Wilkins, Watkins and Page were engaged in their standard evening card game of Whist at the section table, while Newby and Thorne were writing letters and talking quietly on their beds.

Joshua had encountered earlier difficulties with Newby when he took over the section since Newby remembered him from the beginning but his predilection for drinking and fighting had insured the noncommissioned officer burden would never be placed on his shoulders. Joshua had readily given Newby credit in public for teaching him his trade and Hiram Newby had slowly but steadily supported Joshua in his leadership.

Joshua looking over his charges would tell anyone that this was perhaps the finest gun crew in the entire Army as they had trained together enough to be able to service the gun at second nature.

Their particular Napoleon had number 003 stamped on the right trunnion and he insured that they never allowed it to leave their sight. It was rumored to be the most accurate gun in the Company.

"What's the news Corporal?" Newby asked as Joshua shed his shell jacket and forage cap on his bed.

"Well gents it sounds like we are not long for Texas." All the men looked up and Lyttle looked up from his reading of "Great Expectations" and asked, "Is Texas leaving the Union too?"

Joshua nodded adding, "Word we have is to be ready to take the guns with, I want you all to insure the carriages and caissons are ready to roll at a moment's notice. Insure the wheels are tight and the axles are greased and keep a good eye on the teams to insure we can rig for travel at the drop of a hat."

He paused and looked over his section and added, "Seems that Texas may want to have our weapons. Captain Hunt is hell bent that nobody gets these guns."

Private Watkins set his cards down and asked, "Corporal, has Tennessee seceded yet?" Joshua shook his head, "All I have heard is South Carolina, Texas, Mississippi, Florida, and Georgia so far."

Private Page looked quizzically and asked, "Corporal, how you feelin' knowin' your own home state had done left the union?"

Joshua honestly answered, "It makes me feel real funny inside Page, but I took a vow to the Army and so did you."

He remembered renewing that vow last year as he signed up for another 5 year enlistment.

Joshua sat on his bunk and recalled the Sergeant's meeting; O'Keefe had given so much complicated information. While he wanted to share it all he thought it best to give them on certain information for now.

Some he would tell the section and others he would leave out. Lots of orders were flying around fast and furious, and rumors abounded as well.

Captain Hunt had stated that Major General Twiggs had been relieved by the War Department earlier in the week but no one could confirm the orders. There had also been word that Texas militia was beginning to encircle Fort Brown as they had at San Antonio. The Captain had also revealed that all Army units in Texas were making their way to Fort Brown and Galveston in order to be evacuated by ship.

Major Fitz John Porter was glad on the gusty March morning that he had not joined the Navy. He had been aboard the steamship Daniel Webster since the 25th of February and the chartered vessel had arrived off Brownsville in stormy seas today on the 3rd of March.

The captain had informed Major Porter that the seas were too rough to cross the sandbar into the sound formed by the mouth of the Rio Grande but they had received flag signals that a harbor pilot would come out by lighter to meet them tomorrow.

Porter wondered how many troops had been able to make their way to Fort Brown. The War Department instruction provided to him specified that he was to collect up 5 companies of artillery and return them to New York with all due haste.

In his mind he knew he could get 3 Companies of Men aboard and no more. More ships had been chartered and were on their way to pick up troops at various points on the Texas coast. Unfortunately none of these plans took the early spring weather into account.

The next day a harbor tug pulled alongside the Daniel Webster and 3 men boarded, with some difficulty due to the rough seas.

"Good day Major, I am Colonel John Ford, of the Texas Volunteers and this gentleman is Mr. Nichols of the Texas Commission of Public Safety," the military attired boarder announced, by way of introduction.

Major Porter nodded and deliberately abstained from offering his hand.

"I am Major Fitz John Porter representing Lieutenant General Scott, My duty is the evacuation of Federal Troops from Texas, starting with those assembled at Fort Brown, then I am to make arrangements with the appropriate authorities for evacuation of troops from the Garrisons at San Antonio, Fort Duncan, and Fort Ringgold."

The men went into the dining room of the steamer and continued their discussion.

The Texas delegation was concerned that no provocative actions would occur and that the Federal Troops would agree to the negotiations initiated by Major General Twiggs.

The mention of the name enraged Porter, "I hope you gentlemen are aware that General Twiggs was relieved of his authority effective of the 11th of last month! Under what authority did he negotiate with the Texas Commission?"

It had become common knowledge that General Twiggs had intentions on resignation from the Army and some suggested he had entered into a separate deal with Texas for a commission with the State.

Colonel Ford replied, "This we were aware, however your War Department named a successor who was in Western Texas and unable to conduct meaningful negotiations. As there had not been an orderly assumption of responsibilities; and owing to the earnest interest of the people of Texas to have your forces vacate our soil, we were compelled to negotiate as soon as possible!"

Nichols could contain himself no further and blurted out, "And the patience of the people of Texas will promptly be exhausted! The agreement was the evacuation of troops and troops alone. The contents of the Arsenals will remain!"

Porter seethed inside. Word had been that Twiggs had readily surrendered 10,000 brand new Model 1855 rifled muskets, more than the rest of the Federal Army had combined.

He countered, "My orders state I am to evacuate 5 companies of Artillery with their weapons along with all Federal Troops in Texas. The War Department will hold you accountable for their safety."

Colonel Ford had heard enough and stood, "Texas does not answer to your War Department, Major. I will ask you to remember the generosity of the people of Texas that have allowed you safe passage up to this point. I will coordinate with your commanders and yourself once we have returned to Fort Brown. If you are so inclined we will take you there now."

Porter nodded, he realized the hopelessness of his situation, his mission was urgent and clear. He would have to swallow his pride for now.

When Major Porter met with the assembled Company Commanders at Fort Brown he was filled with admiration for their spirit and the manner in which morale had been maintained.

The Texas Militia, consisting of heavily armed men in no common uniform that he could ascertain; were arranged along all approaches to the fort, neither hostile nor friendly. They coldly watched as each additional unit marched into the grounds of the Fort.

The Cavalry Commanders had the best knowledge of the coastal country and had advised Porter of a better location north of them at Indianola where the access to Matagorda Bay was easier even in bad weather. Porter understood and decided to have them scout a location for a camp; he would attempt to get word to Colonel Waite.

He then proposed to coordinate this option to Colonel Ford who had been provided an office inside the fort to enable coordination. After all if Texas did not approve of the plan, it would be "provocative."

The next day in honor of Mr. Lincoln's inauguration, Captain Hunt ordered a 21 gun salute fired from his men employing blank charges, so when reville was sounded and the flag was raised, the battery obligingly fired the salute in perfectly timed sequence.

The salute resulted in anxious negotiations for the remainder of the day between Major Porter and Colonel Ford of the Texas Volunteers as the salute had been regarded as a "provocative act" by the Texas militia.

Captain Hunt refused to apologize for his salute when challenged later by Colonel Ford and had explained, "I was drilling my battery, Sir."

The next day Major Porter assembled the Company Commanders together and briefed them on the approved evacuation plan, "I have received approval from the Texas authorities to move the units currently gathered here with the exception of one company of infantry from the 3$^{rd}$ Regiment, we will move tomorrow at dawn for Indianola. The cavalry reports there is a good location with dry ground and plenty of forage for the horses near Green Lake. We will call this location Camp Witherill. All inbound units from the Texas interior will either come here to provision at Fort Brown proper or move direct to Camp Witherill depending on their supply situation. I will move with you to Indianola and establish my headquarters there."

Following the evening Sergeant's meeting where Captain Hunt provided concise and urgent guidance, Joshua hurried to brief his section.

"We move at dawn with everything we have! We will maintain tight intervals and the men will ride on the caissons and limber chests. We do not expect hostile action but remain ready. First Sergeant O'Keefe wants each man armed with his short artillery sword on his side," Joshua paused a moment studying the eyes of his gun crew and added, "Just so we are protected and not "provocative" in our defense."

The next morning the company moved out, once they were away from Brownsville the situation seemed calmer; the fervor only seemed to pervade the populated areas. Joshua could not help but notice however; the frequent appearance of civilian clothed outriders in the distance as they marched. They were under constant watch.

Major Fitz John Porter had arranged for the Daniel Webster to move up the coast and rendezvous with the troops at Matagorda Bay.

In the intervening time Captain Hunt did his best to continue drilling the men on the guns. He had the uneasy feeling that they might have to use them before they cleared Texas.

Much to Hunt's and the other officers' disdain the troops encamped at Camp Witherill received a visit from Colonel Van Dorn, late of the 2$^{nd}$ U.S. Cavalry, who upon resigning his commission a scant month ago wandered about the evacuation camp talking to the officers. Henry Hunt had heard the rumors that nearly 300 of his fellow officers had resigned their oaths but he'd be damned if any of them wanted to "recruit" him.

Colonel Van Dorn had approached him and Hunt had refused to respond. He had seen Van Dorn before in Mexico and had actually admired him, but now something deep inside him was filled with revulsion against the man.

He instead turned to First Sergeant O'Keefe and directed "First Sergeant, show the Colonel around the company area and then show him another place to visit!"

O'Keefe smirked and replied, "Aye Sir, I'll take him to the Cavalry, I am sure they are a missing him by now!"

Captain Hunt conferred with First Sergeant O'Keefe on insuring an orderly camp was kept and wanted him to keep the men busy with the horses and artillery drill at least 3 times a day.

He was concerned it might be necessary to remain ready to use the guns as the Texas Commission of Public Safety had confiscated the muskets of the infantrymen. Only the officers had been permitted to retain their sabers and side arms.

Of course M Company had the Napoleons and the formerly silly short swords. O'Keefe mentioned that he had seen the men becoming very keen about sharpening them.

Colonel Van Dorn finished his visit to the evacuation encampment and found Major Porter near the edge of the bay looking for the arrival of the Daniel Webster.

Van Dorn greeted him having heard of him, "Well good afternoon Major Porter!"

Porter turned and recognized Van Dorn who had applied Federal Army shoulder boards to a gray Texas Militia frock coat. "Afternoon Sir, and no I am not interested in joining your rebellion!"

Van Dorn laughed and observed, "Major I think you speak for all the men here."

Porter was inwardly relieved to hear this and stated, "Sir, despite our differences I am very grateful that you are permitting my men to remove from Texas unmolested."

Van Dorn thoughtfully replied, "That at least is the situation now, Major. Politics may dictate otherwise in the future."

Van Dorn decided to make issue with M Company, "Major why does that Artillery Company have their guns with them? I thought it was understood that all arms in the arsenals would be left in Texas?"

Porter quickly replied, "Sir, Those guns are specifically mentioned in my instructions to be returned. They are pieces that were never levied to Texas State by the War Department. Only those weapons that were provided to Texas by the government into the Arsenals of the State are to be left to you. These guns came under Army control and will depart under Army control! Those are my orders."

He paused and added, "4 other Companies have instruction to do the same."

Van Dorn thought a moment and asked, "And what if we were to dispute that position?"

Major Porter replied calmly, "Then we will fight you with those guns, I do have full limber chests and caissons, Colonel."

Van Dorn nodded and said, "Do not be troubled Major, Texas has plenty of her own artillery."

He imagined that the 5 regular batteries would have made quite a prize but he already understood the outcome of the negotiations between Twiggs and the Commission. Twiggs had stupidly neglected to remember the equipment of the Artillery Companies. As a Southern Officer he was resigned to honorably agree to the points of the negotiation.

Major Porter decided to look to the camps to insure the Commanders were in possession of sufficient supplies, he expected more arrivals so space would become at a premium, he resolved to convene regular meetings in the evenings to insure sanitary conditions were maintained until the steamers arrived to start the evacuations.

As he rode from camp to camp of the 5 companies he began to notice that Texas Militia men were taking up positions about a mile distant from their outermost picket positions. He was relieved to see the bearded Captain Hunt drilling his gunners; he was beginning to understand why the Captain was so well regarded in the Army.

Soon he would collect up a cavalry escort and make the long trip back to Fort Brown to provide Major French with the same instructions to remove himself and his batteries of the 1$^{st}$ Artillery to this camp as well.

By mid-morning on the 17$^{th}$ of March the Daniel Webster hove into view in Matagorda Bay, the assembled soldiers cheered at the sight.

Major Porter greeting the small landing party boat and held quick consultations with the steamer's First Officer on the beach. The logistics of moving the guns aboard the Daniel Webster would be a challenge but the ship's First Officer felt if they could obtain a coastal lighter to assist; then the guns could be managed.

When Porter asked about the horses, the First Officer shook his head, "Not enough room, particularly since you are loading the guns."

Major Porter trudged back across the beach to a small party of Company Commanders who had followed him to greet the landing party.

Porter looked up and announced, "Assemble your men, One Troop of cavalry will remain in camp to receive the elements of the 1$^{st}$ Artillery when they arrive. Leave the tents up; bring only your equipment to the beach for the lighters."

He looked to Captain Hunt and delivered more specific information, "Hunt, you will bring only gun carriages, limber chests and caisson chests, the rest will be left behind due to limited room on the ship."

Hunt nodded and asked, "The horse teams?"

Porter bluntly replied, "Left behind."

When Captain Hunt briefed the men, they were dismayed, Sergeant O'Brien asked aloud, "Sir, do you really intend on leaving these fine animals to these Texans?"

O'Keefe grew red in the face and barked out, "Shut yer goddamned trap, O'Brien! The Captain ain't got no fookin' choice! Do as yer fookin' told!"

He too was saddened by the abandonment but it was better than seeing them killed like he had witnessed in Mexico.

By late afternoon the lighter had passed through the sandbar and due to its shallow draft it could approach the beach to permit the loading of gun carriages with wooden pilings arranged to roll them over the gunwales of the boat. It was still beastly work requiring teams of men using the prolongues and brute force to get the heavy guns loaded, one per trip to the Daniel Webster.

As the lighter pulled abeam of the Webster the crews then had to dismount the tubes and the wheels from the carriages in order to hoist them aboard the vessel employing a specially rigged cargo boom on the foremast. The loading of the guns took the remainder of the day into the early evening.

When morning came, the men of M Company fed and tended to the teams one last time at their picket line. The drivers were extra solicitous and talked to the horses as they curry combed them in the early morning light. Then Captain Hunt called them to formation and marched them to the beach.

Major Porter saluted M Company and assured the men that he would have the cavalry look to the horses. The men then waited for the completion of loading of the infantry companies of the 3$^{rd}$ Regiment and then the lighter came for them. After two trips the entire rank and file of M Company, 2$^{nd}$ Artillery Regiment was aboard, bound for New York City.

As the Daniel Webster raised anchor and blew her steam whistle, the men on the railing noticed a commotion in the nearly empty camp.

One man cried out, "The horses!" The horse teams had snapped their picket rope and were galloping to the beach dragging the remnants of the picket line behind them.

The confused animals milled in the light surf and shrieked in distress at being left behind. Some reared magnificently and galloped up and down the beach.

Two more determined animals actually entered the water and swam towards the boat for a while.

Joshua felt tight in his chest at the sight and looked over and saw Sergeant O'Brien and Private Newby at the rail, openly crying.

Most of the company stood at the ships railing watching the pitiful sight, clearly distressed to have left them behind.

Captain Hunt, also looking wet around the eyes observed, "Perhaps we could learn something from such dumb loyalty."

He wondered what awaited M Company now. He looked over to First Sergeant O'Keefe standing by his side.

O'Keefe who also looking a bit wet in the eyes, observed, "More shit."

Hunt nodded his head, "The shit is just beginning First Sergeant."

# New York City
# March 1861

After a very busy and difficult debarkation from the Daniel Webster at Fort Hamilton, Captain Hunt assembled his men and remaining equipment.

As he quietly took inventory of what he now was missing, he resolved to himself that he would dedicate some of his time to add to the Artillery Manual of Instruction some procedures for amphibious operations.

The movement of cannons in rapid embarkations and debarkations left much to be desired.

The Commander of Fort Hamilton, Colonel Brown, had received the 3 Companies of grimy and weary men; with a military band to give them a hero's welcome.

Hunt was puzzled and taken aback by the fanfare in front of great crowds of civilian onlookers. What had seemed a humiliating disaster to him was received with great celebration as a victory by the citizens of New York.

He was preoccupied with finding the Ordnance shops and refitting his Company, He had 4 guns, ammunition chests and a company of men. He detailed his quartermaster sergeant to form a detail of drivers to recover the cannon, still under guard on the barge office pier, if he could locate some team horses.

The Fort Hamilton quartermaster quickly assisted and also provided billeting instructions for the troops. M Company was to receive the barracks recently vacated by A Company, 2<sup>nd</sup> Artillery who were leaving as they arrived.

Fort Hamilton was a hive of activity; Joshua stopped a soldier and asked about what was going on.

The hurried man replied, "There are orders for units to go out to reinforce harbor forts in all the secesh states."

Joshua asked quizzically, "Secesh?"

The soldier explained, "The ones leaving the union!"

M Company milled around after entering the sally port of the 3 story fortress. First Sergeant O'Keefe finally arrived after consultation with the Ft. Hamilton Quartermaster Sergeant and called for a formation.

He stood on one of the limber chests that they had brought in and announced, "Now listen up! The Captain wishes to inform you that we will spend two weeks here to refit. You can expect to go somewheres else at the end of that time! There will be a Sergeant's meeting tonight at 7 o'clock, in the meantime get your gear in your bays and insure you got a good count of heads! Supper will be served in the main mess in an hour!"

He turned and pointed to Quartermaster Sergeant O'Rourke, directing, "Get the detail moving to bring in the guns, when you return with them park them where I stand."

Joshua quickly looked around to insure he could account for his crew; he quickly spotted each and noticed that Private Wilkins was talking to a civilian; this seemed odd, as they had passed through a guarded sally port so he went over to investigate.

Seeing him approach the civilian extended his hand, "Good Afternoon Corporal I am Jonah Claven of the New York Times."

Joshua realized the pressman had seized upon the only New Yorker in the Company and smiled, "Good to see you sir, sorry about our appearance."

The reporter smiled and asked about where they had come from. As Joshua explained, Sergeant O'Brien came over and related the story of the loss of their horses. Claven scribbled furiously as the men talked.

Then as suddenly as he had started, he closed his book and rushed away shouting, "Thanks gentlemen, welcome to New York, I have to meet my deadline!"

Wilkins beamed, "He got my name, now my folks will see me famous! Mentioned in the Times!"

O'Brien smiled and shook his head, looking at Joshua he whispered, "Rumor is we will be getting liberty into town soon. "

After the Company had been settled in and the guns and equipment were secured Captain Hunt received a summons to meet with Colonel Brown.

"Henry, it is good to see you again! You will have to brief me on the problem in Texas," the commander of Fort Hamilton was clearly a very busy man.

"Sir, I would like to thank you for the generous welcome we have received, I appreciate the assistance of your staff in insuring our needs were met," Hunt had anticipated the standard Army neglect and had been pleasantly surprised.

Brown smiled and observed, "Henry we understand how bad it was for you. I will warn you now that we are receiving orders hourly from the War Department for units to reinforce the coastal forts along the east and gulf coasts. At each a political siege is underway. I expect you to receive orders as soon as I declare M Company refit."

He offered Hunt a cigar from a box on his desk, Hunt gratefully accepted.

Brown continued after lighting his cigar, "When did you last see your children?"

Hunt quickly replied "two years ago, sir."

Brown replied, "I will give you 7 days leave to go visit them. It's Washington, correct?"

Hunt quickly nodded, "Yes Sir, My brother in law Lieutenant Colonel Nichols cares for them, but what about my men?"

Brown smiled again puffing out a cloud of smoke, "Assign them to a single Lieutenant, Captain. Our standard refit plan is ample liberty for the soldiers, The Mayor of New York is anxious to drain them of their money. Our paymasters can advance them pay if necessary. Every day the situation is becoming more and more serious. We are finding that it helps to let the men blow off steam. Just get word to the noncommissioned officers to advise them to stick together in groups. We may be in the North, but New York is full of Secesh sympathizers and they are itching to make trouble."

Hunt, lit his cigar and asked, "Sir, can you find us horses?" Colonel Brown nodded.

Colonel Brown continued, "We have an entire herd of fine animals just in from Ohio, but we have issued most of them for the troops going out this week for now. Where you are likely going; you will not need full teams. I will get you what I can."

Captain Hunt thanked him and returned to find the First Sergeant. After he had insured he had an Acting Commander he would make arrangements to travel to Washington, it had been far too long.

First Sergeant O'Keefe convened his evening Sergeant's call. From the copious amounts of smoke in the Casemate bay of the fort it was apparent that lots of cigars had been found.

The liberty rumor had obviously found legs as there was a great deal of joviality among the sergeants.

O'Keefe gave a rare smile and announced, "Alright, Alright, listen up you assholes! We will start controlled liberties tomorrow. I want you to spend the rest of this evening helping me get a guard mount established for tomorrow and next week. Lieutenant Platt of 3<sup>rd</sup> Section is the acting commander until Captain Hunt returns. Insure the men stick together in a minimum of pairs. The town is full of pro-slavery bludgers that have been waylaying and robbing soldiers! Tell them no travelin' alone. Also tell them that we still shoot deserters!"

He looked over his noncommissioned officers, he was proud of the leaders he had built. They were finest leaders he had seen and he was glad to have them.

Giving them one last look, he waved them away, First Sergeant O'Keefe was not optimistic about their future, he could smell war.

At morning formation the First Sergeant announced to M Company the pass policy. The men cheered the news as he droned out the first and second guard mounts for the day.

Joshua had volunteered to man the first mount to permit his crew to enjoy some time off. Lieutenant Platt had also agreed to take the majority of Officer of the Day watches in order to permit the officers some time off.

O'Keefe then warned of a busy week after the liberty and advised the men to make the best of what remained of this week. Little did they realize how busy the second week of April would become.

As the morning wore on and the men left Fort Hamilton in groups and pairs, Joshua bid each group the best of luck in the city. He noticed his crew was sticking together led by Wilkins, the "New Yawker"; they had the decency to thank their gunner for the chance to go as a group and asked if they could bring him something.

Joshua replied, "Bring back things to read." Joshua took a piece of paper out and decided to write Lottie a letter,

*"Dear Lottie,*
*I apologize for taking so long to reply to your last letter, we have gone from*
*Texas now as the people there, like home, have decided to leave the union. We*
*are now in New York refitting and awaiting orders. I am happy to hear you are*
*in school in Charleston and hope that someday I can be close enough to visit. It*
*troubles me to read the news these days as I am shocked that America seems to*
*be spinning apart. I have been proud to serve my Country but sometimes I feel*
*that I no longer have one. I am far too invested in my duty to my soldiers and*
*my Company now to lightly ignore oaths I have taken. I pray that*
*I am not asked to serve against my home as I pray my home will not wage war*
*upon my Oath. This whole thing fills me with a hopelessness that I cannot*
*explain. Thank you for your letters, they brighten my day and remind me of*
*better days. Take care and*
*keep me in your prayers.*
*Joshua."*

When he had finished he folded the paper into an envelope and addressed it. Lieutenant Platt watched him and as he addressed it he noted that it was going to South Carolina.

He remarked, "Corporal, you will have to write "Care of Fortress Monroe transfer" on the top of that. All mail going to seceded states is transferred through Fortress Monroe now."

He thought a moment, "I will check with the Fort Hamilton Adjutant, it may need to be checked by a censoring officer as well."

Joshua was surprised but nodded that it would be alright. He could hear the taunting he would receive in his imagination for having a "secesh" lady friend.

Platt just smiled and assured him, "No worries Joshua, we saw how you stuck with us in Texas when it got bad. Is she pretty?"

Joshua nodded, he resolved to ask her in his next letter to send a daguerreotype image if she could go to the trouble of getting one made.

He decided when he got liberty to do likewise in the city despite the expense to obtain one. He spent the rest of his 8 hour guard mount walking the quadrangle of the massive stone fortress.

He was relieved to be able to see their 4 guns, none the worse for wear after 3 years of campaigning. He found his with the 003 on the trunnion and ran his finger along the engraving on the muzzle. He began to make mental calculations of what his section was missing in terms of equipment and resolved to work tirelessly to replace it all as soon as he could. It was an honor to be a part M Company, it had become his home.

When his relief arrived, a caisson driver from 2$^{rd}$ Section, Joshua started to walk back to his empty bay when he was summoned by O'Keefe. "Timmonds get a frock coat on and grab your purse!"

Joshua looked in the direction of the call and saw the First Sergeant, O'Brien, Mills and O'Rourke.

O'Brien shouted out, "Yeah, we need a Corporal to do our fighting for us!"

O'Keefe waved him to follow in a hurried fashion.

Joshua was unused to the casual Billy O'Keefe as the others called him. He noticed that O'Keefe's Irish brogue was more pronounced when he was not "On Parade"

The men laughed and joked as they passed out the sally port into the giant maze of Brooklyn. O'Keefe was letting Mills know his promotion was due and he would let him know when they would give him his Section Sergeant stripes.

O'Brien clapped Joshua on the back as they walked and congratulated him on doing so well in Texas. O'Keefe surprisingly praised him as well and informed him that he was going to buy him a pint.

As they walked through the incredibly bustling and crowded town, most people seemed to be intent on going where they were headed but a few would look up and shout curses.

O'Keefe remarked, "It is quite odd to me that these good citizens behave so much like you Southerners, Timmonds!"

O'Brien piped up to share in the joke, "Yeah, Joshua this trip we are taking with you is a loyalty test, it is. I've got a gold dollar riding that you skip tonight!"

Joshua, getting in the mood, retorted, "Sergeant, you should be watching Mills, I hear he is from near here!"

The men laughed and continued until they found a properly Irish pub, "The Harp." Pushing inside, Joshua noticed of course that the establishment had obviously been blessed by Fort Hamilton as it was nearly full of soldiers. The pub was full of M Company soldiers and C Company infantrymen, their fellow Texas sufferers.

That evening Joshua got his education on being Irish, The men argued among themselves as to the Irishness of "Timmonds" and finally after several more rounds commonly agreed that he most likely was and thereby knighted him as a honorary "Dirty Irish" and made him swear to inform all when a Catholic Chaplain was found in the Army.

As the men half carried each other home that evening, Joshua found that First Sergeant O'Keefe liked to give advice when he was very drunk.

"Don' ever get into no arguments with the men, boy'o." He lightly poked his finger on Joshua's chest and added, "You gots the makings of a sergeant in you lad, jus' don' let any of them boys get all friendly wid ya! Get them to do your will!"

The First Sergeant stumbled along quiet for a while and added, "If ya make friends with them they just die, be their boss boy, be their boss…"

As they got nearer to Fort Hamilton his utterances became more and more unintelligible, Joshua could make out "Chapultepec" a few times but not much else. The old man was thinking about Mexico more and more it seemed.

The week of light duty and liberty flew by. Most of the men in M Company no longer had enough pay to do very much drinking anymore. Joshua had carefully wrapped and addressed the Tin Type image he and Sergeant Shepperd had arranged to have made in town. Joshua would send his, proudly arrayed in his frock coat, and shoulder boards, to Lottie. Hopefully she would reciprocate.

Captain Hunt returned, looking cleaner and with his beard trimmed much neater and began to resume gun drills and focused on refitting the Company. He arranged for First Sergeant O'Keefe to hold a formation to promote Sergeant Mills to Section Sergeant for the 1$^{st}$ Section of guns for M Company.

Hunt shook his hand and promptly put him to work. He had received orders from Colonel Brown. They were going to Florida, within days and without horses.

Hunt met with Colonel Brown that afternoon, quite frustrated by his assignment as "Foot Artillery" to reinforce Fort Pickens on Santa Rosa Island at the mouth of Pensacola Harbor.

"Sir, this is a waste of my company's capabilities!" He was amazed that M Company had been relegated to a static fortress mission.

Colonel Brown was sympathetic but emphatic, "Captain Hunt, I understand your frustration but the reinforcement is critical, the desertion of Captain Winder has left a Lieutenant and an undermanned company of artillery facing a rebel brigade with heavy artillery that could move to take the Fort at any time!"

He pulled out a map of the area, pointing to the spit east of the Fortress, "Providing you horses is meaningless on a sand island less than a mile wide, you will not be required to maneuver. This position is where you will occupy with the 3$^{rd}$ Infantry Companies; your ammunition supply will be stockpiled at the redoubts that my engineers will construct for you there."

He paused and added, "There will be plenty of naval support as well."

Captain Hunt studied the map and asked, "Will the Ordnance shops here be able to manufacture the ammunition I will need for the light 12 pounders?"

Colonel Brown assured him it would commence immediately. He also informed him that Captain M.C. Meigs would be his operations officer. Brown instructed

Captain Hunt to coordinate the loading of the Steam Tug R. L. Mabey which would be used to transfer the troops and equipment to the steamer Atlantic for the trip to Pensacola.

Joshua rushed the crew along as they collected and packed their equipment. They would take only the guns and limbers.

The crews were astonished as he relayed the brief that he had received by First Sergeant O'Keefe, "We are to reinforce Fort Pickens in Florida. We will operate as Foot Artillery and will occupy redoubts with the infantry once we go ashore. Our objective is to defend the Eastern approach to the Fort to assist the infantry against any assault by State of Florida troops. The Captain has said we will load today, and we expect to land in Florida in 5 days."

As the men gathered in Fort Hamilton's quadrangle and loaded the battery wagons, Quartermaster Sergeant Mills arrived in another wagon filled with boxes of fixed cartridges for the Light 12 pounders, "Listen up Sections, once we get to the pier, each section will secure 4 boxes one of shot, one of shell, one of spherical case, and one of canister. This depot ain't got any Bormann fuses so we will have to use inserts and paper ones!"

Corporal Shepperd shouted out, "Did you get friction primers?" Mills nodded, "Yep, and the good ones."

As the day wore into early evening the order to move to the Pier was given and M Company was on their way. Horse teams were loaned to get the guns and limbers to the pier and once that task was accomplished they were led away.

By late that evening they had boarded the Atlantic for movement to Florida. First Sergeant O'Keefe was particularly venomous when asked how he liked the new mission. Many of the men made it a point to ask him. The company was told by the First Officer of the Atlantic to expect a 5 day trip.

After the First Sergeant had given evening reports for the sections to him Captain Hunt went topside for a breath of night air.

On the darkened deck he was surprised when a man walked up to him, "Major Hunt?" he asked, Hunt nodded.

"Allow me to introduce myself Sir, I am Captain Meigs, of the Engineers. I am pleased to see you with us. I have heard of your unique battery."

Hunt laughed bitterly and replied, "Yes, the Foot battery!"

Meigs laughed and replied, "Yes, sorry about that, but I meant the light 12 pounders. I should very much like to see them tomorrow if you would care to show them to me."

Hunt replied that he would be happy to.

Meigs bid him a good evening and reminded him that Colonel Brown would be holding an Officers meeting at 8 am the next morning to discuss the mission.

Hunt nodded, Meigs seemed to be a good man. He had rumors that he was well connected but he did not know how. He decided to make a point to get to know him better, it might be useful.

# Fort Pickens, Florida
# 18 April 1861

Lieutenant John Worden, of the United States Navy, realized that his best dress uniform shoes were surely ruined now. He was walking the approach to Fort Pickens from the landing where Florida State Militia troops had dropped him off in a small rowboat.

The sentry at the landing was not expecting a friend and directed him to the gate. He peered at the Fort, as the day began to warm up; he realized he still had quite a distance to walk. He reflected as he walked towards the fort, on his activities of the past week.

It had all started with the sudden and mysterious summons to the Navy Department on the 3rd of April. He had met with Mr. Wells, himself, the Secretary of the Navy; at 10 pm.

Mr. Wells had produced for him orders signed by President Lincoln, himself, to carry to Captain John Adams aboard the sloop-of-war Brooklyn off Pensacola. The orders were intended to countermand orders from President Buchanan that had halted the reinforcement of Fort Pickens.

Gideon Wells patiently explained the larger situation, whereby both Forts Sumter and Pickens were under siege, and at hazard of being taken, that reinforcements for both bastions had been arranged for and dispatched.

The ad hoc truce arranged between President Buchanan and a resigning Florida Senator, a certain Mr. Mallory, had resulted in a stalemate where a Captain with a squadron of ships loaded with troops was sitting off Pickens with the wrong orders.

Worden remembered asking how he was to get there, and was surprised by Secretary Wells giving him instructions to go by train.

Wells explained it would be faster than by sea and since secession was a political move, most businesses to include the railroads still operated as normal.

Worden had then asked how should he dress and Wells had emphasized that he would quite naturally go in his uniform as a direct agent of the Secretary of the Navy. Wells also provided him directions to call on General Bragg of the Florida States Troops in Pensacola, word would be sent to General Bragg by the U.S. Government via telegram to permit your passage to Fort Pickens.

As he walked down the sandy road towards the fort he remembered the long and lonely 4 day train ride from Washington D.C. to Pensacola.

It had been like routine business travel through Virginia and North Carolina but the environment began to change for the worse on the trains through Georgia and Alabama.

He remembered how he felt urgently compelled to destroy his written order from Lincoln in the washroom of the train on the way from Atlanta to Montgomery.

Georgia State Troops riding in the same car made the realization that his insignia on his hat read "U.S. Navy", he remembered that being an officer was the only deterrent to them attacking him.

His walk took him by some old sand ramparts that had been constructed to guard the approaches to the fort from the eastern stretch of Santa Rosa Island and he decided to mount one to see beyond the dunes. Peering to the South, he could barely make out ships masts in the gulf, beyond the Fort.

Worden had found it odd, that General Bragg had civilly received him and had issued him a pass through the Florida Troop lines without question.

General Bragg emphasized that the pass gave him 24 hours safe passage through the lines, He even provided the boat and crew to get him across the sound.

Worden had nearly fully unbuttoned his frock coat as he approached the fort in the humid Florida heat and he trudged forward towards the main sally port until he was hailed by a sentry on the fortress wall.

He wearily shouted out, "I am Lieutenant Worden of the United States Navy with an urgent message for Captain Adams of the U.S.S. Brooklyn, please take me to your commander."

The sentry disappeared and a few moments later the gated sally port was opened.

A rather tall young bespectacled man greeted him, "Welcome Sir, I am Lieutenant Slemmer of G Company, 1st Artillery."

Worden asked, "Is your commander available? I have an urgent message to deliver."

Slemmer replied, "You are looking at him sir."

Lieutenant Slemmer had no earthly idea of the older man's rank as Navy uniforms, with their sleeve stripe rank system, were a mystery to him.

Slemmer motioned to Worden to follow him to the shade of his office. So the business at hand could be discussed.

As they walked across the interior of the fort, Worden noticed the artillerymen had been sleeping by their guns inside the shady open casemates.

They eagerly shouted out, "Are the reinforcements coming?"

Slemmer trudged on ignoring the shouts only commenting to Worden, "We are somewhat anxious Sir, those ships out there were cheered by us when they arrived. They have sat there for nearly 10 weeks doing nothing. I have fired signal shots on occasion but they do not respond. We have no idea what is going on aside from repeated demands for surrender being delivered by General Bragg from Florida."

They arrived at the office of the commander in the nearly empty barracks building and they sat at a table in the Lieutenant's open windowed office, a light breeze from the ocean air made it more bearable than outside in the sun.

Worden explained his mission and the orders to reinforce the fort, despite his discomfort at revealing the message before delivering to Captain Adams.

He was shocked when Slemmer asked him what day it was. "12$^{th}$ of April, tomorrow is Saturday" he had replied.

Slemmer explained that he had no contact with the fleet off shore, and only one small rowboat. Sadly he had no means to convey him to the fleet.

Worden asked him if he had a signaler in the fort.

The young officer explained no, he had only those elements particular to a heavy artillery company. Slemmer complained that he had lost 2 officers and several men to desertion when Florida had seceded. He described how he had been left in charge of the company after his Captain had resigned his commission along with the First Lieutenant to join Florida troops.

Worden nodded and understood his nervousness at them knowing precisely how ill equipped and undermanned they were at Fort Pickens.

Worden admired the young gangly lieutenant who had clearly done the right thing in horrible circumstances and had decided to make his stand here. He realized this mission while odd was worthwhile; he would bring relief to this heroic young man.

Worden looked at him and directed, "Give me a detail of two smart men; I will create signalers for you. We will need two good lanterns and spy glasses."

Lieutenant Worden asked for a scrap of paper and a pen; reaching back into his memory from his midshipman days, he hastily scribbled down the Alphabet and the corresponding 4 element code for each letter.

His trainees would also need a scrap of paper with the 4 digit signal patterns to correctly identify the numbers sent and received.

Worden explained to Slemmer as he scribbled and he noticed the young officer was fascinated.

Worden explained that each time the Fort had fired their cannon before; that signalmen in the masts had been scanning the parapets to find the fort's signalers. "I imagine they had been quite anxious to correspond with you!" he explained, "This time we shall give them what they search for."

Worden received a Sergeant and a Corporal for his trainees, after lunch he began to train them in how to hold the lanterns and the movements that were to be made to create the sign for 1, 2, 3, and 4. He patiently explained how to hail the distant signalman and then how to repeat messages back to confirm communication.

He periodically would send Lieutenant Slemmer on errands with instructions to provide a table, paper and pencils and a spy glass to facilitate the communication.

As the sun began to set West of the fort Worden had his two new signalmen rehearse sending each a simple message while Lieutenant Slemmer recorded the transmitted number patterns that Worden directed his signaler to send.

When he compared the result he was satisfied they could accomplish the task. Now he needed the night.

Aboard the Brooklyn as the stars made a magnificent show and the quarter moon emerged, Captain Adams decided to go topside for a smoke, He chatted with the idle helmsman who dutifully manned his unnecessary station according to staunch Navy tradition; despite the fact that the ship sat at anchor.

The men on their watches did their best to stay awake; it had been a long and boring 10 weeks off Pensacola.

Suddenly a flash was seen on the parapets of Fort Pickens followed by the boom seconds later.

The signalmen instinctively trained spy glasses from their watch stations in the masts of the Brooklyn.

A young signalman shouted down to the deck below, "The fort is hailing us and they have a signalman! Send up Torches!"

Captain Adams found himself interested by this development and ordered the deck officer to return the cannon signal from one of the starboard carronades.

As the smaller gun barked and flashed the torches were hoisted to the crow's nest in a bucket that had been lowered on a rope. The men began to quietly call out the numerical codes and scribbled down the raw data on a chalk board. As they worked they wondered why it had taken so long for Fort Picket to start communications. They hoped it was still Union men who were sending the message.

On the parapet of Fort Picket, Lieutenant Slemmer was amazed at how quickly the fleet signalers had responded once the professional protocol was followed,

163

he resolved at that moment to learn more about the other arms and specialties that his own Army produced. Weaving them together could make life much easier.

Worden observed, "We have succeeded in communicating gentlemen, now we will wait for a reply."

They continued to train their spy glasses on the motionless boats in the evening half-light.

On the Brooklyn the chalkboard was lowered to the First Officer, he glanced at the numbers and had a petty officer take it and translate the communication. Soon the man reappeared with a scrap of paper.

The First Officer went below decks to the Captains lighted and shuttered cabin, with the Captain following him.

Once they were in the light, he glanced at the message and said, "Sir, here is the communication from Fort Pickens."

He handed the paper to the Captain it read;

> *"lieut. worden usn urgt msg f. capt adams snd stmr ft pickens imy odr fm secr wells"*

The Captain read the abbreviation quickly understanding the meaning, he looked to the First Officer and said, "I think Secretary Wells has sent a courier to Fort Pickens with a message for us, they need a boat to get him to us."

Captain Adams looked at the message again and recognized the name. "Well I'll be damned, he sent John Worden, amazing! Send in a gunboat and insure they run in quiet and dark!"

The First Officer nodded and went topside to instruct the watch officer to signal the fort that a boat was being sent.

On the parapet of Fort Pickens Worden noted that lights emerged on the masts of the steamer and alerted his detail.

The men dutifully recorded the response and Lieutenant Slemmer after a few minutes of comparing his translation by lamplight proudly announced, "Sir I think they say "Sending gunboat."

Worden smiled and said "Good work men! Lieutenant Slemmer, dispatch a detail with a lamp to guide the boat in, I strongly suggest you guide them to a point masked from the shore batteries on Pensacola, we need to do this quietly!"

The smaller gunboat detached itself from the squadron at anchor and made its way stealthily to the sandy shore of Santa Rosa Island shielded from view of Pensacola.

The Captain of the small gun boat was relieved that no apparent notice of the activity had occurred, the Florida batteries appeared to be asleep.

He dispatched a small surf boat to pick up the courier and once he had secured him they silently returned alongside the Brooklyn.

Worden bounded up the gangway and saluted Captain Adams and said, "Sir, Secretary Wells conveys his regards! I have orders to convey to you from President Lincoln to land reinforcements immediately and in full strength. Your squadron is to support the landing and remain on station. 3 more ships bearing reinforcements should arrive shortly and they are to be landed as well. Mr. Wells was emphatic that you understand that President Buchanan's earlier order is countermanded!"

Captain Adams replied, "Thank you John, It is good to see you in good health, may I see this order?"

Worden, crestfallen, replied "No sir I no longer have the written original as I was required to destroy it on the train in Georgia when state troops were questioning me in regards to my presence!"

Captain Adams smiled, "I guess I will rely on the word of a fellow Academy man."

He turned to the First Officer and said, "Swing out the davits and lower the oar boats, let us get this landing underway, send for the Army and Marine commanders, I will consult with them in my quarters!"

He looked at Lieutenant Worden and asked, "John what additional instructions do you have?"

Worden replied, "Sir, I am to  return overland back to Washington. I have a pass from the Florida State troops commander back out through Pensacola."

Captain Adams was worried as the landing would breach the truce and instructed the First Officer to hail the gunboat captain to prepare a special boat crew for the messenger.

They would land Worden first with the reinforcements and get him across the sound to Pensacola, he would have to walk through the lines before sunrise.

Worden thanked him and asked if any messages were to be conveyed back.

Captain Adams said no. He was sure the additional ships arriving would have further updates. He was also fearful that John Worden would not get far away, fast enough, to evade capture.

Charlotte Markley was fast asleep in her upstairs bedroom of the l'Ecole Buissonniere School on Legare Street in midtown Charleston.

Tomorrow she would have a light day with only a single piano class.

The Headmistress would permit the older girls the afternoon to wander Charleston and she had been anxious for tomorrow to come.

At 4 am she was awakened by the bells being rung at Saint Michael's church. It was an odd pealing of bells as they were only chimed 4 times, as she started to doze off again, a window rattling boom shook the fair April night. The sound wave reverberated in the crisp spring air.

Rising she wrapped a shawl about her shoulders and peered out to the bedroom window.

The sky above the rooftops lit like from lightning when another rattling boom was heard.

Thinking a moment she realized that Fort Moultrie lay in that direction. Another loud boom and flash came from where she recalled the harbor entrance lay.

She pulled on a robe and ran downstairs.

Madame Corvet' had an excited look as she came in the front door off the side porch, "My goodness they are bombarding Fort Sumter!"

Charlotte went back upstairs to the small rooftop stair and climbed out on the small widow's walk on the top of the boarding school roof, other girls from the bedrooms below had already gathered there and as she looked around she could make out people on the roofs of most of the houses in the neighborhood.

Charlotte was frustrated that the view was poor, she noticed a glow where Fort Sumter lay, and could make out flashes coming from Mount Pleasant and the James Island area. They could occasionally see a Whirling sparkling track of the fuses of the explosive shells as they arced through the air.

After watching for an hour and talking excitedly to her schoolmates she suddenly realized with a sinking feeling, the gravity of the event.

There truly was to be a war. Her mind shifted to Joshua who had only recently sent her a photograph of him in his Army uniform. Now; it was the wrong uniform.

She sadly returned to her room and took the picture, so proudly displayed until tonight, and placed it inside her cedar chest.

Joshua was assisting his crew in repacking the limber chest on the sunny deck of the Atlantic.

The weather had improved significantly as they rounded the coast of Florida and the balmy conditions made them all lazy.

Fortunately Captain Meigs had been able to convince the navy to provide Bormann fuses to Captain Hunt in exchange for the archaic paper fuses provided at Fort Hamilton.

Once he had procured them he had instructed the crews to remove the iron paper fuse wells from the spherical case shot and shell loaded in the chests and replace them with the iron fuse bases to support the Bormanns.

He did not trust unpacking the actual fuses until they were safely ashore.

As they worked the task the sailors began to announce that they were approaching Pensacola.

The men rushed to the rail to look at the distant fort surrounded by masts of the earlier relief force.

From what they could make out the ships off shore were unloading forces ashore. Joshua found it curious that no firing of guns was occurring.

M Company was put ashore last, after the companies of Infantry all had been landed. It was almost evening of the 13th of April before the first flatboats containing the "Foot Battery" grounded on the light surf of Santa Rosa Island.

The men of the company used the prolongues to tow the guns across the sand to a small redoubt east of the fortress walls.

Captain Barry found Captain Hunt in the twilight and had him follow him. They were to meet with Colonel Brown at the Fort.

Captain Meigs greeted the men when they came into the now well-lit and busy barracks building. He paused to inform Henry Hunt that the request memorandums that he had written while underway had been left with the Captain of the Atlantic. Post

The Captain had promised to post it as soon as they made landfall in the Dry Tortugas to take on coal.

"Hopefully your request for Horses will be heard."

Colonel Brown discussed their dispositions for defense of the fort on a large paper map spread on the table.

To Hunt it was clear that the largest threat would remain the eastern approaches of Santa Rosa Island. Forces from Florida could easily cross Pensacola bay at any point to land infantry without interception from the Navy and threaten the fort.

His fixed position on the redoubt facing east of the fort was to be critical to that defense. Captain Barry's mobile artillery would serve as a reaction force to respond to wherever Colonel Brown needed them.

Hunt grudgingly accepted his mission as sound since his Napoleons had twice the effective range of Barry's 6 pounders.

Hunt was anxious to get back to his men.

Later that evening a few desultory and ineffective shots were fired from the floating battery across the harbor entrance towards Fort Pickens, war now existed in Florida.

Lieutenant John Worden sat and read a Pensacola newspaper and attempted to appear as unobtrusive as possible.

He had been successful in returning through the lines early that morning and had even managed to walk quickly enough through Pensacola on a quiet Saturday morning; he had fortunately moved fast enough to catch the 9 am train to Montgomery.

General Bragg found himself summoned by a courier at his temporary home along the bay waterfront. He had not planned on coming into work early that day.

The courier announced, "Sir, begging your forgiveness for the disturbance, but Captain Winder has determined that Federal Troops have landed to reinforce Fort Pickens!"

He sat for a moment and took in the news.

He found a piece of paper on his roll top desk in the parlor and dipping his pen, he began to write, "Return this to Winder, consider a state of war between us and the Federal troops at the fort."

He had a habit of talking out loud as he wrote, "Close off all communications with Santa Rosa Island. Attempt to locate courier sent yesterday from Federal Navy Department, apprehend if found."

He wanted to know the message that had been delivered in detail.

Worden noticed that the train was coming to a slow halt. He looked up in the car and all he could see out the windows was open country and woods, so he resumed his reading.

The train then came to a complete stop and he heard some talking taking place over the noises of the engine.

He looked up when he heard the carriage door open and two men and the conductor entered the car. The two men were clearly officers of the Alabama Militia wearing fine gray uniforms with buff faced collars.

They walked directly to him and asked, "You sir, are Lieutenant Worden of the U. S. Navy?"

Worden nodded, he knew inside that he had not made it to safety.

The older officer directed, "Sir, you will accompany us as you are now under arrest for engaging in espionage against the sovereign State of Alabama." Worden rose and gathered his belongings and accompanied the men. He would remain imprisoned for a year.

Joshua and his crew had spent the remainder of the month of April feverishly improving their positions and training on the guns.

The expected attack had yet to materialize although the number of fortified batteries increased facing Fort Pickens.

By the end of April, Lieutenant Slemmer and his battery had been replaced by another heavy artillery company of the 1st Regiment.

The requisitioned horses for Company M never showed. Captain Hunt grew more and more frustrated by the inaction.

By this time the news of Fort Sumter had filtered in with the delivery of mail, much delayed, by the Navy.

Joshua and his crew had become masters of the game of Dominos; the box of bones would become a crew tradition.

Hunt had remarked to First Sergeant O'Keefe, "I find nothing more grating than to be a shooting war with nothing to shoot at!"

O'Keefe had responded, "No worries Captain, I suspect you will have your fill of shooting soon enough."

## Schuylkill Arsenal, Pennsylvania
## 19 April 1861

Captain Gibbon scanned the telegram sent by the War Department providing warning to the Arsenal to begin preparations to support President Lincoln's call for 75,000 volunteers to muster to fight the insurrection.

Gibbon shook his head at the immensity of the task that lay before him.

Taking up a pencil he made a quick estimate just for sack coats to equip this many soldiers with the Army basic 5 year campaign allowance, 75,000 times 8 came to 600,000 sack coats in Army blue wool.

He called his clerk in to alert him to be prepared to take a reply back to the telegraph station in Philadelphia.

He pulled out a clean sheet of paper and drafted up his response. He needed guidance of the basis of issue and when expected production was to be delivered by.

He also requested additional purchasing agents to be dispatched to the Arsenal to assist in the ordering of raw material for uniforms and equipment for the prodigious number of men he would be required.

Thinking for a moment he realized that this call up exceeded anything that had ever been requested from the arsenal system.

The Arsenal at Schuylkill did not produce arms, it produced everything else; shirts, socks, shoes, coats, hats, pants, raincoats, tents, knapsacks, canteens and leather gear.

Every item that clothed or supported the life of the soldier was manufactured and stored here.

Gibbon determined to make an estimate of the total cost and then abandoned the notion; it would distract him for hours in that pointless endeavor.

Returning to his reply he asked that additional purchasing agents report to the Arsenal preferably next week.

The image of the wool cloth the order would require emerged in his mind, "2.4 million yards!"

He concluded that this endeavor would require every producer in the loyal states would be required to alter production to government orders in order to meet this magnitude of demand.

He also decided to add comments that suggested to the War Department that overseas purchases of raw material be considered in order to expedite production.

This included raw cotton as he expected the formerly organic asset to rapidly become scarce as his army of seamstresses in Philadelphia consumed the woven material on hand.

Gibbon then summoned his warehouse operations manager. He would need a complete update on all stocks currently on hand; he explained to the manager that they were to be prepared to respond to orders in a first come first served basis as normal for now but to expect prioritization to be changed. He wanted to understand what had already been produced and stockpiled at the Arsenal warehouses.

Two weeks later in Lowell, Massachusetts a government purchase agent called on the Sales Manager of the Merrimack Manufacturing Company.

Lowell was a city of factories and factory workers who since the revolution had been harnessing the power of the many rivers that crossed the Bay State.

Most of the families that had established the firms in the valley had roots to the English textile industry. Many had fled to America during the English Industrial Revolution to escape the strangling government regulation, and inflexible domination of the specialist's guilds.

The action of leaving England, in itself, was illegal; as trade secrets considered vital to the Crown, were compromised by the action. This issue had become one of the causes of the War of 1812.

As the Manager and the Government purchaser discussed the requirements, the Sales Manager suggested the agent visit the Dye Plant to insure that the proper hues of uniform color be obtained.

An initial order was agreed upon at this first meeting of 500,000 yards of blue wool fabric of medium 13 ounce weight.

The Sales Manager quickly calculated that this order would likely insure the future of the mills for a century. After meeting with the Government purchaser and agreeing to meet again to finalize the contract, the Sales Manager rushed to meet with the President of Merrimack. This would be large news.

The purchasing agent retrieved his horse and rode the half mile to another complex where the skeins of processed wool yarn were dyed; the sales manager had directed him to seek out a Mr. Ladd.

As he approached the large brick building he noticed the horrible smell.

Archibald Ladd was a 6th generation dye master. His father's father had left England after the Revolutionary War to ply his trade in America.

The hierarchy of the guilds of garment dyers had driven him away to seek his fortune elsewhere.

The government purchaser found him on the smelly processing floor where large dip tanks of "moad" or dye baths were arranged.

The agent tipped his hat and offered his hand to Ladd.

When Ladd reciprocated is when the agent noted the man's arms and hands were a dark brown color. Years of supervising the process had left their mark.

The agent produced color samples of government sky blue for trousers and navy blue for coats, "Sir, the sales manager will contact you regarding a large government order for uniforms due to the rebellion. Here are samples of the two specifications for cloth we will order."

Ladd nodded, "I understand sir, I am familiar with the Army color schemes although it has been a while since the firm has produced it. What sort of quantity will be required?"

The purchase agent replied, "500,000 yards."

Ladd let out a low whistle, and remarked "Now my arms shall be blue!"

The agent wrinkled his nose as he followed Ladd to his small windowed office on the corner of the dye building floor, "Pray tell, why does it smell so bad?"

Mr. Ladd laughed, "Wool does not take dye easily, your color base must be dissolved in an alkaline bath, we at The Merrimack Company employ cattle urine."

Ladd noticed that the agent left quickly, the smell did that, he became preoccupied with the quantity of indigo they would have to assemble.

He recalled reading that the South was breaking away and was personally angry about the betrayal of Fort Sumter. Many of the men in the plants had been mentioning a desire to join the army to set things right.

It only made sense that Mr. Lincolns declaration would result in government orders, he just wondered if there was enough material to produce an order that large.

He walked outside to their warehouses across the road from the Main Dye building and unlocked the swinging door to where the indigo was stored.

The dark musty room was full of burlap wrapped cakes, he sorted through what he had trying to estimate how much was available, as he sorted through cakes with indecipherable labels applied by the East India Company he came across cakes that made him grin.

They had been marked *"E.J. Markley Charleston District SC."*

Ladd remarked out loud, "I will use these cakes first! The slaves that made this shall be freed by the uniforms produced with it!"

Making his estimate of stocks he knew he needed much more. He would draft up an order to drop off to the main purchasing office.

In the meantime he would finish the current orders and switch the entire floor over to blue.

By the end of the week the workers on the Dye building floor were dipping long rods of white spun wool in the indigo moad tanks, Ladd watched as the skeins first turned yellow, then green, and finally increasingly dark shades of blue as the air contacted the dye.

He periodically would check the work and direct repeated dips to obtain the right color. Once this had been achieved the skeins were rushed over still dripping to the weaving floor to be milled into bolts of cloth.

The finished bolts were to be rushed to the Schuylkill Arsenal.

Captain Gibbon finished up a meeting with several purchasing agents working the shoe project.

He knew the production of army brogans would be the biggest challenge. To simplify production he decided to reduce the specification to wooden pegged soles and to make both feet on a common straight last.

He remained concerned that with leather supplies being what they were with the other accoutrements being made as well that shoes would be a challenge to meet the numbers that would be ordered. He had sent agents all over the Northeast to contract cobblers into the "cause" he hoped it would suffice.

The process of manufacturing uniforms was proceeding much better. He was aggravated that he had encountered a button shortage and it required changes to reduce the sack coat to only 4 for the time being, thinking on the modification he shrugged, they might not look as fine as other armies did, but at least they would be uniform.

Near the Industrial complex of Schuylkill, at the Phoenix Iron Company, Superintendent John Griffen, resolved to improve upon his wrought iron cannon design.

The war news and the presidential call up caused him to speculate that the ordnance requirements of an additional 75,000 troops would at a ratio of 1 gun per 1000 troops would result in at least 75 additional field guns being ordered to support the newly raised force.

Griffen remembered his father relaying the story of a horrific government display of a cast cannon which burst aboard a ship. This was a failure that apparently was common and it had nearly killed President Tyler in 1844, surely a company as modern as the Phoenix works could provide better to the Army.

Griffen had patents on his rifled wrought iron gun design; that had been satisfactorily tested by the Army in 1857 at Fortress Monroe.

While the ordnance officers were greatly impressed by the effectiveness and strength of the piece, the tests had resulted in no orders.

Griffen turned a portion of the works away from the rolling of iron railroad rails and focused on a newer method of making the wrought iron gun.

He consulted with his designers to form the tube from rolled iron sheet coiled around a central mandrel that once brought to the required thickness was then brought to welding heat and roll welded together.

This was a change from the original design employing the longitudinal foundation of rods welded together around the mandrel and then spirally wrapping that foundation with additional layers of wrought iron strap.

The method from his original patent resulted in a high number of rejected samples due to the large amount of forge welding required. The rolled sheet process would cure that and it was faster.

The super strong barrel was then plugged and wrought closed on one end and a minimal cascabel and knob was wrought to close the tube. Trunnions were then welded to the center of gravity and the finished product was machined to a very business-like taper. He estimated that it would prove to be the safest iron rifle in the inventory.

Perhaps the army would like these better than the Parrot design. He resolved to find out.

Colonel Symington accompanied his visitor, Major Waite, from the Ordnance department as they toured the Allegheny Arsenal grounds.

Waite had visited to explore the possibility of expansion of the Arsenal by War Department direction.

Mr. Lincoln's expansion of the Army would soon require massive increases to ammunition production.

The two men climbed the steps onto the stone loading dock of the Laboratory where a small crew of nimble fingered young girls and ladies worked under the careful supervision of the laboratory supervisor.

Symington explained to his visitor, "We prefer the ladies as they have demonstrated superior dexterity in the repetitive task of rolling and tying musket cartridges."

He picked up a standard "Buck and Ball" cartridge from the work position of the laboratory and showed it to Waite, "They can produce about 1 cartridge every minute."

Waite looked over the operation and remarked, "We will need to expand it immensely."

He looked around a bit more and asked, "Can you expand sir?"

Symington thought a moment, observing, "We currently employ 300 employees out of Lawrenceville at our current rate of production, given the resources I would expect we can."

Waite continued to walk around the premises then he asked to see the magazines for powder storage.

The two men walked down the cobblestone streets to a row of brick warehouses.

"These barrels contain the musket grade powder we get from New York, we have never been very happy with their packing methods so we insure they are stored in rain proof buildings, my operations can empty a barrel in half a day." Symington observed.

Waite, paused and took some notes, and added, "Sir, the War Department wants us to think in terms of millions of rounds. As training requirements alone would deplete our current rates of production."

Colonel Symington nodded, "I think we could manage that, I will meet with my foremen to discuss the expansion."

The two men repaired to the Colonel's office for some coffee and a smoke, no fire or any sort was permitted in the vicinity of the magazines and the laboratory.

Waite lit a cigar after filling his cup from the pot on the office clerks stove.

Waite expressed his concern about the Army being able to produce the powder required to support such a massive increase in production.

Symington was puzzled and said, "I should think we managed fine for the war with Mexico."

Waite nodded, replying, "That was with Virginia, all of our usable Calcium Nitrate is mined out of Virginia, now that they have seceded we have little to no source of supply."

He continued, "We have already sent agents to England to attempt to procure Indian Saltpeter to make up for it."

Waite shook his head, "The rebels now control one of our most vital mineral resources! I imagine they are extracting the stuff like mad, even as we speak."

Waite remembered touring the caverns when stationed at Harper's Ferry as a Lieutenant.

He was amazed at the primitive conditions the "Peterseekers" worked in. He recalled also how much work went into the production of so small an amount of product. It took hundreds of such operations to provide Nitre in the quantities needed by an army. Perhaps importing it was the answer.

Waite emphasized to Symington that they were to frequently conduct quality inspections of the powder before processing it into cartridges owing to the variability of supply.

This included the use of the pressure test guns to insure the powder possessed sufficient potency to match the sights of the newer rifled muskets.

The two men sat and smoked and discussed the new Minie bullet and Symington got up to show Waite some samples of the cartridges that would be made to accommodate the 1855 rifle musket.

By June 1861 Colonel Symington would have nearly 800 workers making ammunition at Allegheny Arsenal.

This was also the month he learned that of all his male relatives; he was the only one who still soldiered for the Union.

He had begun to consider retiring.

The honor of being an ordnance officer was beginning to lose its gleam to him, he reflected on the resignations of Mordecai and Huger; both friends and fellow Southerners, perhaps it was time to move on.

# 8 THE ARLINGTON LINE

## Columbia, South Carolina
## 4 June 1861

Governor Pickens looked out at the sea of eager faces as he stood on the impromptu stage that had been emplaced for him to address the men.

Beside the Governor, stood Colonel Wade Hampton; South Carolina's representative warrior. Following the bombardment of Fort Sumter, Hampton had resigned his seat on the State Senate and tried to enlist.

Governor Pickens had gotten news of this and insured that the State's richest planter was granted a Colonelcy as was fitting for such a man.

The men of the Legion had just finished two days of inspection and acceptance reviews of their drill for mobilization as Confederate States troops to face the growing number of Federal troops massing before and occupying parts of Virginia.

He noticed that Hampton had retained the Legion Flag but also had provided the Richmond Depot flags, consisting of the three stripes, 2 red and 1 white with a field of blue containing the stars of the Confederate states. He also noticed that the Companies had retained their South Carolina Militia flags each with a slightly different variation of the Palmetto tree and the crescent moon. Looking out he saw the 2nd South Carolina Cavalry, made up of militia companies from across the state. He also saw the Infantry Regiment and men of the Artillery battery that supported the Legion.

Smiling, and proud of this contribution, he addressed the men,

> *"My fellow citizens of South Carolina, I stand before you humbled by this demonstration of selfless patriotism, on your part, as I see you stand here, willing to defend the ideals that we citizens of the South hold dear! You sons of South Carolina have declared your readiness to face those who threaten the principles and wisdom of our ancestors. I ask the Lord's blessings on your formations and your officers that you may prevail over the hirelings who seek to destroy us at the bidding of men who think themselves kings! Show them that the South is prepared to stand her ground for what is right and just. Defend the Sovereignty of Virginia as you would your own home. I look forward to the day when you return to your homes in peace and victory!*

The assembled men gave a loud "Hurrah!" despite their weariness and the stifling heat of the sandy pinewoods where they were assembled.

Soon they would be loading the mounts of the cavalry and the cannon of the artillery into trains for the long journey to Virginia.

In the crowd of men composing the 2nd South Carolina Cavalry were the members of the former Wassamassaw Cavalry.

Louis Markley and Jacob Timmonds had agreed to join together when the advertisements in the Charleston papers appeared in May.

Tom had reluctantly decided to finish his studies at the Citadel in Charleston as he was so very close to completing a degree.

Captain Winters had been accepted as well but with only the commission as a Lieutenant, which bothered him somewhat.

Colonel Hampton had provided the captaincy of the Company to a family friend, J.C. McKewn of Beaufort, so the Wassamassaw Cavalry had now become D Company 2$^{nd}$ South Carolina Cavalry.

The men did their best to cheer Winters up but he remained sullen, yet determined to go fight in any capacity.

Louis and Jacob excitedly gathered up their gear after the speech from the Governor, they would have to get the horses and the tack prepared for loading and the long train ride to Virginia.

Louis asked, "Have you heard from your brother lately?" Louis liked to ask Jacob this question as frequently as he could; knowing the reaction it would elicit from Jacob.

Jacob, sensing the taunt, remarked, "I hear he is sweeping Mr. Lincoln's floors."

Both boys laughed at the joke, even though for Jacob it was a bitter feeling to have a brother that forgot his home.

He was indeed curious but Mr. Markley and Lottie seemed to be the only ones getting news from him.

The last anybody knew he was sitting in a fort in Florida.

Governor Pickens, having seen off the Hampton Legion then rode in his carriage with his entourage to another sandy encampment under the pines.

There he would provide the exact same speech to Colonel Micah Jenkins and his 5$^{th}$ South Carolina Infantry Regiment. The 5$^{th}$ was another one of 9 regiments that South Carolina had donated to the cause.

Pickens had great respect for Jenkins as well; the young man represented to him the product of South Carolina's system. Jenkins, a recent graduate of The Arsenal and Citadel schools had been readily able to raise a formidable Regiment of men from the Militias upstate.

The governor knew from experience that this was no small feat, as the people from upstate were not so easy to inflame as the low country citizens.

Pickens envied the groups of younger men, remembering his days in the Army. He sighed as he approached Colonel Jenkins and his staff, realizing now that he had the burden of an entire state on his shoulders.

Before he began his address Jenkins had asked him for a private moment away from his staff, and the Governor's entourage. The two men walked a distance from the forming regiment.

"Sir, I cannot express my appreciation enough for your support for me and my Regiment, but I must trouble you again in regards to our weapons."

Governor Pickens shrugged and replied, "Micah, we have provided you with the best we have from the arsenals that we have assumed. The State did not receive the levy of rifles that other states obtained."

Jenkins, fearful of angering the governor, decided to persist, "Sir, the Regiment was raised on the assumption of becoming a regiment of riflemen, it is a waste sir, to send these men into battle with smoothbore muskets. I must implore you to communicate with Mr. Davis that we should have rifled muskets of the latest pattern available if we are to be effective!"

Governor Pickens assured the earnest young Colonel that he would do what he could and closed the discussion, "Let us go greet your soldiers!"

As the governor addressed the Regiment that like Hampton's Legion; was freshly sworn in to the Army of the Confederate States.

A young private from Jamestown, South Carolina craned his neck to get a glimpse of the Governor. He was thrilled to be included in this grand cause, his father had advised him to avoid being too anxious to see battle, but he had hardly listened.

The boy was William Cross; his father was a teamster who had served in Mexico.

His close friend Roland Sykes, who had grown up on a small hardscrabble farm outside of Georgetown asked, "What'n the sam hell you lookin' for Billy?"

"That's the Governor of the State, you fool!" Billy said in a fierce whisper.

Roland was non-plussed, "Puts his pants on just like us. Easy to be grand when you ain't gotta go off an' fight."

Their Sergeant walked up to the two men and reminded them of their manners, and both swiftly stood still and tried to listen.

After the ceremonies above the Saluda River had been concluded, the officers and sergeants had directed the immediate dismantlement of the encampments.

All units were to be moved to the rail yards as quickly as possible.

The men would be issued rations at the rail yards and would spend the night there until transportation could be sorted out for the long train movement to Virginia.

After a hot march over several miles the rail station came into view.

Billy was expecting something much grander, instead he only saw a large complex of brickmaking plants and the rail terminus that served the brick plant operation.

The Rifle Regiment had it easy, once they arrived they were marched to an open area vicinity of the rail yard and directed to set up a hasty camp, which meant no tents.

Quartermaster wagons were shortly brought by and the men were issued cornmeal and salted ham for rations and told to stick close by and await their call.

Jacob and Louis rode their pets to the same rail yard with the 2$^{nd}$ Cavalry and found a short train with cars awaiting them and the 6 pounders of the artillery.

To their collective dismay they learned that this train could only accommodate the guns and the horses.

A small detail of men was selected to accompany this train to watch the property of the Legion; another larger train would "be along shortly" to pick up the ranks.

After all the units had closed on the rail yard in Columbia, a messenger made the rounds looking for the Colonels.

He found Colonel Hampton in his tent holding court with his Regimental Commanders over cigars and bourbon.

"Sir, Major Wadsworth from General Bonham's staff, the general requests all Brigade Commanders to meet with him this evening, if you could follow me I will direct you to the place!"

Wade Hampton rose with a groan and handed his glass to his adjutant and put on his hat and followed the Major out and across the rail yard to a small Methodist Church on the near side of the rail yard.

Judging from the crowd about the place he figured he had been the last to be found.

As he walked into the structure he could see Jenkins and General Bonham talking quietly while they waited.

Seeing Hampton, Bonham beamed and greeted him, "Colonel Hampton it is a privilege to be in your company, Sir! I suppose you had grown weary with the Senate."

Hampton laughed, and observed, "Yes, this will be much better, you cannot settle differences with sabers in the Senate, you know."

General Bonham laughed and motioned to his aide to bring a map forward so they could consult.

He directed Major Wadsworth to hold the map for him so he could address the Commanders using it as a guide. He pointed out points of interest as he talked,

"Gentlemen, consider me a provisional division commander for the time being until we get to Virginia. I would like to acquaint you to the larger situation in Virginia and this will explain the haste in which we find ourselves at the moment."

Putting his finger on Washington City, he continued, "General McDowell is forming a vast Army of Mr. Lincoln's 75,000 volunteers and he is under great pressure to attack Richmond as soon as feasible.

McDowell has pushed forces across the Potomac and seized the Arlington Heights and the City of Alexandria. It is the belief of General Beauregard that he will attack either toward Harpers Ferry or the railroad terminus at Manassas."

He pointed to a point on the map halfway between Washington and Manassas and continued, "Approximately in a line from Harpers Ferry to here, which is a line from Vienna to Fairfax, Virginia is what General Beauregard is calling the "Arlington Line."

"We will likely be employed at any place between Harpers Ferry to the front at Fredericksburg. I expect we will receive further orders when we arrive at Richmond. See Major Wadsworth if you would like to review this information tonight or later on the train."

Bonham paused and added, "I will apologize now for the train situation, the railroad agents can give me no clear timeline of when the series of trains assigned to us will arrive. Seems that one thing the South has plenty of is willing souls, what we do not have enough of is railroad engines, I will warn you now, I expect a mess."

As the sun set over the brickyard, the trains had yet to arrive.

Billy Cross and his messmates sat and watched their "up-stater" Eugene Gerrard, everyone called him Gene, cook the cornmeal with the ham chunks in a recently liberated frying pan.

Their cook fire, made of Loblolly Pine limbs smoked badly but it got the job done.

Everyone had suggestions but Gene got angry when receiving advice so they decided to just watch him come up with the dish.

He added a little water and the concoction began to look a lot like grits, dirty grits, with ham chunks.

While Billy and Roland ate hungrily, George, who hailed from Columbia pulled out his bible and read psalms out loud to the mess.

He had been a lay pastor who had decided to join up. George could quote the Psalms from memory but he read them anyway, that way no one could accuse him of making the verses up.

While most of the boys were not churchy, they did enjoy his wonderful voice and they began to enjoy the evening bible readings.

As Billy decided to turn in, he rolled and thanked Gene for the good supper, and pulled his blanket about him even though it really was not very cold.

They had been sitting by the rail yard for 6 hours with no sign of trains. Perhaps they would show in the morning.

In the 2$^{nd}$ Cavalry area, the men of D Company had located a table and had a boisterous Faro game developing.

Louis had decided to engage a new acquaintance by the name of Archibald Ribedeaux who claimed to have been a riverboat gambler.

They had sensed that he was a dandy because he always sported a red silk tie under his Shell Jacket.

Jacob watched over Louis' shoulder as he had never been exposed to cards. The boys of the mess had learned the game from Ribedeaux; and now that they were fairly familiar with it, money had started to enter into the contest.

Louis was holding his own against the house and he was getting Archibald worked up.

The men were unhappy about being separated from their horses by the train situation but the Captain had explained the problem and they trusted him.

Jacob nervously watched Louis make his bets and play the cards and ultimately he took Ribedeaux's money.

They parted friends, Archibald knew he would win it back on a later date when the Markley boy ran back into bad luck, that was the way it goes.

The cavalrymen laughed and joked into the late evening around their small fires, some produced spirits and passed them around, by midnight most got to sleep, still no trains had arrived.

The whistle of the steam engine woke the drowsy men at 4am in the morning, the men awoke to a damp and muggy morning.

They were forced to gather their equipment in the dark and were moved like drowsy cattle to the cars.

There were no passenger wagons, only boxcars.

Fortunately the train was large enough to accommodate the two regiments even though they were crammed fairly tightly into the cars.

The men would spend the next two days aboard that train moving from point to point across South Carolina, North Carolina and Southern Virginia.

As they rolled along the country side they took turns peering out the open box car doors at the changing countryside and noticed that Virginia was becoming significantly more forested and wooded than the conifer dominated South Carolina.

The small villages seemed to be very civilized and nice as well and often crowds of well-wishers were seen gaily waving to the soldiers as they passed through the towns.

The train moved slowly and sometimes made indecipherable stops for long periods of time.

The soldiers adjusted to the travel and had established latrine holes in the corner of the box cars where they could relieve themselves when necessary.  The noticed that there was no need to make the holes in some of the cars.

After another day and night of travel, the train stopped, it was after sunset and Jacob could hear shouts and the sounds of heavy wagon wheels outside.

He listened closely and began to hear the orders, "Second Cavalry unload here, Second Cavalry unload!"

As he jumped off the car and walked with the others on the tracks he saw the rail station sign "Richmond."

The First Sergeant cried out, 2nd Cavalry soldiers assemble on me. They were going to retrieve their mounts and reassemble the units.

Billy Cross asked if the 5th Infantry was going to get off and he was told, "Stay put!" so they did.

They would be riding the train some more.  He was a little sad to see the South Carolina boys getting split up like they were.

The men of the 5<sup>th</sup> South Carolina Infantry had another day and night of travel, finally at midmorning the train came to a stop.

The soldiers got out in bright sunshine and looked around. They were in a broad valley surrounded by rolling terrain, but in the middle of a very busy rail station, complete with round house for reversing engines and tracks merged on the rail yard from all directions.

The sign outside the depot read, "Manassas Junction."

As Billy Cross fumbled to put on all his gear and sling his musket, he heard his First Sergeants voice, "B Company form up on me, on the double quick!"

The Regiment formed up on the road that led off to the East. Soon the soldiers could see Colonel Jenkins, on his horse riding the line of companies to get to the head of the column; his adjutant rode alongside with a small map and was gesturing towards the east as well.

As he rode by B Company, Billy heard him say "Fairfax Courthouse", he calculated that would be their destination, he noticed that everybody and everything seemed to be in a hurry.

As the soldiers of the 5<sup>th</sup> South Carolina marched off the rail yard they marched on to a grassy pasture of the side of road where two other equal sized regiments were arrayed in marching order.

Clusters of officers on horseback were conferring and he noticed that the Colonel and his adjutant trotted ahead to join the gathering, as the other men saw the Palmetto adorned banner of the regiment enter the pasture.

The men of the other two regiments raised their hats and shouted "Hurrah for South Carolina! Welcome boys!"

As they approached closer Billy could make out "Mississippi on their flags.

Gene Gerrard remarked as he marched, "Well I'll be! We are to be a part of a Mississippi Brigade!"

Colonel Jenkins leaned over to shake the hand of his new Brigade Commander; all of the officers remained mounted.

The Brigadier General introduced himself, "Good day to you sir, I am David Jones, Colonel Jenkins, it is my pleasure to introduce you to Colonel Burt of the 18th Mississippi Infantry and Colonel Featherston of the 17th Mississippi."

After the officers had exchanged pleasantries and complained of the heat for a few minutes, General Jones got to business, "Gentlemen we have a ways to march today. My orders from General Beauregard are to move to Fairfax Courthouse as expeditiously as possible and to construct a line of defenses to deny approaches to Centreville. We will march through Centreville to get there. I have sent an advance party to conduct a reconnaissance of Fairfax a little while ago so we will establish our dispositions based upon what they recommend. It will be a long march so I suggest you insure your men get water at the creek just east of here: it is called Bull Run."

The men of the 5th were instructed to ground their gear and to draw rations from the quartermaster wagons parked hooked to their teams on one side of the pasture.

Each man got a pound of cornmeal and a pound of salt pork to put in their haversacks.

The sergeants instructed the men to return to their gear and prepare for a march, they also warned them to conserve water until they could fill their canteens at Bull Run which lay about 6 miles to the East.

Billy Cross and his messmates had managed to stow the rations and put all their marching order back together when the group of mounted officers broke up.

The General trotted to the exit of the pasture and shouted out to a brightly dressed Sergeant, "It will be a long march so let's start off with the old 1815!"

With that command the section of musicians began to beat and roll on the drums and the fifers picked up the key as the regiments began the long and dusty march to Centreville.

Billy and Roland were delighted by the musicians, they had seen and heard them at the ceremonies in Columbia but now they had their own Brigade Band.

It seemed to make the march easier having a tune to do it by. Many in the regiment took to whistling along with the band as they marched.

The Division paused at the stone bridge of the Warrenton Turnpike to allow the soldiers to fill their canteens and their caps with water to splash on themselves.

It was shaping up to be a rather hot June day.

The march became a long and dusty one as they climbed the hill to Centreville, which was several long rows of white clapboard structures providing the support a village does to a small farming community.

Just to the East of town, General Jones called for a rest halt.

Some of the townsfolk from Centreville came to talk to the men as they rested, most were very apprehensive about the news of the "Yankee Invasion."

Billy was queried by a man and a women, but all he could do was shrug, "Don't know much Ma'am," deferring to the woman, "I just got here myself, I reckon you should ask a feller with a horse."

As the men rested in the sparse shade outside of Centreville, General Jones assembled his regimental commanders, "Gentlemen I apologize for the rush I have placed you in, but General Beauregard is greatly worried. The word we are hearing from our contacts in Washington and in the papers indicates that General Scott and Lincoln are pushing Erwin McDowell to move on Virginia as soon as he can. Way we see it here, is Lincoln called up 90 day Volunteers in mid-April. It is now June and them volunteers are running out of obligation. Some of them will be done and heading home by July. General Beauregard wants several layers of defenses in case they come this way. From his reckoning three major rail centers are likely targets, Phillipi, Harpers Ferry and Manassas; if you want to bring large amounts of troops into Virginia to attack Richmond from Washington then you will need one of the three to support an army. We are to fortify at Fairfax, and digging takes time, so that's why we are running to get there."

Colonel Featherston nodded, and asked, "Say General, where are you from?"

Featherston asked because Jones still wore a federal blue frock coat with federal rank epaulets.

"South Carolina originally, Orangeburg to be precise," Jones replied, he turned and noted the broad smile on Jenkins's face.

"Nothing against Mississippi, mind you but it made my heart leap to see a South Carolina regiment march in!"

Jones laughed and added, "Now I don't feel outnumbered by these Mississippians!"

The Colonels all laughed and they then reluctantly rose to resume the march.

Billy watched and began to reassemble the equipment on his back as the mounted officers moved back to their units, he heard the roll of the drums begin again and the three regiments reluctantly rose to walk in the June dust some more.

It was early evening when the troops arrived at Fairfax, as the marched in, sore of foot and bone tired, they noticed an artillery battery of 4 guns sitting by the road.

A Captain standing in the road motioned the 5$^{th}$ off to the right side of the road on a bare hill just east of the crossroads and the town.

"Make camp here! Form a detail from each company to fill canteens, the well is behind you by the barn!" The Regimental Sergeant Major had accompanied the advance party and now had his First Sergeants scurrying the men to make camp. Tomorrow would prove to be a busy day.

The Divisional Engineer made it a point to visit each regiment in order to explain the design of the defensive line.

He consulted with Colonel Jenkins and then walked the line with the Company Commanders pointing out the locations for positions.

He learned to his horror that the South Carolina Militia had little experience with field fortifications.

Finally he assembled the Soldiers at each location with the First Sergeants and instructed them.

"We will focus you on getting as much done as you can using your available time! First thing you will construct are called *Lunettes* that is French for half-moon."

He kicked his toe in the dirt to demonstrate the concept, "you make a U shaped wall of logs and stack dirt in front of it."

He saw that the men were nodding in understanding. "I want to see at least one per company constructed."

He waved his arm across the hillside and continued, "In between your *Lunettes* we will construct and emplace *Chevaux de frise* or what I call Spike Horses, It is made of a log with wooden spikes inserted into the log so it is a long porcupine. These are to stop cavalry advances on your position. Now first sergeant; assemble a detail to cut logs from the woods to our front for the positions and the *Chevaux de frise*, we will assemble a wagon detail to assist you."

The engineer captain then proceeded to the 18$^{th}$ Mississippi who would be tasked to build a redoubt with the artillerymen to defend the approach road to Fairfax.

He would teach them how to weave *Gabions*, or baskets of saplings that would be filled with dirt to protect the cannon from the fire of enemy cannons.

The Mississippians would prove to take great delight in their weaving skills by the end of the day.

Billy, Gene and George were placed on the detail to scratch out and dig post holes for the timber frame of the Lunette.

They had stripped down to shirtsleeves in the hot morning and by noon had 6 short poles standing upright chest high, "This here fighting Yankees is hot work," Gene complained as he tamped dirt down around the pine log, oozing thick sap in the June heat.

"Working like a darky ain't what I signed up to do!" pronounced George as he brought the next log for the first run of logs at ground level.

Billy just smiled and shoveled dirt against the logs that were being stacked to form the back wall, "I am a thinking we might be glad to have this here fort, if a bunch of Yankees come down that road."

The men of the mess agreed but continued to work and complain, none the less.

The day was getting hotter but clouds on the horizon indicated a coming rain.

A party of men from A Company were slowly producing the *Chevaux de frise*. It proved to be slow work.

The Engineer Captain had produced a brace and bit with a large borer, which he carefully kept an eye on, and showed the men how to drill a pattern of holes in each log.

Axmen then sharpened smaller diameter trunks into spikes that were inserted into the holes. By late afternoon they had 10 of the obstacles produced to place in front of the *Lunettes* on the right flank of the Brigade.

The men were proud of their work and looked forward to night and supper.

That night the Engineer met with General Jones and the Colonels and discussed additional measures, "Gentlemen, we need to insure we know where every well is on these heights and assign a detail of men to address each. From Centreville radiating out, there on only a certain number of wells and springs in this country, if we have to leave this area under pressure I have orders to insure we clog the wells and the springs before leaving. If the Yankees come through this country we intend to make water hard to find."

The General and the Colonels nodded, understanding from the recent march they had made.

"I also want you to form a party of axe men and equip them with a wagon and good tools, when we are notified by our cavalry screen that they are coming up the turnpike we are to push them out to fell trees across the pike at as many locations as they can. It will give us a chance to separate the infantry for their artillery."

Colonel Jenkins rose and thanked the Captain, "Sir, we are honored to have had your assistance, my men have learned much today."

Billy and his messmates lounged in the darkness around their mess fire under rubber blanket "shebangs" suspended from their newly constructed fortifications and listened as George read from the Gospels, he had not gotten far until he noticed his messmates were asleep.

## Washington, District of Columbia

## 14 July 1861

Major Hunt watched as his company slowly departed from the cars of the train.

His remaining soldiers were the image of the trail worn veterans; all had Florida suntans and indeed looked to be a leathery bunch. He was concerned that on the return to Fort Hamilton in Brooklyn 2 days ago, that nearly 20 men had decided not to enlist.

First Sergeant O'Keefe had explained to him that the men had been discussing the news that the Volunteer Regiments gave veterans promotions and bonuses for being regulars and there were men that could not resist the opportunity.

Hunt realized that men he had known as fellow captains were now general officers in volunteer regiments and once again agreed to himself that O'Keefe was a veritable well of worldly wisdom.

From Fort Hamilton, they had little time to rest, after attending to administrative details and reports that needed to be submitted. M Company was ordered to depart by rail to the Capitol.

Fort Hamilton had just completed the move of the 7th New York Militia and every available force was being rushed to Washington. Hunt had been promoted to wear his brevet rank from this point forward.

He reasoned that his tiny battery being moved from place to place, always at a rush; would be better served if he wore the rank of a field grade officer.

The artillery service constantly found itself piecemealed and relegated to afterthought, he hoped someday he could change this. The promotion order was against the 5th US Artillery Regiment, now being formed.

Hunt often wondered about the portent of the order.

The departure from the reinforcement mission to Fort Pickens had come suddenly on the 28th of June. M Company and Captain Barry's A Company were ordered to New York.

The complex movement would move the troops to New York and the guns to Washington. The troops would have to find their guns when they arrived at the Washington Arsenal.

Hunt hoped that the newly minted Brigadier General Meigs; now the Army's quartermaster, would remember to protect the Napoleons from being issued to some thrown together volunteer unit.

As the First Sergeant assembled the men into formation and made corrections to their appearance.

A Lieutenant approached Major Hunt, "Sir, I trust you are Major Henry Hunt?"

Hunt nodded, and the young man continued, "Sir, I am directed to show you the way, you are ordered to report to the Washington Arsenal and encamp there to draw your artillery and horses!"

M Company, 2nd Artillery started their march from Union Station to the Arsenal passing by the gleaming white Capitol where the partially completed rotunda dome was being erected. Joshua looked in awe at the edifice.

"That is quite a castle!" observed Private Mulcahy with a low whistle.

"I heard the British burned it down in 1812," added, Private Wilkins.

"We will try to prevent that from happening again! Now look sharp and remember we are being looked at!" Sergeant Mills barked.

Joshua liked working for Sergeant Mills and Lieutenant Benson they were both competent men who did not look down on the common soldiers.

He was grateful that Sergeant Schwartz had decided not to re-enlist in New York, word had it that he was going to join a Pennsylvania Regiment of Volunteers to obtain promotion.

It was a warm sunny day and the city was utterly full of military activity. The parks and grassy areas between the Capitol building and the Potomac were full of Army camps.

First Sergeant O'Keefe called the march, "Left, Right, Left! Stay in step you!"

The Company passed a group of gaudily dressed "Fire Zouaves" who were sightseeing in town, "Mind the Africans!" O'Keefe shouted out, the men hurled curses in return.

"Fookin volunteers, makin a fookin circus out of the Army!" O'Keefe muttered under his breath.

The artillerymen snickered as they marched through the busy panoply of military units massing in the city.

Crowds of curious civilians watched them as they marched, one of them called out, "What State are you boys from!"

First Sergeant O'Keefe roared back, "The United ones!"

The Lieutenant continued to point the way through the streets.

Soon they turned parallel to the Potomac and the Brick buildings and wharves of the Washington Arsenal appeared before them.

As they entered the grounds it was apparent that the arsenal had become a large and busy artillery park.

Rows upon rows of guns and limbers, caissons and battery wagons line the yards. Solid shot and shell gleaming in the sunlight were neatly stacked in long pyramidal forms.

Long rows of unmounted cannon of every conceivable caliber were stored on iron rails. To the North of the compound were long rows of tents.

A Captain approached Major Hunt as they marched in past the sentry post.

"Major Hunt I presume?" he asked as he smartly saluted.

 Hunt returned the salute, "Yes Captain, I have orders to come here to draw my guns, we had them shipped from Fort Pickens two weeks ago."

"Yes sir we have been expecting you, sorry to say they have not arrived yet but we expect the ship shortly."

The Captain pointed to the tent camps, "Sir you can put your men in the camp there, have your quartermaster sergeant form a detail to draw rations. We will commence issuing you the battery equipment you will require in the morning. If you would be so kind to follow me, sir, we have orders for you at the Commandant's office."

George Ramsay looked up from his pile of requisitions on his desk as the adjutant knocked, seeing Hunt enter, he rose to greet him, "Henry Hunt, good to see you lad!"

Hunt eyed the huge piles of paperwork on Ramsay's desk and the table behind and replied, "Looks like you are fairly idle these days, Sir!"

Ramsey only grinned in response. Hunt imagined that George Ramsay was likely the oldest Major in the United States Army. Ramsey was 59 and had entered West Point at age 12, in 1810.

Ramsay rummaged through a stack of papers on his desk, "I have orders for you and your battery, here somewhere."

After a moment of sifting he produced it, "Ah here it is, you are to refit here as a Light Artillery Battery, mounted, upon refit and provisioning you are to be assigned to General Tyler's Division for movement into Virginia."

Hunt listened and nodded asking, "Sir am I to remain with only 4 guns?"

Ramsay nodded, "Yes Henry, you are to collect the guns you possessed in Florida, I already have my ordnance workmen preparing your fixed loads, you shall be able to draw full caissons and limbers with boxed spares for your battery wagons."

"You also will draw horses from me in the morning so be prepared to provide a detail of drivers."

Hunt replied, "Sir, thank you, who do I talk to about soldiers, I come from New York short 20 men of a full company?"

Ramsay thought for a moment and suggested, "Consult with my adjutant, I think he will have to put you directly in touch with the War Department."

Sergeant Mills and Joshua took a 4 man detail over to the paddocks behind the Penitentiary on the grounds where the team horses had been kept, each section was to select and collect 12 horses for the limber and caisson teams.

At first Mills toyed with the notion to get a matching color, but he could not find horses he liked to match so they abandoned vanity for character.

Joshua was disturbed by the condition of their feet, the animals had been collected by buyers all over the Northeast and while they meet the standard size and weight of an Army horse, some had apparently never been shod.

"These are gonna be a lot of work, Sergeant." Joshua pulled up the feet of one particularly well-mannered gelding, digging a finger under the frog of the hoof and smelling the finger, "Yep, a lot of work!" He said while making a face.

Joshua had his detail; Privates Lyttle, Newby, Page and Watkins bring the bridles they had drawn from the quartermaster and after selection of the animals.   Joshua had each man bring 2 horses back to the Company Farrier at their camp.

Farrier Sergeant Mueller, loyal to M Company to the end, was delighted with his new wagon and forge and was anxious for some work.

The privates brought the pairs of team horses to Sergeant Mueller's operation and picketed the horses for shoeing, after the selection for his section; Joshua came and assisted Mueller with the farrier work. With 74 horses to shoe, he was glad to have the help.

The two men worked rather feverishly as a team throughout the remainder of the Monday to shoe as many of the horses as they could, by early evening they had 12 of the animals finished.

Joshua resolved to report to Sergeant Mills that they would require some help if they were to have the job complete by Wednesday.

Sergeant Mills discussed the issue that evening with Quartermaster Sergeant O'Brien who visited the ordnance Sergeant for the Arsenal.

The next morning another farrier and wagon had been loaned to M Company.  By the end of Tuesday they had 44 of the 74 horses shod.

Late on Tuesday afternoon, Lieutenant Pratt came by to check on the teams, he paused to discuss the progress with Sergeant Mills, "The rest of the Army of Northeastern Virginia is moving out today by order of General McDowell," he observed.  "I guess we will have to catch up to them."

Major Hunt learned the same, during a visit by Colonel Ripley who visited the Arsenal to check on preparations to support the offensive. "We've learned that your guns will arrive tomorrow Major."

"Sir, I have become accustomed to late, short and piecemeal, I have yet to meet General Tyler and am not sure how I should find him,"

Major Hunt was becoming concerned that M Company would miss the best chance he would have to properly employ the Light 12 pounder in action.

Colonel Ripley suggested that he send a Lieutenant across the Long Bridge to Fort Albany on the Arlington Heights where Tyler's Division Headquarters was established, "This Officer can act as your liaison, and bring you word back to where to meet the command once we have you fitted."

Hunt agreed and tasked his newest volunteer, Lieutenant Presley Craig, his new brother in law who had joined them last night, with the mission. Presley had volunteered at Hunt's visit to see Mary the previous night. He was short a lieutenant as Lieutenant Benson was clearly sick with the measles.

Craig eagerly accepted the new task and secured a horse and galloped off to Fort Albany.

Major Hunt worried a little about sending Craig, as he still could not walk well yet due to a recent foot injury. The young man anxiously wanted to be a part of the fight and he had convinced Hunt and his new wife Mary that he could meet the challenge.

Lieutenant Craig quickly covered the distance to the Long Bridge but had to wait on a regiment of Infantry that was crossing.

He quickly followed them and walked the horse slowly across the bridge, as he could not travel any faster than the Infantry.

Once he reached the guard posts and the gun positions on the Arlington side he was able to bypass the Infantry regiment and made his way up the heights passing the imposing earthworks of Fort Runyun.

"Sergeant I am looking for General Tyler's First Division, do you know their location?" Craig asked the sentry at Ft. Albany.

The Sergeant pointed down to a collection of wagons on a field adjacent to the redoubt, "Sir, those wagons are the trains with baggage for the First Division; they will know the route and destination. The General and his staff departed here two hours ago."

Lieutenant Craig then rode down to the supply wagons that were preparing their loads and assembling teams to depart, The Division Quartermaster informed Craig that his destination was Centreville where the Division Rear would establish once it had been captured from the Secessionists. "Everybody is going to Centreville, son! You go there and you'll find us!"

Craig asked the Quartermaster to pass word to General Tyler that M Company would be moving up Wednesday night or Thursday.

The Major agreed to notify the General as soon as he was able.

Lieutenant Craig then slowly rode back against the traffic back to cross the Long Bridge, The amount of men and equipment flowing out of Washington was astonishing, he wondered how any army could resist such massive power.

Henry Hunt pored over maps he had obtained from Ramsay and looked at the best means to travel to Centreville.

 It was now late Tuesday and he had drawn all the equipment and horses he required but he still needed 4 guns, limber chests and 20 men.

The equipment was still moving up the Potomac. The men he had learned were enroute from Carlisle Barracks; there was no time to train them.

First Sergeant O'Keefe tapped on the pole of his tent, "Beggin' your pardon sir, Have you word on my recruits?"

"First Sergeant, it appears we will train them on the march, I've only now received word that they will leave Carlisle Barracks in Pennsylvania tomorrow morning,"

Hunt shook his head, "As usual First Sergeant we will make do."

O'Keefe grinned, "Capital Sir! Do you remember how to tend a vent?"

Hunt laughed at the old joke and replied, "Sure thing, you confiscate an infantryman!"

The two men talked into the night as O'Keefe reviewed the morning report and the status of the refitting of the Company, he also brought the Guidon to show to the Major.

O'Keefe had the seamstresses that did contract work for the Arsenal repair the rips and tears the proud banner had endured on all the previous campaigns.

Joshua spent the evening cleaning and examining his pendulum hausse and insured the instrument was in good working order and the leather pouch for it was soaped and oiled.

He thought about what it meant to go up that road soon. He wondered where his brother was. He wondered what the Markley's and Lottie thought.

Thinking about it, he realized he had received nothing from her since April. He felt like he was in another world. He wondered if he would ever see his home again.

Major Hunt decided, after looking at his watch, midnight, to take a few moments to write Mary, his wife he never seemed to be able to see.

> "*Dearest Mary,*
>
>> *I apologize for not visiting more. It is very hard for me to be so close to you and still be so very far away. In a fortnight I expect us to be committed to the battle in Virginia against my own countrymen. Never in my career did I envision ever being called to arms against citizens of this land. We are as ready as one can expect. I trust you will be patient with my sudden separation. Please give my regards to Family and*

*inform them I am keeping a close eye on Preston. I pray that I am permitted to see you after this fight. There are those who estimate this struggle will be over soon, but I am of the opinion that it is just the beginning of a long and difficult argument.*

*If my prayers are not heard I wish to express to you my gratitude for you undying devotion to me and my difficult calling. It has been pure joy to me to have your company; your patient understanding has enables me to pursue this calling. Like others, many others, I have to attend to my duty as I see it. Sadly I am my father's son and like him the Army enjoys my first attentions. Please remain in good health and faith.*

*Love always*

*Henry"*

Major Hunt quickly sealed and addressed the letter; he remained and would always remain very private in regards to Mary.

She was the only person on earth that truly understood him. Hopefully he would see her again.

Late on Wednesday afternoon the Quartermaster of the Arsenal summoned Major Hunt.

 He was to send teams down to the wharves, the ship bearing their guns had arrived.

Joshua took half his crew and rode the teams down to the Wharves where a large black steamer was docked. The ship was in the standard Union Navy trim, all black and very businesslike in appearance. As they arrived at the wharf, two guns had already been lowered onto the wharfs deck.

He checked the trunnions and found to his relief, number "0003".

He assisted Newby and Watkins in lifting the lunette to the pin tail of the limber and prepared the gun and limber assembly to be moved. He quickly walked around the gun to insure no damage had occurred in shipping, he noted that the salt air had started to cause a green tinge to occur around the dolphins and at the edges of the rimbases but overall she appeared to be none the worse for wear.

Kansas, Texas, New York, Florida and now Virginia. He reflected that he had gotten around a fair amount since leaving Macbeth.

By 7 pm the entire company was, equipment wise; complete.

Major Hunt instructed First Sergeant O'Keefe to conduct a Sergeants call at 9pm to brief preparations for movement they would depart as soon as possible on Thursday the 18th of July.

Very late that evening a courier arrived at the Arsenal bearing an order from General Tyler for Major Hunt. As Hunt lit his lantern to read the dispatch, he noticed that the man was very dusty. He glance down at the dispatch in the lamplight and read,

*"To: Commander M Co 2nd US Arty*

*From, Cdr 1st Div Move with all possible dispatch to Centreville VA employing route of march Chain bridge, Vienna, Germantown, Centreville. 1st Div occupies Centreville. Upon closing Centreville report to Col Richardson 4th bde no later than 19 Jul.*

*Tyler, BG"*

Hunt thanked the young officer, and asked, "Can we get you anything?"

The young man responded, "No sir, we got them secesh on the run, come up quick as you can."

Hunt turned back to his map and analyzed the route, it looked to him that General Tyler was directing him to bypass the supply wagons that were likely clogging the main axis to the Army, the order made sense.

He called out to the First Sergeant, who was in the next tent.

The next day on First Sergeant O'Keefe's urging Major Hunt decided to delay the departure for one more day just to see if the Army could succeed in provided the replacement soldiers that had been promised from Carlisle Barracks.

Since General Tyler's order specified no later than 19 July to Centreville; which lay only 29 miles distant, it would be an easy distance to cover as they had learned in Kansas.

O'Keefe wanted to allow the men to sleep in and have an easy day, as he put it, "Some of thems may be dead by Saturday."

O'Keefe promised to close the deal with an inspection that afternoon as a way for the soldiers to repay him for a morning of sleeping late.

Major Hunt thought about the First Sergeant's suggestion and decided; after recalling his letter to his wife, that it would only be fitting to draft up something to say to his men.

Some were likely not to live out the rest of the week. He found a sheet of paper in his tent and started to draft up a speech for them.

The next day was a lazy one. Water call and feeding call for the horses was continued as normal and

Major Hunt wandered among the drivers as they chopped and mixed the feed for the animals and curried and combed them. He noted that the men were expectant and asked many questions about what the morrow would bring.

Major Hunt regretted his lack of information.

At 4 pm First Sergeant O'Keefe had the bugler call *Boots and Saddles* that caused the men to fall out and form into a company formation. He announced a surprise that led to Private Newby being promoted to Corporal and to be the Color Bearer for M Company.

Newby actually had blushed a bright red at the news but eagerly moved forward to accept the honor. His 8 years of mixed service was to pay off after all.

After Newby had accepted the leather guidon sash and proudly accepted the swallow tailed guidon; First Sergeant O'Keefe called the company to attention.

Major Hunt moved to the head of the formation and accepted O'Keefe's salute and announced "Post!"

At the command Lieutenants Platt, Craig, Thompson took their positions at the head of the sections. He noticed Craig was still using a crutch to get around.

"Stand at Ease!" Hunt called out.

He produced from his frock coat pocket a scrap of paper and looking at it for a moment; he returned it to his pocket and started,

"Men,

*I have watched most of you perform your duties for over 7 years, from Fortress Monroe to Kansas, to Texas, and Florida. In each instance I have always told others that you represent the finest artillery battery in the Army! We have been tough and uncompromising to you. And you have always answered that call and have done your utmost to make M Company an organization that people noticed. The Army noticed and you possess a new weapon as proof of that notice. We move to battle tomorrow, against a foe we never wished to have, our own countrymen! In this difficult challenge we face I ask you to focus on your oath and your duty to the United States. A hard action now on your part may bring a swifter end to this argument. Hopefully we will sway these people so earnest for war, away from that path.*

*God help us if we do not achieve this! This evening I want
each of you to take some time to write those who you hold
dear, a message that you are about to embark on something
crucial, something important, and something noble, the
preservation of our Union, that you are offering your life
for! Look to each other over the next few days, help your
comrade when he stumbles or loses heart. For better or
worse we travel into hazard as brothers in arms.
Remember that as you perform your duty!*

*I thank you for being here today and it is my honor to lead
you!"*

Hunt called out to the First Sergeant to take over the formation.

He was resigned that he had done all he could to prepare these men
for what they soon would face.

Soon, much wisdom would be passed to the survivors of this
endeavor. He earnestly hoped it would not be costly.

The next morning before the sun rose, M Company, 2<sup>nd</sup> Artillery
Regiment departed the Washington Arsenal enroute to Georgetown
and the Chain Bridge.

As they passed the Columbia Pike crossing the Long Bridge, on their
way to the Chain Bridge, they noted the fortuitous choice.

The Columbia Pike was jammed with the quartermaster wagons
resupplying the 32,000 men that General McDowell had entered
Virginia with.

Soon the Company reached Georgetown, being short 20 men enabled
all of M Company to ride either on the teams or on the limber chests,
caissons, or on the battery wagons.

Unknown to Major Ramsay, Major Hunt had secured two extra unauthorized wagons, and teams in order to carry ammunition, rations and tentage for the company. It was a habit he was later to expand.

Joshua was excited to be entering the fray. As they rode toward Vienna he was astonished at the amount of equipment littered the roadsides on the route up.

He estimated he had noticed over a hundred rucksacks on the way up.

An abandoned woodstove elicited comment from Wilkins, "looks to me like a general was willing to make do with a little bit less!"

Joshua was happy that the horses pulled the full limbers and the 12 pounders easily and did not seem to be troubled by the load.

As they ascended the hill towards Vienna, Joshua noticed that trees had been felled across the roads and had been cut away by the troops that preceded them.

The evidence of such activity reminded him that they were in an unwelcome place with people out there who wanted to stop them.

They stopped in Vienna to water the horses at mid-day and had to clear a well in order to accomplish the task, the effort took nearly two hours to accomplish.

The rebels had filled the wells with timber and trash and the waste had to be cleared by the men before they could hoist buckets of water up for the horses and men.

The column turned left at a crossroads and the covered the approach to Germantown.

Joshua was shocked to see that someone had fired the town. The houses that had lined the road were reduced to ashes and residual flame. No sign of the former inhabitants was apparent.

The sun began to set West of Manassas; it was nearly dark when the Company pulled in short of Centreville.

As they pulled into the approaches to the village they could see the imposing works that the rebels had established in front of the crossroads.

Major Hunt directed the First Sergeant to make a camp off to the left in a vacant field as he rode ahead to attempt to find the headquarters of the 1$^{st}$ Division and General Tyler.

Joshua formed a detail from his section to take the canteens and find a well in Centreville for water; most of the canteens of the men were emptied on the long ride up the turnpike to join the division.

First Sergeant O'Keefe had instructed the non-commissioned officers to put together watering details to find water for the men and the horses.

The well in town was surrounded by men, a Sergeant standing by the well explained when he saw Joshua, "Sorry lad, but this one is a mud hole, with 30 thousand men all trying to get the same thing it is taking an hour for the water level to rise enough to fill the bucket. They say there is a spring back northeast of town."

The detail from Lieutenant Thompson's section found the spring and small creek deep in the woods a mile south of the camp.

The drivers led the horses on the long walk through the tangled woods to the brook; the watering of the animals took until well past midnight.

At the Sergeants meeting midway through the evening, First Sergeant O'Keefe discussed an early morning plan to get the horses watered, he sent Quartermaster Sergeant O'Brien on a mission to find some empty salt pork barrels that they could store water in the wagons with.

It might be a touch salty but it would be better than nothing. The Sergeants worked up a detail to fill the barrels for spare water for the canteens, most of the sections had been able to fill theirs but it was muddy stuff, particularly after watering 80 horses there.

General Tyler made introductions in his cramped headquarters tent by lantern light. "Hunt, I would like you to meet Lieutenant Edwards of the 3$^{rd}$ United States Artillery, I am going to place a section of his Parrot guns, consisting of 2 twenty pounders under you. The boys did a good job for us on Thursday, this will give you 6 guns, counting your 4 for covering Blackburn's Ford Southwest of here."

Major Hunt shook Edward's hand and then asked, "What is our object sir?"

General Tyler pointed to a bearded Colonel in discussion with another Colonel, "You will support Colonel Richardson there, in making a demonstration towards Blackburn's Ford. You will learn more once I brief the others."

Tyler turned to the gathering of Officers in the headquarters tent, "Gentlemen! Gentlemen! I would like to see the Brigade Commanders around the Map Table here."

The gathered officers stopped their sidebars and the Colonels assembled around the hand drawn map on the small table in front of General Tyler.

"Gentlemen the plan that Major General McDowell wants us in the 1$^{st}$ Division is supporting and diversionary in nature."

With his hand he indicated the trace of a serpentine stream named "Bull Run" on the map from the Warrenton Pike to a ravine labeled "Little Rocky Run", "We are to deceive General Beauregard into believing that our main attack will come via Blackburn's and Mitchells Ford, and the Stone Bridge across Bull Run."

"After we collect forces tonight and tomorrow, General McDowell will conduct a night march North and West to Sudley Springs Ford and turn the Secessionist's left flank."

Tyler gestured with his hand along the Warrenton Pike, "Three Brigades, Colonel Keyes, General Schenck, and Colonel Sherman will proceed early Sunday Morning to the Stone Bridge, here."

Tyler pointed to the bridge crossing Bull Run, "Colonel Richardson, you will repeat the push to Blackburn's Ford as you did on last Thursday."

Major Hunt from his back bench position adjacent to Major Barry, who upon seeing him had expressed a silent happy greeting; noticed that General Tyler gave Richardson a hard stare.

"I will expect all commands in position by 6 am and we will commence artillery fires at 6:30. Since our lines will be somewhat far apart in this effort, Colonel Miles of the 5th Division will take acting command of Colonel Richardson's demonstration on Blackburn's Ford."

Tyler looked over the room and noting Major Barry on the back wall of the tent, introduced him, "Gentlemen, Major Barry in the back there is the Division Artillerist, and he has apportioned to you the requisite artillery to accomplish your missions, please defer your questions on the guns to him."

"Gentlemen, I am concerned about the lack of good water at this location, I have directed my quartermaster to find us a solution, I anticipate this situation to improve one we have defeated the secessionists on Sunday."

He looked to see if the Quartermaster was present, but could not see him, "I have heard there are springs Northeast of Centreville and at the Cub Run so use those for now."

PLAN of the 1st BATTLE of BULL RUN Virginia 21st J...
Topography from U.S. Engineers official Maps.
Union Army — — — Artillery ++++++ - Rebel Army —— Rebel...

Tyler opened his pocket watch and announced, "Gentlemen, my watch shows 12:30 after midnight now, please adjust yours accordingly. You can expect modifications to emerge on this plan tomorrow after I have met with General McDowell, so plan on a final meeting tomorrow at 4 pm back at this place."

Tyler bid his commanders a good evening and they departed in sidebars with one anotherMajor Barry, free to talk, patted his dusty friend on the back, "Henry, damn fine thing to see you made it out, I was beginning to worry that you had resigned to work for Beauregard."

Hunt smiled, "The way the Army has been treating M Company, I should think they wanted me to."

He then looked at his friend and asked, "Did the General ask for your advice?"

Barry shook his head, "Of course not Henry, just piecemeal us out like usual, absolutely no massing, except for your operation, consider it a personal gift. Make it a point, please, to look out for Edward's section of Parrots. They did a hell of a good job pulling Richardson's chestnuts out of the fire on Thursday."

Major Barry described the blundering action where Colonel Richardson under General Tyler's prodding had actually attempted to cross Bull Run at Blackburn's Ford and had blundered into an estimated 4000 rebels supported by artillery.

The entire affair had nearly turned into a disaster, and General Tyler had spent most the morning with General McDowell explaining his actions.

Hunt smiled, and asked "Where do you expect to be?"

Barry responded, "With my pair of Company E's on the right along with my lonely 30 pounder."

He looked at Henry with a serious look in his eye, "Henry do not take your position for granted, there are a lot of rebels down in there and they are supported by a fair amount of artillery on the heights beyond. Your light battery is the perfect economy of force element to cover our back door, just be prepared for Beauregard to try something there."

Barry added, "The firing of the 30 pounder is the signal for you and the rest of the division artillery to start your diversionary firing. Your front has rebel batteries about 600 yards south of the ford, Edward's told me they cannot range you if you follow his recommendations for positions, His Lieutenant is a young fellow named Benjamin, he knows the spot.

Hunt replied, "Many thanks for that William, I do not expect to receive much useful intelligence other than what you can provide. It appears that our mobility is once more to be ignored."

Barry nodded and added, "Only a Major at this point Henry, perhaps with more rank we can change things."

Hunt nodded and sadly observed, "Sorry friend but I must return to my company."

Once outside the tent, Henry Hunt waited for a moment for his eyes to adjust, it was a clear and warm night and he had a giant aching in his back and feet, He found his new horse and rode back to M Company's camp, and found a Cadet Meigs awaiting him.

"Major Hunt, Sir, Colonel Richardson is having a meeting, please follow me!" Hunt followed the eager youth.

As they trudged through the dark to Colonel Richardson's headquarters, Hunt asked, "Tell me Cadet, you are not a relative on Montgomery's?"

Cadet Meigs, "Why yes sir, his son sir, he was delighted that Colonel Richardson agreed to assign me as your liaison officer, sir!"

Hunt grinned in the darkness, and remarked aloud, "You cannot sling a dead cat around this army without hitting a Meigs!"

Entering into the crowded tent, Colonel Richardson nodded at Hunt and proceeded to explain the plan for Sunday morning.

Hunt rubbed his eyes and took occasional notes. The plan seemed rather complex with the potential of having 3 Colonels to answer to with the provisional command being placed under Colonel Miles of the 5th Division.

He also learned that one of the 5th Division's brigades under Colonel Davies would also back stop Richardson's Brigade.

He expected to get lots of orders on Sunday. After the meeting had ended he rushed back to find the First Sergeant.

Joshua walked the picket line and patted the horses, it was a clear and warm night and he was too anxious to sleep.

The horses gave quiet whinnies as he moved the line, touching them; he resolved to wake early so they could be watered in time to take care of all the other preparations.

First Sergeant O'Keefe had let them know one by one that Sunday morning early they would move in range of the enemy. He hoped he would be ready for what lay ahead.

# 9 A FIRST GREAT BATTLE

## Blackburn's Ford, Virginia
## 20 July 1861

Billy Cross and his messmates spent a lazy morning under the shade trees, cleaning their muskets and stocking cartridge pouches and cap boxes with paper cartridges and caps. Gene excitedly continued to talk about the skirmish from a fortnight ago.

"For a while, I could not tell who they was, hell some of them had on gray like us!" Gene exclaimed he had been assigned duty as a skirmisher once the Federal troops had appeared on the clearing on the hill above the Ford.

Roland returned from the river bank with a cap full of black berries and added in a low falsetto, "Pardon, us gentlemen but noting the similarity of our attire, art thou aligned with our cause?"

The men of the mess laughed. The heat of the day was starting to slow down all movement and make men avoid the sun. A lone crow flew over squawking in the heat.

"They pushed them boys' right into us and they never counted on our skirmish line being right at the edge of the wood!" Gene laughed at the memory, "Boy they was sure surprised."

Billy had thoughtfully remarked, "Sad thing some of em had to die just before gettin' a drink by the Run."

Billy recalled the stealthy wait as they watched what he thought were about 600 men, approach behind skirmishers moving towards the broad creek called Bull Run. The approaching troops looked to be quite tired and hot.

He recalled waiting in the shade as the creek was heavily wooded on both banks, and Thursday had been a damned hot day. The Captain had had them douse cook fires and silenced his buglers and drummers, when he had noted the dust of an approach drifting up from the woods on the hill between the ford and Centreville.

After the troops had emerged from the woods, Billy remembered watching a smaller group almost as big as B Company fan out and form a line of skirmishers roughly a quarter mile from the rest. As they quietly watched and waited two cannon approached and unlimbered on the hill.

As Billy waited and watched, he noticed on either side of him the river bank on the Manassas side of the run was full of men doing the same waiting and watching, all in the shade with plenty of water to boot.

When the eyes of the men in the skirmisher ranks could be clearly seen; the Sergeants passed the word down the line in sharp whispers, "Cap your muskets, no firing until orders!"

The pair of cannon on the hill had begun to shoot at various targets, Billy remembered the first shot had hit Mr. McLean's house by the Ford, he recalled the crashing and breaking sounds that the cannon shot made as it plowed through the clapboard structure.

Sergeant Otis, an old hand from the war in Mexico calmed his men, "Just searching fire boys, they don't see us or have no idea where we is."

The next shot passed through the trees above Billy's head, the solid projectile making ripping and splintering noises as it tore through the treetops, the round kicked up a great spray of dirt and dust just short of Mr. McLean's rickety wooden barn. Leaves and twigs from the disturbed branches had gently rained down on the waiting men.

The troops on the ridge above started to sound drums and fifes and deployed on line with their bayonets gleaming in the hot sun, Billy was amazed to see them form up like they were on parade, as he focused on the spectacle he had realized he had forgotten to watch the Skirmishers to the front. The spread out line of advancing skirmishers had now approached to about 50 yards from the trees; the bright afternoon sun was causing many to shade their eyes with their hands.

All along the line the cry of "Fire!" was echoed along the deeply shaded riverbank. Hundreds of muskets had answered the order in a near simultaneous roar. Billy had hardly noticed the recoil as the heavy charge of 3 buckshot an a single 69 caliber ball exited his musket, he had quickly rolled onto his back and dug out a new cartridge from his leather pouch and bit the tail of the cartridge and awkwardly poured the charge into the musket's muzzle, he had then crammed the remainder of the cartridge, paper and all into the muzzle and pulled the ramrod from its channel and rammed the load home. Billy then returned the long ramrod back to its channel. He rolled up to his knee and with fumbling fingers dug a cap out of the cap pouch on his belt and capped his musket. No sooner had he finished when Sergeant Otis had commanded the men to fire again. After the second discharge the smoke hung thickly in the trees, the strong rotten egg smell of burnt powder filled their senses. Billy could see the skirmishers walking backwards up the hill, firing and shouting as they retreated back up the hill. The musket balls were impacting in the water of the creek and passing through the tree tops but no one around him had been hit.

Captain Sykes walked the line shouting "Everybody up, everybody up, form a line!"

Billy recalled them fumbling with their gear and the Sergeants roughly forming the men in a column, they had formed and ran through the knee high water at Blackburn's ford where there were less slippery rocks and then turning by column left, back into the woods on the northern bank. Colonel Jenkins appeared on his horse in front of the long mass of men as the commanders formed them in a front, indicating the location of the front by running along the line with their swords in both hands.

The command was again shouted out along the line, "Load!"

Billy again repeated the loading process this time much interfered with as his messmates on either side of him had been now shoulder to shoulder in tight ranks. Once all the men had loaded and replaced their ramrods; Billy noticed that the first Regiment of troops from the hill were now only about 200 yards away.

The massed troops waiting for what seemed like an eternity, the Federal troops continued to advance until they were 100 yards distant and the drumming stopped.

Captain Sykes then cried out "Present!" A moment later, he shouted "Fire!"

The entire 5th South Carolina Volunteer Infantry Regiment fired simultaneously in a thunderous sputtering roar and 645 charges of buck and ball sailed into the tight ranks of the Federal Soldiers, Billy saw several men crumple and fall. On the hill beyond through the smoke, he saw more regiments in both blue and gray uniforms forming on the sloping hill behind.

Again the command "Load" was shouted.

Billy was in the process of loading when he hear the command "Present!" and "Fire!" off in the distance. As he feverishly tended to his musket he heard something buzz angrily past his ear, and a thud sound beside him, Private James fell on his musket and clutched his thigh. He quickly got up and ran into the creek. Sergeant Otis had shouted "Close Ranks!" and Billy had a new neighbor.

Captain Sykes then cried again "Present!" then "Fire!"

Their next volley caused many more men to fall or move to the rear than the first. Billy had then noted that the formation in front of them was breaking and moving back up the hill.

From the heights behind the South Carolinians, the batteries of the Washington Light Artillery now opened fire on the Federal troops descending the hill towards Bull Run. Billy could see the shells bursting above the heads of the advancing troops in the distance, and he noticed men falling.

Captain Sykes then echoed the command from Regiment, "Fix bayonets!"

The men had clumsily removed the wicked spike bayonets from their scabbards and affixed the sockets over the lug on the muzzle of the muskets.

Suddenly two white bursts of smoke appeared in front of the Regiment with a loud crack, and two groups of men fell. The federal battery on the hill had noticed the flashing of the bayonets in the sunlight and directed their fire at Colonel Jenkins men.

The order was given to advance and the 5th South Carolina departed the shade and moved to confront the approaching regiments coming down the hill. Overhead Billy could hear the rustling of the Washington Artillery's shells passing overhead in response to the Federal battery's fire. The shots plowed up plumes of dust well short of the Federal guns on the hill.

A sudden volley of musketry to the right of Billy's company, about half way up the hill suddenly captured everyone's attention.

Sergeant Otis shouted, "Watch that boys!   That's Early's Virginians on their flank!" Another very loud sputtering volley of musket fire emerged from the close ranks of the Virginians emerging from the ravine.

The sudden appearance of another Regiment emerging from the deep wooded ravine of Little Rocky Run, which flowed into Bull Run south of Blagburns Ford, shocked and surprised the advancing Federal troops.  Billy watched as men in groups and clusters began to break and run back up the hill.

The Regiment loosed one more volley at the retreating Federals and then were ordered to return to their positions on the far side of the run.

By 3 pm in the afternoon the Federals had broken and retreated back into the woods towards Centreville.  The artillery pieces from behind them and the federal guns on the hill continued their pointless duel for another hour.

Men in singles and groups began to shout "Hurrah!"

Billy had heard one man shout, "Come on back! Lots of water down here boys!"

As Billy thought about Thursday's action, while wiping down his musket, he recalled he had not felt frightened; he had been too busy following orders.

He recalled how angry they had been when they got orders to abandon the works they had been so busy building in late June. When the first Federal troops had appeared on the Centreville road before Fairfax on Wednesday the regiment was ordered to slowly retreat.  To the men it seemed like cowardice, and they grumbled and protested "running away without a fight"

Captain Sykes would only offer to them the explanation, "We will stand when the time is right Boys, only then."

He realized the genius of the orders directing the clogging of the wells in Fairfax and Centreville. Water was what everyone wanted on a day like this, and they sat on the best supply with a full Division supported by artillery. Even though it was terribly muddy, it still was water.

When they visited the dead and wounded that Thursday evening on the field in front of them they noticed the wounded that could speak begged for water and the dead all seemed to have empty canteens. The sergeants directed them to pick up weapons and cartridge boxes, they had hoped to obtain new federal arms but only found 1842 muskets just like theirs.

Billy remembered feeling sick and guilty as he stared shocked at the dead men. One man, whom he had stared at for a long time, had half of his head shot away. The remembrance of the sight brought back the sick feeling.

Captain Sykes walked his line and checked on the men with the First Sergeant.

He remarked to Billy and George, "Stay alert boys, there's still 40 thousand Federals up that hill."

George had asked Billy what he had been so quiet for.

Billy remarked vacantly, his reverie broken, "I just wonder, is it a sin what we done the other day?"

George had answered as he closed his cartridge pouch, "Naw Billy, you are fighting for your people, your kin. Them men you were shooting at came to our home and they mean us ill. Defending your home is no sin!"

Billy argued, "Thought the good book says, "Thou shalt not kill" after all."

George patiently explained, "I have heard that the Hebrew translation really said, "Thou shalt do no murder" this here is a declared war, it's different."

Billy had felt a little better having George's counsel. He was a Lay Pastor after all. He suddenly wanted to hear him read the bible some more, as the habit had brought them all comfort. He was happy that the Federal "hordes" as he had been hearing for months, appeared to be no better soldiers than them. He could not get the image of the dead man from his mind.

Billy became anxious to write his father, he had now; like his father before him, seen an engagement with an enemy, and he knew this would make Abner Cross extremely proud.

At the Richmond freight yard, 95 miles from Manassas Junction, Wade Hampton's Legion had begun to load the Infantry regiment and equipment on the trains. The men had been extremely frustrated in the $2^{nd}$ South Carolina Cavalry because they had to search 2 days for their horses.

The animals had been misdirected enroute and it had only been due to the foresight of assigning men from the Regiment to act as stevedores that had prevented them from being lost. After much arguing and insistence the cars containing the horses had been linked to a train bound for Richmond.

Wade Hampton had met with his Regimental Commanders and briefed them on the orders he had received from Beauregard, "Gentlemen, we have been directed to make haste for Manassas. "Old Bory" has directed Johnston to bring his troops out of Winchester to Manassas and we are to reinforce as well. It sounds like the Federals want to take Manassas and we believe them to have 40 thousand troops encamped 15 miles from Manassas now. For now we only have rail cars for the infantry, The Cavalry and Artillery will move to Manassas by road."

Hampton paused to light a cigar; he took a puff and checked to see if it was lit and continued, "I expect this to become a confusing thing as we are as green as the Federal volunteers are. Make double sure you check everything and make damn sure people understand your orders."

Hampton gave further administrative instruction to each of his commands, he remained unhappy with the quality of weapons the Richmond Depot had equipped his cavalry with, sabers, single shot horse pistols and M1842 musketoons, which were little better than shotguns, but he resolved himself to make do.

He remembered the ordnance officer's response to his protests; "they are necessary for standardization of resupply. Nobody has Hall Carbine cartridges anymore!"

Rumor had it that orders had been placed for fine English weapons that should arrive soon, if, indeed, they would even be needed.

Louis and Jacob had rushed from camp to the freight yard when word arrived that the horses had been found, they had quickly hunted down the boxcar with a "20" painted on the corner that they had loaded the horses in. Jacob was relieved to see his horse was still there and apparently doing well. Had they been lost, the order had been given that they would be infantry instead, and the thought of walking did not appeal to him.

After the Infantrymen of the Legion had loaded aboard the trains that afternoon the men lounged in the straw covered boxcars, there was some surprise that there were no coach cars, but war required sacrifice so they settled for what they got.

Back in the Cavalry camp Louis held up his 1842 carbine and remarked, "Ain't this something, we was better off with our Halls!"

Lieutenant Winters remarked, "I read where the Army said they were perfect for Cavalry as they provided no ill affect to friend or foe."

The men snickered a bit at the observation.

Winters grinned and added, "We need to load them with Buckshot and that should work for our purposes anyway, remember we have speed and shock on our side, just keep a keen eye out for dead officers and pistols, we need Colts more than musketoons."

Word was passed that they would start the march before dawn; it would be a long march for the Cavalry.

The infantry train was moving fast and by 9 pm in the evening of the 20th they had arrived at Manassas Junction. Colonel Hampton ordered them to detrain where they had stopped.

Manassas Junction was a chaotic scene as 20 thousand men from Johnston's force were clogging the rail yard that evening. "Old Bory" now had men in numbers to match his foe.

After some struggle to rig a ramp to unload the horses of the staff, Colonel Hampton saddled his horse and moved off to search for General Beauregard's Headquarters.

He received word from several officers he encountered that General Beauregard was situated in the direction of Blackburn's Ford in the McLean House, a brick house a mile from the run. It was 4 hours past sundown but he resolved to find his commander.

After stopping a galloping courier, Hampton finally ascertained the direction to travel in the dark.

He paused a moment to look at the great comet that had appeared in the sky, it was very visible at night now. He wondered if it was a portent from the Almighty. Riding on he noted a faint light and found the farmhouse surrounded by horses.

As Hampton entered the house, he saw General Beauregard gathered with several other officers gathered around a map. As his eyes adjusted to the dim lamp light he recognized General Bonham and General Bee.

"Colonel Hampton is a pleasure to see you again!" Beauregard greeted him warmly, "Come, join us we are discussing our dispositions, we expect company soon."

Hampton had taken a great liking to the cocky creole General, he had done a magnificent job preparing Charleston for the reduction and taking of Fort Sumter, it was only fitting that he be given command of the Army of the Potomac.

Beauregard spent a few minutes to illustrate the past few days to Hampton.

To much laughter he described the ruined supper at the same house they were in now during the evening of the fight at Blackburn's Ford when a Federal shell had churned through the headquarters and lodged in their hearth.

"Colonel Hampton I intend to hold you and your Regiment in reserve until the remainder of your Legion arrives, I expect McDowell to make a move in this direction in the next few days. I am relieved to have General Johnston's force arriving; I should think I now have numerical parity with the Federals."

He pointed to the map on the dining table and showed him the path of Bull Run, "The fight on Thursday made it clear that McDowell wants to make an attempt on our right, but we have to watch all the crossings on this six mile stretch of the run. He might try a different approach now."

Beauregard assigned Hampton to a pine woods area near the headquarters for a bivouac site and instructed him to maintain a Liaison Officer with the headquarters. Hampton agreed and with a salute, went back out into the darkness to gather in his small force.

To his relief, the sky had darkened and a light rain had begun to fall.

## Centreville, Virginia

# 20 July 1861

Joshua was assisting his section as they removed the wheels from the gun to regrease the hubs, the steel of the rim reflected the bright sun, the movement up the road had polished the iron to a bright gleam, and it reminded him of a freshly used plow. They had finished the wheels of the Caisson and the Limber and were finishing the Gun.

Lieutenant Craig had come by several times in the morning as he had been assigned to watch over Joshua's Crew and Sean Mulcahy's gun as a section. Major Hunt had assigned him as a temporary fill as Lieutenant Benson was sick with the measles.

Word had spread through M Company might be moving early tomorrow morning. First Sergeant O'Keefe had assembled the Sergeants after water call and briefed them that the Company was to accompany General Tyler's Division to a place called Blackburn's Ford. He explained that a hot fight had ensued there last Thursday as they were marching up so the light 12 pounders were needed there to range secessionist batteries that commanded the heights south of the stream called Bull Run.

"I regret to inform you, that we have been relegated to a supporting action in this scrap," O'Keefe had announced, "the main army is to march north and then west to attack the rebel left flank. We will keep watch on the back door of our fine general's army to prevent the secesh from doing likewise on our left."

O'Keefe looked his noncommissioned officers each in the eye and added, "One more time, check your caissons and limber chests, insure you have full loads, insure you have a full barrel of water in the battery wagon for the crews and we will sound water call for the horses earlier than usual tonight. I expect us to move at 3 am or so with the rest of the army, so get your men some rest later this afternoon."

Sergeant Mills and Joshua walked back to their section camp after the meeting, Mills was annoyed by the news, "Here we are regular artillery and we are being relegated to a supporting effort of this fight!"

Joshua philosophically remarked, "Well sergeant, we don't get asked we just do as we are told. I heard you say that many a time."

Mills smiled, "Yep that would be correct Josh, just like you to remind me of things I said as a Corporal!"

As they arrived at the camp, Joshua noted that his crewmen were oiling and laying out the harness leathers for the teams. He was inwardly proud of their industry, the excitement of the coming action, supporting action or not, had energized the men.

Lieutenant Craig at that moment rode up, "Sergeant Mills, I need a courier!"

Joshua immediately volunteered, "I'll do it, my section has pretty much everything in hand."

Craig handed him a folded message, "Corporal this is from Major Hunt to General Tyler, he is in the camp south of Centreville, have his adjutant take it to him as soon as possible."

Joshua took the note and strode off in the direction of the small crossroads village as Lieutenant Craig rode back to Major Hunts tent. The officers had been in there all morning.

It took Joshua some time to determine exactly which camp was 1st Division Headquarters, he was amazed at the dazzling array of units encamped, and the spectacular array of uniforms worn by the various units that made up the Army of Northeastern Virginia. Troops were wearing both blue and grey, he saw an officer stride by wearing a Scottish kilt, and many men wearing various types of "Zouave" uniforms. He thought to himself that at artillery distance it might be hard to tell who was who with this variety of uniforms.

He finally found the tent; intuitively going to one with lots of horses picketed around it, and delivered the message to the Adjutant.

"Corporal stand by and I will check if there is anything for Major Hunt," the young officer disappeared back inside the tent. Shortly he returned and shook his head. Joshua saluted and left.

As he walked back through the bustling camp in the dusty heat, he paused to look at signalers in a small makeshift tower waving red flags with a white dot in the center, they were facing towards Washington, He had no clue what their motions meant but they periodically would stop another man would lower a note to a Sergeant standing below.

As Joshua continued he noticed a tent with a cross attached to the ridgepole in a camp that had a large green Regimental color with a Harp embroidered on it, it also had large letters sewn on that read "69th NYVI". As he walked by the tent marked with the cross he saw an older man there wearing a plain black frock coat with a green scarf moving boxes within, he walked over and knocked on the upright pole and when the man turned to look at him he saluted.

"Begging your pardon sir, but are you a preacher?" Joshua was slightly nervous walking into another Regiment's camp.

The old man smiled and replied in a thick Irish brogue, "Aye son, a Priest is the title you should use, are you seeking absolution?"

Joshua not knowing what "absolution" was, shook his head no, "Sir, I am with the 2nd United States Artillery, and we've got a lot of Irish soldiers, they are looking for a preacher, I mean priest, sir."

The old priest smiled, "Son, I am Monsignor Merrill of the Diocese of New York City; I'm doing my 90 days with the Regiment. We are having a Mass here at this tent at 5pm. Your men are welcome here if they need absolution. I am afraid since we will be moving early in the morning that I cannot come to your location."

Joshua quickly thanked the Priest and strode back down the Warrenton Pike to his encampment, he had found what he had hoped to find.

He quickly checked in with his section when he arrived and he gave instructions to the crews about watering the horses and feeding them early, and provided them with warning that the Company would be leaving in the morning before dawn.  He then went to the First Sergeant's tent.

O'Keefe and Quartermaster Sergeant O'Rourke were inside smoking their pipes.

"First Sergeant, I am ready to accept my honorary Irish appointment!" Joshua announced with a flourish.

O'Keefe raised an eyebrow and looked at O'Rourke, "You've found a Catholic Chaplain?"

Joshua nodded, "He says he is something called a "Monsignor" whatever that is."

O'Keefe, laughed out loud and exclaimed, "Holy Shit, boy'o that's a fookin wonder, it is.  When is his Mass?"

Joshua replied, "5 pm First Sergeant, with the 69<sup>th</sup> New York."

O'Keefe patted him on the shoulder, "Good work lad!  Good work indeed, if you gentlemen will excuse me now I must go consult with my Major."

At a quarter until the hour of 5 pm, First Sergeant O'Keefe organized a small formation of the 30 Irish soldiers of the company and marched them up the pike to the encampment to attend the worshipful mass of the "Fighting 69<sup>th</sup>" Regiment of the New York Volunteer Infantry, for the rare occasion to attend a Mass put on by the army.

After watching them form under the supervision of the First Sergeant and march away Joshua smiled.

Major Hunt approached him and after returning his salute, he grinned and said, "That was a fine thing to do Corporal, something I will not soon forget. You see the army has never been inclined to support the needs of the Catholic soldiers, we had too many problems in Mexico."

He looked at Joshua for a moment and asked, "How are you feeling about tomorrow, son?"

Joshua thought a moment and replied, "It feels funny, sir. I heard Lieutenant Craig talk about the South Carolina Regiments that are over there. I can only hope my brother is not with them. I heard that he was in the cavalry."

Hunt nodded in understanding, "I know how you feel Timmonds, I have some very good friends that are commanding troops for them, good friends from the Academy and battle in Mexico. I cannot set my vow aside that easily."

Joshua nodded, "I understand sir, I cannot either."

Joshua quickly excused himself, saluted and left. Being with the Major made him very uncomfortable, but he genuinely admired the man, he was utterly professional and had been seen on several occasions fighting more senior officers than himself for the men. He resolved to do his utmost for his commander.

When he arrived back his section, he noted that the men had the harnesses all laid out to hitch the teams after they had watered the horses, Sergeant Mills had already alerted them to the early morning move.

Private Thorne was frying chunks of fresh beef in an liberated "secesh" frying pan for the crew.

The smell of the fresh meat made Joshua very hungry, "Thorne, when's supper?"

Thorne looked up and smiled, "Soon Corporal, I will need some of your hard tack though."

Joshua gave him two of his hard crackers from his haversack and he added them to the sodden mess among the beef chunks.

Thorne then announced, "All you's gimme about 5 minutes then you can come beggin with your cups, we'll make salty mud coffee after we eat."

Joshua was pleased at what a good mess cook Thorne had become. He had been very quiet until they had started the march, now everybody knew his calling.

Just as the sun was setting, the section of Parrot guns under the command of Lieutenant Benjamin of the 1st United States Artillery arrived at M Company's camp.

The soldiers curiously looked over the enormous 20 pounders, they had only seen the Parrot rifles at a distance. The M Company and G Company artillerymen traded notes on their respective piece. To Joshua's amazement the G Company boys had never heard of the light 12 pound gun and they were amazed at the range. Joshua found himself amazed at the range of the Parrot, twice that of his gun.

The G Company gunners showed Joshua and his crew the Schenkel Shells that the gun fired. He was interested to see how the shell was like a giant Minie ball, with a large Paper Mache cup on the rear of the iron shell.

The men talked for an hour as the G Company rifles had been in the fight on Thursday. They assured Joshua that M Company should follow them, "G Company knew just the spot to be!"

The First Sergeant had the company bugler call Water Call in the early evening and the company drivers began the long process of watering and feeding the teams. Once they had completed the task,

Sergeant Mills instructed them to proceed with harnessing the teams to the limbers and caissons, the horses would sleep in their traces.

At the Sergeants call after dark First Sergeant O'Keefe was brief.

"We will move by split sections with the G Company rifles and Lieutenant Platt's section leaving at 2 am. They will follow Colonel Richardson's brigade down to positions overlooking the ford. Lieutenant Craig's section will depart at 2:30 with the battery and forge wagons in tow."

O'Keefe stopped to light his pipe again with a match, and after a puff, continued, "This moving in the dark will be a fookin' mess so don't be rough on the horses, last thing we will need is a crazed team in the dark with infantry on a narrow road."

O'Keefe went through a few more administrative details and advised the Sergeants to try to get the men to sleep. He knew it was a fruitless endeavor as the entire camp around Centreville had the air of a festival on this particular evening.

"I know the men are anxious to see some action," he observed, adding, "It will only be later that they will wish they hadn't."

Major Hunt and Lieutenant Craig sat together in Hunt's tent. Hunt was concerned that his new brother in law remain mindful of his safety as well as possible.

"Presley, I am glad to have you despite Mary's protests, but you need to be mindful of your foot!"

Craig waved the comment away, "Henry, I am a soldier just as you are, I know the risks."

Hunt smiled, "Well, be mindful to keep moving, sitting on a horse makes you a fine target. There would be hell to pay when I return to your sister if something was to happen to you!"

"Major, don't you worry over Mother or Mary's concerns; I would not miss this fight for the world!"

Hunt and Craig had a last shot of brandy and a cigar before trying to get some sleep. As expected neither could.

Boots and Saddles was sounded by the bugler at 1:30 am. The soldiers quietly dressed and collected up their bedrolls and equipment and stowed them on the saddles of the team horses.

Joshua checked his crew and the stowage of equipment on the limber and the gun. The night was clear and in the early morning calm the great comet that had adorned the sky since midmonth could be seen low over the Northwest horizon. Joshua felt it to be a sign of some sort as did the other men.

First Sergeant broke up one set of particularly enthralled observers, "Get back to makin' ready gents, it's a sign all right, it is a sure sign I will be kickin' yer asses if you don't quit dawdlin'!"

Cadet Meigs rode over to M Company in the dark and after quick consultation with Major Hunt, quietly led the section of G Company and M Company over to Colonel Richardson's column. Once he had placed the 4 guns into the march column, he returned to guide the rest of the Company in the rear of the Brigade.

The movement proved to be agonizingly slow. The column moved and stopped, often waiting for long periods. As the column began to descend the hill crest they entered dense forest and without the starlight it was impossibly dark.

Due to the slow speed and darkness, Joshua directed his drivers to dismount and lead the teams at a walk through the thick woods, as they trudged along in the dark quietly soothing the horses; he imagined it was nearly 4 or 5 am by now.

William Barry and Lieutenant Edwards, traveling behind General Tyler's leading brigade were having a clearly worse time. In order to get the two batteries and the 30 pounder into the position designated by General Tyler, the detachment had to descend the hill from Centreville and then move laterally off to the right. The 30 pounder Parrot Rifle weighed nearly 3 tons and was becoming more and more difficult to maneuver as they entered the ravine called "Cub Run". It took nearly 4 hours to get the two batteries and the siege gun across the suspension bridge over the run and up to the positions overlooking the stone bridge. The gun crews had been required to manhandle the heavy piece up the opposite bank after the nerve wracking bridge crossing. Major Barry had fully expected the bridge to collapse under the weight.

Once Barry had the guns in position he was then required to ride to Sudley Springs Ford further North to rejoin General McDowell's command group. As the Army of Northeastern Virginia's Chief of Artillery he had to dedicate his energies to the commanding general's primary object. As he felt his way through the early morning darkness he hoped that they would indeed roll up Beauregard's left flank. He was beginning to grow concerned that sunrise was less than an hour away, and he still had a long ways to go.

As he followed the column at an excruciatingly slow pace he began to note the redness of the rising sun off to the East. Instinctively he knew the plan was going to be greatly off schedule.

Two miles ahead of Major Barry, Colonel Burnside and his brigade had resorted to forming parties of ad hoc engineers to clear and widen the road for the artillery and wagons to transit the rough track through the woods. Behind them rode General McDowell. His fine meal of fresh beef from late last night had him feeling greatly ill. The general had opted to ride in a carriage as he had been required to make frequent stops. It was clear to him in the dark woods that they were likely not going to reach Sudley Springs before daylight.

As his wagon passed a wider opening in the deep woods he was
hailed by a Captain mounted on a horse, "Sir, Captain Woodbury,
with General Hunter's Division. I beg to report we have encountered
a delay! Our guide recommended to Colonel Burnside that he take
another track away from the run as our march would be observed by
rebel batteries after the sunrise. The track through the woods to
approach Sudley Springs is poor and we have parties being required
to widen the road for the artillery."

General McDowell, hearing this news, suddenly forgot about his
abdominal pains and summoned his adjutant, "Bring me my horse
and find Major Barnard!"

The flanking effort had been delayed by the movement across Cub
Run of General Tyler's Brigades and artillery and in the dark the
forward progress was hard to determine. Now that the dawn half-
light was beginning to brighten the landscape McDowell began to
realize where he was.

The General secured his horse and his Engineer and made haste to
reach the head of General Hunter's column in the woods ahead.
General McDowell was surprised at the dustiness of the movement
that he had not noticed in the darkness. General Beauregard's scouts
were sure to be seeing the same.

A half hour later, Major William Barry arrived at the commander's
empty carriage dutifully following the marching infantry in the
woods.

"The General has rode ahead on horseback to consult with General
Hunter!" shouted out the orderly driving the carriage.

Barry nodded and spurred his horse on through the long dusty
columns of marching troops; the morning sun had clearly lit up the
woods now.

On the Army of Northeastern Virginia's left, Colonel Richardson moved his brigades forward and directed them to form on line at the edge of the woods that opened up on Compton's Farm, the troops moved in the early dawn light to the right and left of the road that descended the fields and farmhouses along the road that crossed Blackburn's Ford. He directed Lieutenant Benjamin to occupy the position he had established on the 18th and had Lieutenant Platt place his section on the left of the road by a barn looking into the hollow of Bull Run.

Henry Hunt was impatient to rejoin his forward section; He greatly feared poor placement decisions by an Infantry officer and two inexperienced Lieutenants. With the light emerging, he wanted to get a look at the ground. It was nearly 6 am now.

# Bull Run vicinity, Virginia
# 21 July 1861

Lieutenant Thompson looked at his pocket watch in the early morning light, 6:15 am. Noting the time he went over to his gunner on the 30 pounder Parrot gun. The sun rising in the East reddened the entire sky, the day promised to be a hot one.

Looking out beyond the stone bridge across the run with his field glasses, Thompson could make out a signal tower erected by the rebels and the tops of tents beyond the wood to the right of the stone bridge.

Turning to the gunner, Thompson pointed and directed, "For your first 3 shots put them into that camp to the right of the bridge, solid bolt to start. Three shots, on my command, if you please."

As the crews loaded the gun, Thompson turned and looked to his right and left, to his right he saw Colonel Sherman's brigade forming on line forming the right of Tyler's Division on the left was Colonel Shenk's brigade forming on line slightly forward of Sherman's. He understood his first 3 shots would trigger a diversionary bombardment over the stone bridge and behind them at Blackburn's Ford. He hoped that Major Hunt would be looking out for Lieutenant Benjamin; he was proving to be a fine young officer.

As he looked over further to his right he became concerned about the amount of dust the main attack was generating on the approach march to Sudley Springs Ford. There was no way the secesh would not see it.

Thompson looked at his watch again, 6:30 am, the time had come, he called out, "Fire!"

The number 4 on gun number 1 yanked hard on his lanyard, the Parrot gun roared. Quickly the crew sponged and reloaded.

Lieutenant Thompson shouted out again, "Fire!"

The gun roared again, Thompson studied the position with his field glasses but observed no effect, whatsoever.

Upon the completion of the third shot, Lieutenant Thompson heard the batteries to his right begin a deliberate bombardment and to his rear he noted muted cannonading at the vicinity of Blackburn's Ford. The fight to crush the secessionists was on. Hopefully General McDowell was at Sudley Springs Ford by now to spring the trap closed.

Captain Edward Porter Alexander sat on the cot of his tent by the signal tower that served as his headquarters at the near left of General Beauregard's defensive line. Alexander was pulling on his boots in order to visit his men in the tower to check what messages had been transmitted over the evening. A Federal attack was expected today, and he reckoned it would be a busy day. Just as he was pulling on his right boot he heard a loud boom and an incoming rustling noise.

The solid 30 pounder bolt sheared through the thin canvas of his tent with a loud shuttling howl. Captain Alexander dove to the floor. He quickly grabbed his leather pouch from under the folding cot and ran out of his tent, forgetting his hat.

Bareheaded he scaled the ladder of the signal tower; he hoped it was not the next target of the Federal gun.

The sergeant manning the tower wryly observed, "Seems them Yankee hirelings don't think much of you sir."

Alexander replied, "That appears to be the case, did you see where it came from?"

The sergeant pointed to the East, "Right there sir, looks like a full division in line and about 7 guns. We just hollered to someone to go get you before they fired the shot."

Alexander looked with amazement and the forming ranks on the slopes below Centreville, just across the run.

The Sergeant observed, "Once it got bright after sunrise, they was just standing there, must have moved in the dark."

The big gun on the eastern bank of the run fired again, the shot ripped through more tents below scattering men and upended a wagon parked by Colonel Evans headquarters tent in a large cloud of dust.

Alexander dug his field glasses out of his leather bag and started to scan the far side of the Bull Run River. Looking to North he noted a large dust cloud emerging from the woods near Sudley Springs Ford. Alexander dug out his message book and securing a lead pencil he scribbled out a message, which read;

*"COL Evans, Look to your Left, you have been turned! CPT Alexander"*

Alexander shouted to a soldier standing by below, "Soldier! Get this to Colonel Evans below!"

Captain Alexander wadded the message into a ball and dropped it from the top of the tower to the soldier below. He then turned to the Sergeant beside him, "Send this message to General Beauregard, Large dust cloud vicinity Sudley Springs Ford. Troops stationary to our front vicinity stone bridge, Warrenton Pike in Division size."

The Sergeant nodded and taking up his flag, signaled the hail to the tower southeast towards the McLean house, where General Beauregard's headquarters was situated. He then proceeded to send the message in Wigwag, with his large red flag to the far tower.

The third shot ripped through the heavily timbered river bottom by the run to seemingly no effect. Alexander noted that other batteries had begun to fire on the Federal side as well.

Major Hunt arrived at Lieutenant Platt's section when he heard the first shot of the 30 pounder two miles to the Northwest. He looked at his pocket watch, 6:30 am. Looking over the placement it was clear that the approach from Blackburn's Ford was adequately covered by Lieutenant Benjamin's Parrot guns, he did not quite understand the object of Lieutenant Platt's placement.

Hunt quickly directed Lieutenant Craig to pause by Platt's section and await further orders, Hunt decided to ride the ground himself, clearly the Infantry colonels were guessing in regards to massing guns for effect. "Impersonating Artillerists" was his term for such ad hoc actions.

As Hunt prepared to start out, Colonel Richardson approached his location and ordered, "Major Hunt establish your battery here. Have the guns begin firing across the run!"

Hunt replied, "Sir at what object do you wish for us to engage?"

Richardson was in an excited state, "Down by the Run there, there is enemy in the trees and by the farmhouse across the way!"

Hunt saluted and acknowledged the order and directed Craig to unlimber alongside Platt's section to the left. With a nod to Benjamin, the young Lieutenant had his two guns fire into the river bottom timber. Hunt studied the closely spaced shots with his field glasses and noticed no movement at the points of impact. He turned to Platt and instructed him to fire two rounds in the vicinity of Mclean's farm across the way, "Deliberately if you please." As Platt's second round ripped through the old wooden barn by the McLean farmhouse, a small group of horsemen rode away at a gallop from behind the house.

Joshua hustled his crew to reverse his gun to face the enemy at 11 yards to the left of Lieutenant Platt's section, the caisson drivers moved the caissons back about 20 yards away near the road. As the crew assembled their tools and steadied the limber team, Joshua anxiously looked for orders from Lieutenant Craig.

Lieutenant Craig being very new to artillery, remembering that the men were waiting on him; shouted out, "Shot, at the far ridge, 5 degrees elevation! Advance the Charge!" His command got the men in synch with Platt's section who were shooting into the ravine below.

Joshua extracted his Pendulum Hause and hung it from the mount cast on the cascabel of the gun. He quickly slid the sliding sight up to 5 degrees elevation, then straddling the trail he had number 3 and 4 adjust the trail to the left towards a squared off looking object on top of the hillocks overlooking Blackburn's Ford. He imagined the object was the oft mentioned "masked batteries" behind earthworks. Joshua then looked out and estimated the distance to be nearly 1800 yards. He gave the screw several swift turns to align the front sight post of the gun with the rear sight of the Pendulum Hause. He then elevated the gun slightly higher to accommodate the extra distance.

Joshua backed away returning the Hause to his pouch and announced, "Load!" Number 5 showed him the shot in his leather bag as he walked the charge up to number 2 at the muzzle.

As Private Watkins rammed the load home, Joshua announced, "Prick and prime!"

Private Wilkins quickly punched a hole in the bag with his gimlet inserted into the vent, and quickly produced and inserted a brass friction primer. No sooner was it inserted that Private Lyttle stepped over and hooked his lanyard to the small twisted wire loop of the friction primer and backed clear of the wheel and quickly taking the slack out of the lanyard; faced Joshua for the order.

Joshua nodded as he checked the positions of his crew and shouted, "Fire!"

As the gun violently rolled back, Joshua stepped off to his left to see the effect of the shot, on the wooded hillock he saw a spray of dark earth short of the position.

The crewmen laid hands on the wheels and the cheeks of the carriage and rolled the gun back on line.

Joshua then shouted out, "Sponge!" Watkins dipped the sponge end of the rod into the water bucket and quickly sponged the bore.

Lieutenant Craig rode the line on his horse and asked Joshua, "Timmonds what do say the range is?"

Joshua shouted out, while keeping his eyes on the ridge, "My guess is 1800 yards sir!"

When he heard the sucking noise of the sponge staff clear the muzzle, Joshua then shouted, "Shot! Advance the charge!"

As he aimed the following time he used the top of the Pendulum Hause frame as his rear sight instead of the sliding elevation sight. The next shot kicked up chunks of timber and men could be seen running laterally away from the target.

Joshua then shouted out without taking his eyes off the target, "More like 1900 yards sir!"

As Joshua was about to repeat the reload process, he heard First Sergeant O'Keefe shout as he paced the line of guns, "Slow the fook down! Deliberate fire goddammit! Think through each shot and remember yer drill!"

O'Keefe then began to question Sergeant Mill's on the round count of his sections limbers as the crews continued the bombardment.

Troops were still coming down the road from Centreville; Colonel Davies' brigade of Colonel Mile's division had received direction to reinforce the left of Colonel Richardson's Brigade. As the troops marched in column along the edge of the woods of the open farmland on the plateau above Blackburn's crossing, Hunt decided to look over the ground.

He paused to talk to each of his Lieutenants telling each, "I want you to deliberately and slowly engage suspected targets to your front. Do not waste your ammunition by rapid fire! Employ only solid shot for now until something presents itself."

Hunt turned his horse and looked at the troops filing past behind the guns. Seeing a Colonel riding past he saluted and noted the colors indicated a New York Volunteer Regiment. They followed the road that ran along the edge of the woods and entered into a wooded ravine to the left.

Hunt looked to his right beyond Lieutenant Thompson's slowly firing Parrot guns and he could see Colonel Richardson's Massachusetts Regiment and the two Michigan regiments forming lines along the more open right side of the road leading to the ford below. He had placed two regiments to the front and one to the rear. Peering down at the run he saw no apparent movement.

A Colonel rode up to him from the troops turning left and Major Hunt saluted him, "Major Hunt, sir, M Company 2$^{nd}$ US Artillery."

He replied with a quick salute back, "Colonel Davies, Hunt. Keep up the fire Major, this is a demonstration insure you keep a rapid rate of fire."

Hunt, not liking the instruction asked, "Sir, I have noted the deep ravine to the left that I would like to look at, I am concerned that our pieces might be better placed to cover it. I request to reconnoiter the ground to the left."

Colonel Davies nodded, "I am thinking the same Major, proceed with your reconnaissance."

Colonel Evans walked his troop positions along the run, staring as he walked at the big gun on the other side which was firing shot along with two other batteries into the trees where his Regiments were crouched. So far he had lost no men to the slow deliberate fire. It was maddening to him to watch the Yankee regiments forming lines on the slopes leading down to the run. They seemed to be in no great hurry and they had yet to detach skirmishers to feel forward.

He paused to steady his men as he walked the line of his brigade, "Wait for 'em boys, don't show yourselves until you have to."

At 8 am a breathless courier found him in the middle of his Brigade trooping of the line, "Sir, Message from Captain Alexander, had a hell of time finding you sir, it has been near an hour lookin' for you!"

The soldier handed him the crumpled ball of paper wet with sweat from the couriers run.

Peering oddly at the courier he unwadded the ball and read Alexander's message, "Shit, Where is my adjutant?"

He turned and grabbed his Adjutant, "Get the bugler! Sound officers call!"

Evans quickly convened his Regimental commanders behind the center of his Brigade, "We will leave 4 Companies and two guns to cover the bridge, that gaggle across the way ain't nuthin' but a demonstration! Get the rest moving towards Sudley Springs Ford on the double quick, find good ground and get some guns supported by infantry on it now!"

Evans then turned to his adjutant, "Get word to General Beauregard that the Federals are on my left flank and I am turning to meet them. I'll be needing reinforcement as quick as he can send it!"

After his regimental commanders departed, Evans turned to his orderly sergeant and snapped his fingers, "Wet my whistle, Hiram!"

The orderly sergeant had a large wooden canteen on a strap, he quickly filled the tin cup attached with a thong with a dram of the bourbon within and handed the cup to Evans, who downed it quickly and nodded thanks.

Colonel Evans then found his horse and trotted with his 6 companies and 2 guns towards the North. If they wanted a fight he was bound and determined to give them one.

General McDowell was beginning to worry, the flanking march had taken too long to accomplish, He rode his horse across the run at Sudley Springs. The regiments each paused and men filled their canteens as they crossed without regard to the curses of their officers and sergeants. He felt queasy again; he hoped the distress would not strike him again.

Behind him he could hear the steady bombardment of the demonstrations at Stone Bridge and Blackburn's Ford; he looked towards Manassas Junction and noted he had only Burnside's Brigade across.

General Hunter, the 2$^{nd}$ Division Commander rode up and reported, "Sir, once I get Porter and his brigade across, I think we should get on that hill there!" Hunter pointed towards a wooded hill directly in front of the Ford.

McDowell looked at the position he indicated and commanded, "Put one brigade on it and try to push another to the right of it. I will need a place for Heintzelman to maneuver around to flank the rebel rear. Make haste General!"

McDowell studied his watch 9:05 am, he hoped his demonstration had preoccupied Beauregard.

He watched Porter's men cross the ford and form in column on the road as Burnside's men moved in Column into the woods between the run and the hill to his front.

McDowell summoned his Engineer, "Major what is that feature there?"

Major Barnard dug a map out of his case and studied it for a moment, "It is named Matthews Hill, sir there are several more prominences behind it."

McDowell watched with some satisfaction as Burnside and Porter began to move forward, keeping a good alignment of the two columns. He turned and noted Heintzelman's lead brigade had arrived at the ford, noting each man trying to fill a canteen as they crossed the ford. "Can't be helped," he thought to himself, it would be a hot day.

Suddenly a loud sputtering volley erupted before Burnside's Brigade. The Rebels had Matthews Hill.

The distant crackling noise across the run to his right caused Lieutenant Thompson to turn away from his cannonade of the woods by the Stone Bridge; He looked towards the source of the volley firing but could only see distant smoke emerging above the dense trees lining the run. He noticed that Colonel Sherman had pushed skirmishers almost to the run and nothing was occurring, it seemed odd to him.

He turned his field glass to the flat across the run beyond the stone bridge; He noted a column of infantry crossing the Warrenton Pike headed to his right. Rebels were responding to General McDowell's attack.

He shouted to his crews, "Focus your fires on that column there! 2500 yards!"

Soon the 30 pounder was oriented on the distant column, by the time they had gotten two shots off, the column had disappeared behind the trees.

Suddenly he noted another column crossing close to the far side of the bridge as he directed his guns to that point, two rebel guns suddenly fired after remaining silent all morning. The two six pound shot skipped in the dusty dirt past the 30 pounder and one struck the caisson team of the gun.

The round struck on the oblique killing three horses outright as it tore through harnesses, horseflesh and singletree of the caisson, two other horses shrieked and twisted, wounded by splinters. The drivers tried to unhitch them and one man fell, struck by a terrified horses' hoof as it reared. The caisson Sergeant pulled his revolver and shot the horse multiple times to put it down, then he checked on the injured soldier. He looked up and met Thompson's gaze and shook his head.

Sherman's Battery of E Company to the right of Thompson replied with case shot from all 4 guns and the rebel pieces fell silent.

Thompson realized he would need more horses now or he would have an immobile gun. There would be no way to move the heavy siege piece without full teams. He summoned his Quartermaster Sergeant and instructed him to go back into Centreville and find 6 horses.

Thompson spend the morning engaging fleeting columns as they passed across Warrenton Pike, "Shooting them on the fly," he would later describe it. He hoped that General McDowell was getting the word, as he possessed no way to inform anyone.

Major Hunt cantered down the road past the marching companies of the 31st New York Volunteer Infantry pushing out to the leftmost portion of the line. He looked out to his right as he rode sizing up the ground he was on.

As he rode he noted that he was on a finger like plateau that came to a point above the Bull Run River at Blackburn's Ford. The road that he was following, skirted the front of a wood that then dipped into a ravine to the left of the plateau, the ravine was heavily wooded, much like the trace of the Run below. From the midpoint of the plateau he realized a battery could cover the approaches from the ravine to the left and the road that transected it and emerged again on the adjacent knoll. The ravine to the left offered a perfect approach for infantry, should the rebels decide to attempt to flank Colonel Davies and Colonel Richardson's Brigades. He needed to move his battery.

Hunt's mind raced, as he watched the New York Regiment occupy the road leading into the ravine and as he heard the desultory shelling going on back at Compton's Corner. He could have Davies place Green's Battery at Compton's Corner to cover the Ford and his light battery could cover all approaches on the plateau and the next. If the rebels wanted to push to Centreville using this location they would have to use either the Ford or the Ravine that he was looking at now. He realized that since General McDowell was pushing all his force around to flank the rebels that this back door to the Federal rear at Centreville was wide open.

As he turned to ride back to the Battery he encountered Colonel Davies. The two officers stopped to talk while still on their horses in the still green oats growing on the open ground.

Hunt pointed back behind him and said, "Sir, the ravine and that far ridge across it threaten our flank on this ground. I have noted that this road we are on crosses that ravine and emerges again on the ridge across the way. I beg to recommend that we move my Battery to a location near here to control this ground. With the Infantry here and guns we can refuse this flank properly!"

Davies laughed and replied, "Major Hunt that is precisely why I have come here. Colonel Miles has ordered me to position you here with the same intent. He has brought up Lieutenant Green with 4 guns that can replace your pieces overlooking the Ford. Make haste and establish here. I will have troops fell trees across the road in the ravine frustrate passage to here."

Hunt, greatly relieved, saluted Davies and spurred his horse to move M Company. The rising noise of battle to the North disturbed him.

As Hunt departed Colonel Davies ordered the 31$^{st}$ New York to deploy skirmishers with an ax detail down into the ravine.

Colonel Evans started to see his command beginning to break. He had watched with pleasure as his initial volleys had clearly disrupted the approaching columns of the lead Yankee brigade.

Even though he was greatly outnumbered he had good ground and good aim, the slope approaching the hill contained many dead. While they had done good early work stopping the advancing Federals, their combined volleys were beginning to kill and wound more of his men, and looking to his west there was a fresh column approaching. The long Federal line was starting to form a concave around his small force. The converging fire of their volleys filled the air with buzzing musket balls.

His South Carolinians and Louisianans were beginning to waiver, and he noticed men starting break from his formations. The Federal volleys were starting to enfilade his ranks. More and more men were falling.

He anxiously looked over his shoulder and noting dust rising from behind the ridge at Henry Hill, hopefully his reinforcements were near. He realized he needed to buy time.

Evans rode to talk with Major Roberdeau Wheat of the Louisiana Regiment, "Major, rally your Tigers and charge them goddamned Yankee bastards! We got to break them up some so our reinforcements can get up on this ground!"

Wheat first looked astonished as he expected to be ordered to pull back, but he suddenly got an evil gleam in his eye.

He nodded and saluted, and turning his horse he cried out, "Fix Bayonets!" He continued to cry out the command as he rode his line. Once he noted that they had complied he commanded them to charge.

The men of Burnside's brigade to their front were beginning to rally from Evan's initial punishing volleys; suddenly they realized that the southern troops were charging with loud whooping and yelling. This demonstration caused Burnside's lead Regiments to break and run.

Wheat rode apace with his men crying encouragement, the fire from the other Federal Regiments intensified. Suddenly Major Wheat dropped his sword and fell from his mount, shot through the chest. The men of the 1st Louisiana Regiment, staggered by the loss of their beloved commander, broke and ran. Two men stopped and dragged their fallen commander with them.

Evans saw Wheat fall and cursed aloud, the Louisiana Regiment was greatly admired and Wheat was clearly a fine officer. He turned and to his relief he saw South Carolina Regimental colors appear on the small ridge behind him, General Bee had arrived.

At that moment the 4th South Carolina on Matthew's Hill broke and ran, Evans spurred his horse to catch them. Looking to General Bee in the distance he raised his hat in salute and said to himself, "It's your baby now Barnard!"

General Beauregard and General Johnston stood by a wooden table set in the front garden of the McLean House, under a canvas awning. General Johnson was still weary from his long train ride to from the night prior. Beauregard too had spent most of the evening drafting up his offensive plan. He explained the plan on the map on the table after handing the written order into Johnston's hands.

"Sir, I have arrayed my forces with the intent to meet any enemy attack that I expect to occur along the Warrenton Pike emerging out of Centreville, and I have received confirmation of massing there at sunrise," he paused as he heard the increasing crescendo of musketry occurring on their left flank off to the North.

"I have delivered orders for Longstreet and Jones to attack abreast of Ewell towards Centreville while holding McDowell at the Run between Mitchells Ford and the stone bridge."

Concentrated cannon fire was beginning to become apparent to the North to accompany the musketry.

Johnston despaired of familiarizing himself with this country or having the time to read the order he had been given.

"General Beauregard, I fear I will have to trust you to execute your plan as you have developed it, while I am senior and have command, you know the field and the plan better than I."

Johnston turned and listened for a moment to the crescendo of noise from the North, asking "General why is that noise of battle building there when you have planned and anticipated this action to our front?"

Beauregard seemed confused by the question for a moment, but replied, I suppose it is a demonstration to distract me from his intended axis of attack."

Beauregard pointed to the south towards Union Mills Ford and explained, "Soon we should hear sounds of battle across the run as

Longstreet and Ewell push to Centreville, the terrain there is excellent for a flanking march to go unseen by the Unionists."

General Johnston began to feel a great doubt in his psyche; a battle was clearly welling to the North. He studied the map on the table and noted the ford at a place marked Sudley Springs. As he momentarily studied Beauregard's marked troop dispositions he realized despite his fatigue, that Beauregard had left his left flank open as wide as barn door.

Johnston doffed his hat and walked to his horse announcing as he pointed North, "General the battle is there, and that is where I am going."

The Officers met and held a quick conference on horseback at a shady intersection of the farm roads near McLean's Ford, an occasional shell could be heard shuttling overhead as the Federal Cannon on the bluff to the East engaged the Washington Artillery battery locations on the hills behind them.

Brigadier General James Longstreet, who only a year ago was the Paymaster of the Army, and Brigadier General Ewell who had spent most of his time out West in campaigns against Indians, discussed their preparations to begin pushing their Brigades up the ravines of Little Rocky Run near Union Mills Ford and the smaller ravine to the right of Blackburn's Ford.

Longstreet described his plans to Ewell, "Dick, I have already suggested to Colonel Jones' to get his brigade across in front of me. I will need him to capture the Battery on the hill that fires over our heads at this instant. If he can achieve that, then we will have an open path to Centreville. These deep woods give us a covered approach that reaches nearly to Centreville."

Ewell nodded and calmed his mount, which was as restless as he, "Damn general, when we start? Do you hear that great noise to the North, it sounds to me like we are missing this battle?"

Longstreet calmly observed, "Beauregard's orders made it plain that he would tell us when to begin. We have no other choice but to make what preparations we can until he orders his intent. I am anxious of the noise as well."

Longstreet tugged out his watch and opened it, it was nearly noon, hopefully Colonel Jones had gotten his brigade across the run, he wanted to get back to order Jubal Early to move his brigade to Jones' vacated position along the run so he could quickly cross the run when the order came.

Joshua had finished sighting the gun on a road at the crest of the heights beyond the run and awaited another group of horsemen to cross, they had expended nearly all their supply of solid shot in the limber chest and the caisson and his number 5 announced when advancing this round that 4 shot remained. As he waited for a target he glanced behind him and noted Major Hunt approaching back up the road in a purposeful trot.

"First Sergeant! Cease Firing of the battery! Limber the guns." He shouted as he reined his horse to a stop.

Joshua directed Private Lyttle to remove his lanyard and plucked the friction primer from the vent. While he was nervous in regards to moving a loaded gun, orders were orders.

The crews quickly stowed implements and the team drivers quickly brought up the limbers and waited as the crew rotated the gun carriages to mate them to the pin tails of the limbers. Joshua momentarily reflected that they had made a mess of the farmer's oats. Joshua then told Sergeant Mills that he should travel last in the movement as he had a loaded tube. Mills nodded and moved the second section into line ahead of the first section.

Hunt watched as the crews limbered the guns and then waved his arm and trotted back down the road. The 4 guns followed. The supporting infantrymen lounged in the shade of the trees watching the artillery maneuver with idle interest. All were becoming aware of the noise of the growing battle behind them.

After a short pull they arrived in at a spot further down the farm road where Lieutenant Craig waited them on his horse, he quickly indicated the line of the two guns of his section. Lieutenant Platt was already dropping his section to the left. They would be oriented to the left of the knoll and overlooked a thickly wooded ravine beyond the plateau of oats that overlooked the run.

Joshua could still see the knoll he had been firing at, but the ground they oriented on now did not appear to offer very much in the possibility of shots. He focused on readying the gun and soon had his crew established. After he had finished Sergeant Mills approached him and directed him to fire the remaining shot into the deep woods below and then await orders to load. Joshua quickly depressed his barrel until he had aim at point blank over the bluff into the thick woods below. He ordered his crew to reprime the piece and he then fired the round into the woods to clear the piece. He did not bother to monitor effects.

Billy slowly chewed on a piece of cold cooked salt pork as they lounged in the deep woods. His shoes and trouser legs were still wet from crossing the run, they had been ordered to cross the deeper portion of the run near McLean's Ford and the lead company had destroyed the small plank walk erected by Mr. McLean with overuse. He remembered having to hold his cartridge pouch up as he crossed as the run was nearly waist deep in some places on the crossing. As they sat and waited a solid shot tore through the tree tops directly overhead. A large branch crashed to the ground by them.

Gene wryly observed, "Them Yankees cut you some firewood to heat yer lunch, Billy!" The men laughed quietly. They made the most of what humor they could but they all were nervous. Captain Sykes had earlier explained to them that the offending battery would be their express objective once the order to attack had been given.

Gene then remarked, "Listen to that noise beyond. I'm thinking this thing will be played out before it gets to us."

Roland observed in response, "Captain said there is more of them than us, I wouldn't be so certain."

The men watched as Colonel Jenkins held a conference with his captains on the shaded road below where they sat, He motioned with his arm up the ravine and then he crooked it, indicating a turn to the left up the bluffs, clearly they would be climbing the steep left edge of the ridge across from them. Billy looked at the steep bluff with tangled fall down and great rocks and thought to himself "I hope it ain't so hard to climb where he is sending us."

General McDowell used his position near the ford at Sudley Springs to instruct each crossing unit. His messengers from Centreville had delivered consistent news of no action either at Blackburn's Ford or the Stone Bridge, additionally he had learned that Colonel Sherman had found a new ford not on his maps, between the Stone bridge and Sudley Springs, He had directed that messenger to find General Tyler and direct a crossing there as soon as he could. He felt much better now and he watched with pleasure as General Burnsides men appeared to have taken the crest of Matthews Hill. He had the rebels on the run now.

Small groups and clusters of wounded men flowed back towards him, most seemed deeply shocked as they passed by, many of the 90 day men were very close to their mustering out date. Many a letter had been written the night before detailing plans of reunion after "Saving Washington," many had not survived to muster out.

As Heintzelman's Brigade finished crossing; Major Barry and two Batteries of rifled Parrots crossed the ford, Barry seeing McDowell, rode over to consult with him.

"Major Barry, Get those pieces and swing wide off the road to the right. Push them to the next ridge there beyond this one to our front!

I will direct infantry from Heintzelman's trail to follow and support, if you move with haste you can enfilade them with your fires!"

Barry nodded and General McDowell turned and pointed to a white house on a hill in the distance, "Guide on that house there. See if you can find good ground to command the ground between it and the run."

Captain Ricketts and Griffin, commanders of the batteries rode up, and Major Barry rode with them back to the waiting artillery, "Gentlemen we will swing wide of the line forming to our front to obtain positions there," he pointed to the ridge.

A long line of infantry was arrayed to their front and heavy musketry exchanges made the conversation difficult.

Ricketts expressed his concern, "Sir who will support us? That sounds like you want us to bypass the infantry!"

Barry quickly replied, "Move there quickly Captain! I will arrange your supports. We can break them by enfilading fire if we are quick about it. Get up there now! Show them what mounted artillery can do!"

The two Companies spurred their teams and skirted the marching Regiments on the New Market Road and rapidly made their way to the prominence marked by the Henry House. The crescendo of musketry increased as each side added regiments to their lines and exchanged volleys. Major Barry rode back to report to General McDowell and arrange supports.

After returning to his signal tower after retrieving his hat, Captain Alexander peered at the battle building to the North, looking through the telescope on a tripod in the tower; he could clearly see that the main fight was there. The Unionists had arrayed the majority of their forces there and it was clear that General McDowell was attempting

to roll the left flank.  He quickly drafted a message to be delivered
by courier to General Beauregard,

*"No movements or activity noted from Union Mills Ford to Stone
Bridge, minor bombardment only, crossing noted north of Stone
Bridge now at possibly brigade size.  Main fight is vicinity Henry
House.  Captain Alexander"*

Alexander turned to the Sergeant manning the tower, "Get this to a
courier, have him take it to General Beauregard. "

From his vantage point he watched the fight unfold.  General
McDowell had his men arrayed in long lines below the ridge called
Henry Hill.  He noticed then two Unionist batteries swinging to the
right of the line.  Quite exposed they moved to the vicinity of the
House that marked the crest of the hill and unlimbered and prepared
for action with surprising rapidity.

No sooner had the guns got into position when he observed smoke
from a volley emerge from the grounds of the Henry house, several
artillerymen and horses fell,  He watched in horror as the rightmost
battery engaged the house and the grounds at close range, he
watched as large pieces of the clapboard walls were blown off the
dwelling.  Soldiers ran from their positions away from the house.  He
imagined the Yankees were using canister, and he hoped no one was
sheltering in the house.

The two batteries turned their fire onto the Brigades to the right of
General Beauregard's line, with each firing he could observe the
murderous effect on the lines of troops, they were enfiladed.  To his
relief he noted that the larger portion of Beauregard's newly arrived
units from General Johnston were wisely positioning behind Henry
hill and apparently were unseen by the Yankee batteries.  They had
begun to form a long line behind the hill.  Their fixed bayonets
gleamed in the noon day sun.  He watched helplessly as the guns
raked the exposed units forward of Henry hill in the distance.

General Johnston and Beauregard arrived at the knoll where the Portici House sat and immediately both realized the gravity of the moment. To the right General Johnston saw what he assumed to be Evan's Brigade vastly outnumbered and gamely holding a force 3 times their size in the hollow forward of Henry hill, Jackson's Brigade and what looked like an Alabama Regiment were forming on line in the lee of Henry hill and union batteries had materialized by the crest of Henry Hill and had Evan's brigade caught in enfilading fire. Johnston became filled with the urgency of the moment.

"General Beauregard send orders immediately to your right wing to detach reinforcements here now! This is the decisive point!"

Beauregard appeared shocked; he nodded and motioned for his orderly to take orders, "Send word to Cocke, Early and Bonham to dispatch half their available forces to march here without delay!" The orderly saluted and galloped off.

General Beauregard then turned to Johnston, "Sir, respectfully I must ask you to allow me to concentrate on this fight. I would recommend that you repair to a distance by which you can strategically reinforce me. I must insist that as the senior subordinate that I be allowed to continue this fight forward alone!"

General Johnston was taken aback for a moment, but thinking for a moment he was inclined to agree, "Very well, General, If I were you I would do something about those guns on the left."

Johnston then turned to his aide, "Captain James, arrange for some couriers, we will repair to the Portici House, over there where I can see."

At that moment a courier arrived looking for General Beauregard, Johnston asked to see the message; it was a note from Captain Alexander stating the battle was where he stood. Johnston thanked the courier and assured him he would notify Beauregard.

General Jackson studied the unfamiliar ground as he hurried his brigade forward to reinforce the fight to the left. The Unionist line now stretched from the Run from the stone bridge at Warrenton Pike to the right edge of the Henry Hill to his front. In his mind the geometry of the situation was all wrong. He paused at the Portici House knoll and looked over the developing fight. The defending elements were in the hollow short of Matthews Hill; they only manned a front half as wide as the growing Unionist line and were now receiving enfilading fire from the increasing number of troops.

It was clear that those regiments below Matthews hill were lost and would certainly be overwhelmed.

As he carefully looked over the ground he noticed a long and slight depression just short of the crest of Henry House hill where the enemy approaching the ridge could not see or fire into. He recalled Wellington's description of his ground at Waterloo, "Sheltered from influence of artillery and observation" this would have to do, he thought. He spurred his horse to his lead company and directed the Captain where to march.

He quickly got his hot and tired men into a line below the crest of the hill and encouraged them to sit down and rest, other units were coming from the wooded approaches adjacent to the run and he held a short discussion with Colonel Hampton; who he suggested attach himself and his 600 men to his right.

Jackson then had his artillery occupy the rise to the right along with other pieces that were action there. Looking at the battery already in action he recognized a former student, Captain Imboden directing a very rapid rate of fire. Jackson smiled and remembered Mexico.

He looked over the line with satisfaction to take and hold the ridge the Unionists would have to march over the ridge; He could destroy them in detail with volleys without them knowing the extent of his line. It was good ground.

The location none the less began to get hotter as a Unionist battery positioned itself to his left behind the house on the ridge and began firing over his line into the embattled brigade to the front of his right. He could not see the guns but he could see the smoke of their muzzle blasts and hear the shells shuttling over his head as they fired.

As he steadied his men along his lines, he saw an approaching officer on horseback in a fine blue uniform. He was asking for General Jackson loudly as he rode the line.

Jackson rode to him and greeted him; it was Barnard Bee; the man was clearly distraught.

"General Jackson, My Brigade is nearly destroyed, can you reinforce?"

Jackson calmly replied, "General Bee that is why I am here"

Jackson realized that Bee apparently wanted him to move his brigade to his location. The dictum "never reinforce failure" entered his mind.

Bee noticed that Jackson short response indicated no action, reiterated, "Sir, I am overwhelmed, how will we stop them?"

Jackson coldly replied, "Show them the bayonet!"

Bee was obviously angry and rode off shouting "Just sitting there like a stonewall!"

Minutes later while rallying his men an exploding case shot mortally wounded General Bee; what was left of his brigade broke and ran past Jackson's line.

Colonel Cummings was pushing his troops as hard as he could to catch up with General Jackson's movement, as the last regiment in his march; the 33$^{rd}$ Virginia found themselves tangled on the route by artillery from the Washington Light Artillery. They were being repositioned to support the fight to the North.

Cummings spurred his inexperienced men to move at the double quick, but when he realized in the heat of the day, that he was bleeding off a lot of his strength to stragglers, so he slowed the march. As he reached the hill called "Portici," a Lieutenant from General Jackson's staff directed them to enter the woods on the left of the road, he ordered them to move in the woods until they were on the left of the white house on the hill ahead of them.

The 33$^{rd}$ moved down a narrow trail in column through the wood while the sound of the battle rose and fell. Soon Cummings began to note the louder and sharp reports of artillery that judging from the sound was nearby. Soon his guide indicated they were deep enough so Cummings ordered his companies on line and had them march on line to the edge of the wood towards the field that was filling with Unionists below.

As they neared to edge of the wood, he immediately noticed two Federal Batteries sitting exposed barely 100 yards away. In the distance red costumed Zouaves could be seen moving up to collocate with the battery that was busy firing into the flank of General Jackson's line.

For Cummings the temptation was irresistible, he immediately ordered up his men on line and advanced on the battery. The 33$^{rd}$ Virginia Volunteer Infantry wore standard Army blue uniforms, so as he closed to within half the distance, the officers of the battery seemed confused by their appearance but after some discussion they turned their attention back to their task.

Cummings directed his commanders to fire by volley as a regiment on the two batteries, the Captains echoed his command. The volley tore the two batteries to shreds. Half the men fell wounded or dead. Team horses on the caissons struck by the musket balls reared and ran, dragging drivers, limbers, and caissons towards the Federal center. The devastation of the two batteries caused a shock to the right of General McDowell's line.

The Fire Zouaves of the 11$^{th}$ New York, following Major Barry up the hill, rushed to form a line but were unable to present their arms before Cummings second volley sent a hazy grey cloud of musket balls into their tight ranks.  Men in the dozens fell, their fire in response was scattered and had little effect.  Cummings was able to deliver one more punishing volley before the increasing Federal fire forced him to withdraw to the wood.

Captain Porter Alexander watched the battle develop from his vantage point on the signal tower.  The annihilation of the Federal batteries on Henry Hill seemed to have been executed with excellent precision,  the attack appeared to create a lull in the overall firing along the line,  then he notice the Federal troops begin an advance on line up Henry Hill.

He watched in fascination as the union troops recovered the guns only to be attacked and driven off the guns by a small force of cavalry that emerged from the wood.  The guns changed hands two more times as both sides attempted to secure them.

Looking down below the run, columns of reinforcing regiments were moving in dusty marching order towards the fray.  He turned his telescope to the north and began to note scattered and disorganized movements of groups and clusters of soldiers moving back across Sudley Springs Ford, he assumed it to be the evacuation of the wounded.  What he realized was the distinctive fact that there appeared to be no more regiments moving across Sudley Springs Ford to reinforce General McDowell.

He quickly pulled his message book out and penciled out a note to General Beauregard,

*General Beauregard, no further troops are crossing Sudley Springs Ford to reinforce Gen McDowell, no additional movements noted vicinity stone bridge or Blackburn's Ford.  Capt. Alexander.*

He summoned a courier below to take this message to Portici.

He returned to his telescope and watched transfixed as the Federal lines crested Henry House Ridge, as the regiments topped the ridge, a nearly continuous rattling roar of volley fire from Jackson's Brigade greeted them. Regiments of Jackson's brigade then charged the Federal line in an uneven movement he could see the flashing sunlight off of thousands of bayonets. Once Jackson's men topped the crest of Henry Hill, they delivered another great volley.

At that point Alexander started to see the Federal lines disintegrate, first small groups then larger clusters of soldiers broke away from the rear of the regiments. Jackson's troops and rallied elements of other units delivered volley after volley into the Federal troops. Something inside the great mass broke. Suddenly he noticed entire units break and run for Sudley Springs Ford; it appeared that a general rout had begun.

The dispatch rider who had earlier given General Longstreet the order to release Early's Brigade; returned to report new orders from General Johnston, "Sir, General Johnston has ordered a general push all along the line, the Unionists are breaking, He wants you to push with what you have to Centreville.

Longstreet nodded and looked at his watch; it was nearly 4 pm, while the noise of the battle to the North continued it had become apparent that the crescendo of cannon and musket fire was reducing. At least he would do something on this day.

He turned to his Adjutant, "Pass word to Colonel Jones to seize the battery on that hill!"

Below the bluffs of Compton's farm, Colonel Jenkins rode his line in the woods, shouting, "5th South Carolina up! Commanders rally on me!"

Billy Cross and his messmates raised their heads and hearing his cry in the woods, they stood up and put their belts and cartridge boxes back on, the day remained terribly hot, but they had not had it bad so far. The sounds of the distant battle had definitely settled down.

Captain Sykes after a short consultation with Colonel Jenkins returned, "First Sergeant, have the men fall in on the road!  Move fast!"

Billy and his messmates fell in column on the narrow wooded road in column, 4 men abreast.  The order to load muskets passed down the ranks.  Billy dug a cartridge from his pouch and quickly loaded his musket. After he had returned his ramrod to its slot under the barrel the First Sergeant ordered them to march up the ravine.

After they had moved about a quarter mile up the road, Billy heard yells and shouts and then the firing of several muskets in the deep shady woods.

Ribedeaux muttered, "They must have skirmishers in here!"

Billy looked at the bluff on the left, "Still pretty steep, guess we is gonna have to climb up through all that."

Captain Sykes cried out, "Left Face!  Form a line of battle facing left!"  After a pause he cried out, "Fix bayonets!"

The order caused Gene to comment, "Don't none of ya'll be stickin' me with them bayonets, when we are climbing that hill!"

The men of the 5th South Carolina were marched into the thick blackberry bramble to the left of the road so the 18th Mississippi could move past them to occupy the right of the line, the 17th Mississippi would form the left most reach of the line.

Colonel Jenkins once satisfied with the initial alignment ordered them forward with a simple, "Advance!"

Joshua lounged against the wheel of his gun, they had been ordered to cease fire in order to allow the guns to cool, the heat made many on the crews feel faint. Joshua noticed that muzzles of the guns were stained black by the firing. Flies buzzed about angrily attracted by the fresh dung deposited by the horse teams.

Drummer boys from the New York regiment had come by with buckets of water and watered the men in the battery. The enterprising Surgeon of the 31$^{st}$ New York had found a spring in the woods behind their position and dispatched the drummers and his medical orderlies along the line to provide the badly needed refreshment.

Suddenly the skirmishers who had been sent into the ravine earlier in the morning began to emerge from the ravine, and the sound of musketry was heard below in the ravine.

Major Hunt mounted on his horse and rode to the edge of ravine; a skirmisher emerging shouted to him, "There are lots of men moving this way down there!"

Colonel Pratt behind him ordered his regiment out of the woods to form a line, as Major Hunt returned to his battery. As he looked across the field of oats, he began to note rebel skirmishers scrambling over the lip of the ravine onto the field to his front. As they emerged as various points he could see that he had a brigade forming out there, barely 350 yards away.

He turned to his battery and shouted, "Load Spherical Case, 300 yards!"

Hunt to his horror saw the infantry supporting his guns forming a continuous line behind his guns; they would have to fire through his crews to engage the enemy. He spurred his horse over to Colonel Pratt.

"Sir it is essential that you form your lines adjacent to my battery, not behind! They cannot engage the enemy if they are compelled to fire through my position!"

Pratt nodded and shouted commands to adjust the front, the move took several precious moments, he then commanded his regiment to load, they would have to wait until the rebels advanced halfway across the field to effectively engage them with their smoothbore muskets.

The rebels across the way were emerging in greater and greater numbers and forming a front to advance. The great mass of men wore both blue and gray uniforms which stood out clearly against the green backdrop of the treetops of the wooded ravine. Their fixed bayonets gleamed brightly in the late afternoon sun.

Major Hunt returned to his battery and rode the line shouting, "You will dispense with sponging, I will need minutes more than arms! I need you to fire as rapidly as possible."

O'Keefe trooped the line and announced, "You heard the Major, focus on your tasks focus on nuthin' but your tasks!"

Across the field a mounted officer was collecting his brigade in a battle front and the men were clearly capping their muskets and forming in ranks to deliver a volley, regardless of the long range.

Major Hunt was becoming alarmed at the size of the force forming to his front; he quickly moved to the rear of his battery and commanded, "By Battery Fire!"

Joshua had checked the fuse when his number 5 passed, the spherical case shot had been cut for ¼ of a second, it would be a miracle if the shot functioned properly at this range. When the command "Fire" was passed down the line the 4 light 12 pound guns fired simultaneously, immediately in front of the massing troops the sizzling shot burst with loud bangs and white smoke. Joshua noted several men falling.

Without thought he commanded, "Spherical Case, 300 yards advance the charge!" The gun crew quickly rolled the piece back on line, white smoke slowly drifted out of the blackened muzzle.

His number 5 passed him seconds later and barely paused as he inspected the round in the pouch, Private Mulcahy quickly inserted the fixed round seam side down and Private Watkins rammed the charge home.

Joshua shouted, "Prick and prime!"

In an instant, Private Wilkins had pierced the bag with the gimlet and inserted the friction primer, Private Lyttle had the lanyard attached before Wilkins' hands had cleared the breech, he removed the slack and looked to Joshua.

Joshua shouted, "Fire!"

With a yank of the lanyard the battery had repeated the previous engagement; each gunner had expertly off set his aim point a few yards away from the earlier aim point. Four more bursts in front of the troops and more men fell.

The gun crews worked like men possessed, Major Hunt commanded additional rounds of Spherical case and had adjusted the range to 250 yards which was the time limit on the Bormann fuses, they were all cut at nearly zero time.

As the battery finished the 3$^{rd}$ engagement, the rebel Colonel to the front got his first volley off at extreme range, the incoming rain of musket balls was somewhat high but the buckshot from the buck and ball cartridges rained in among the cannon crews and the infantry inflicting minor wounds. Joshua had one impact the barrel of his gun as he set his pendulum hausse to set his piece on the next aim point.

Joshua noticed the rebel troops were reloading, he then heard what he wanted hear, as Major Hunt shouted "Canister, at 200 yards, by battery!"

The load was advanced and inspected by a glance, the crew at the front of the gun, had the round loaded and rammed home in an instant. The gun was pricked and primed before Joshua could finish his command. Again M Companies 4 guns as one roared. The 4 tin encased canister projectiles split open as they exited the muzzles and spread into a wider and wider pattern as the 76 lead balls within were released. The cloud of shot impacted the ranks of the rebel troops as they were attempting reload.

Joshua noticed great gaps appeared in the lines before him as he shouted for the number 5 to advance the next charge. Joshua quickly adjusted his aim after the crew had returned the gun on line and they repeated the point blank engagements with canister at different points along the enemy brigade's front.

M Company fired again and again working their pieces with practiced precision. First Sergeant walked the battery line shouting, "Pour it into them men! Do not let up! Pour it into them!"

On the side of the road that led to Blackburn's Ford, Colonel Davies and Colonel Richardson watched transfixed as the gunners of M Company engaged the rebel brigade that had suddenly emerged from the ravine, Davies realized that no orders were necessary to change the outcome of what he was watching, at last count the battery had gotten at least six shots per gun, and was tearing great gaps in the rebel ranks as they attempted to form on the lip of the plateau. The absolute fluidity of the drill of the crew was intoxicating to watch.

Richardson remarked, "My god that is the most beautiful display of drill I have seen in 20 years of service! It is like something from the Mexican War!"

The two men cringed as the rebel brigade got another volley off in the direction of the battery, but from the distance it appeared to have no effect.

Davies remarked, "It is a damned shame for the New York Regiments, they have to get closer for them to have a chance at contributing to the fight."

Billy Cross limped back down into the ravine.

He remembered climbing over the lip of the bluff, and no sooner had he arrived there, after Captain Sykes had shown him the line was; that a white burst with a loud bang had appeared in the sky before him. Something hard and fast had hit his fingers and knocked him down. As he struggled to rise, he realized he was missing two fingers on his left hand. He looked in shock at his musket and the barrel was bent and the wood was missing from the fore stock where his left hand had been. Captain Sykes lay still on the ground, very still, and everyone that was beside him was no longer there.

Billy sat below the bluff and wrapped his hand with his kerchief, it was bleeding badly. The terrible roar of the guns and the buzzing of shot over the top of the bluff, reminded him of angry yellow jackets looking for something to sting.

He remembered last Thursday and said to himself, "I guess today is our turn!"

Above him he heard a ragged volley of musketry as his regiment returned fire against the terrible enemy and he resolved to rise and rejoin his friends.

He lifted his head above the lip of the ravine, as another blast from the cannon to their front tore a gaping hole in the ranks to his right; he noticed that 8 or more men fell wounded or dead.

Billy picked up a musket and returned to the line, despite the pain in his left hand he managed to load the musket and presented the piece when ordered and fired.

The next volley of fire from the cannon, killed Colonel Jenkins' horse and several men ran over to extract him from the fallen animal.

The guns across the way fired at an unbelievable rate and men were beginning to separate from the rear and seek the safety of the ravine.

Joshua had lost track of time or where he was. He repeated steps and commands that he seemed strangely removed from. The actions of the crews had taken over in the realm of second nature.

First Sergeant O'Keefe trooped the line shouting encouragement; he was somewhat dismayed that an enemy musket ball had destroyed his pipe.

Soon the cry rose from the caisson sections, "We are running out of canister, 1 round left!"

With the last roar of fire, Major Hunt realized that the rebel force to his front had retreated below for the safety of the ravine. In his mind that only meant that they went there to reform, so he cried out, "Shell, 300 yards! Aim low!"

The gunners in the next engagement endeavored to put the shell as close to the earth as possible as the shell passed over the lip of the ravine before the shell burst in order to drive men from the lip of the cover. The command had its' intended effect; driving the rebel troops down to the road at the bottom of the ravine.

Major Hunt rode the line and commanded his gunners to keep pouring shell into the ravine, He was proud that the infantry to his rear had not had to fire a single shot. His new gun had proven itself. Then to his horror he saw Lieutenant Craig's body lying beside his horse, no one had noticed him fall.

Hunt quickly dismounted and lifted his head, Presley was clearly dead, he had a large entry wound in his temple and was a sickly gray color. For a moment Henry Hunt forgot everything, he was filled with the terrible responsibility that he owned this single death. He owned it forever.

Hunt quickly summoned First Sergeant O'Keefe as his crews fired shell into the ravine, "Wrap the Lieutenant in a blanket and place him on a caisson."

In the ravine below, Colonel Jones tried to confer with his Regimental Commanders but the exploding shell overhead continually forced them to take cover. He decided to order a withdrawal. Each Colonel would later describe the effect of the bombardment as "Galling fire". They had failed to take the battery.

An hour later Colonel Jones reported on foot, to General Longstreet that he was unable to take the battery above Blackburn's Ford.

Longstreet looked at him, sympathetically and announced, "It is a small matter, Colonel Jones, we have won the day."

General McDowell was shocked when he noticed large groups of men moving towards him and the Ford. This was no orderly move, entire regiments had broken. He watched as a crazed team of artillery horses towing a wagon without drivers tore past him knocking men over, the battery wagon in tow bounced across the ford spilling implements and equipment.

Looking east, he saw bodies of men crossing the run at all points. Many had abandoned their muskets. He resolved to get back across to rally them; He signaled his aide and escorts to follow him.

McDowell shouted to his Adjutant riding behind him, "Get orders to General Miles to rally the stragglers at Centreville! Ride ahead of us and let him know!"

The retreat began to take a life of its' own and McDowell's grand army, after 14 hours on their feet, in the heat and humidity, the lack of water, and the terror of battle could take no more. Troops now wildly sought the nearest available exit from the battlefield across the run. Officers could not stop or rally them. The rebel troops seeing them break advanced their artillery to points where they could fire into the fleeing masses.

Quartermaster Sergeant Watson of G Company, 1st Artillery led his detail with 6 borrowed horses out of Centreville to replace the horses lost to rebel fire and was amazed to see running troops moving towards him as he approached the Cub Run Bridge. The men were wildly shouting, "Sold out! We're sold out! They are coming up the road!" Watson tried to stop one man to talk to him and the man knocked him down with a blow to the face. The leading pack of men then tore the horses away from his small detail and mounted them and rode away to Centreville.

In shock Sergeant Watson rubbed his throbbing jaw and watched the retreat turn into a solid line of men, wagons and horses fill the road crossing the Cub Run Bridge. Oddly he noticed that civilians in carriages were amongst the terrified men.

Watson flinched when to his left he heard the firing of cannon; the rebels had turned their guns by the Stone Bridge to fire on the fleeing masses crossing the Cub Run Bridge. A pair of 6 pound shot had stuck a supply wagon crossing the bridge and killed the team. He saw large chunks of the horses being thrown into the air. The heavy wagon now blocked the traffic across the narrow suspension bridge. The fleeing masses abandoned their wagons and carriages and began to move on foot across the difficult ravine. He realized then that G Company would not recover the 30 pounder. Watson assembled his detail and walked across the cow pasture back to Centreville.

First Sergeant O'Keefe held a dripping felt covered canteen up towards Major Hunt as he sat and studied the far bluffs across the run, "Here sir, drink some, or this heat will kill you."

Hunt looked down at O'Keefe, "Thank you First Sergeant. I am proud of them they are shaping up well."

O'Keefe nodded and asked, "Do you think it is over, Sir?"

The sudden quiet after 9 hours of fighting was puzzling. Hunt studied the heights beyond once more with his field glasses but saw no evidence of movement across the ford. The pounding of hooves behind them caused him to turn and he saw a messenger on a lathered horse approach Colonel Davies. Major Hunt turned his horse and rode over to them. The messenger was greatly agitated, "All is lost Sir! General McDowell's army has been destroyed! You must repair to Centreville immediately to form a defensive line with Colonel Miles." Hunt noticed the men of the 16th New York were hearing the discussion and began to talk and mutter excitedly.

Colonel Davies responded, "Very well we will proceed to march back to Centreville."

Colonel Platt approached on his horse, and Davies ordered, "Gentlemen, it appears that things have gone badly over there. Get your men up and ready to march back to Centreville. Major Hunt, I will put your battery to the rear of our column, I will need you to be prepared to act as a rear guard."

Hunt nodded, he was shocked by the news. He had been certain of a victory today. The great work of his men and the death of Presley meant nothing after this news. He grimly moved back to his battery to order them to limber the guns. As they pulled the Company on line in the oat field, he looked over the prone victims of his action across the way, then back to his grimy and businesslike gunners and their blackened pieces. He realized then, this was to become a long affair.

He then looked to Lieutenant Platt and First Sergeant O'Keefe, "Move the Company to Centreville! At a walk!"

# 10 EPILOGUE

The panicked rabble of the Army of Northeastern Virginia reached the outer line of forts in Arlington by the night of the 21$^{st}$. Pieces and parts of units came in throughout the night into the day of the 22$^{nd}$. It would take nearly two weeks to collect up the retreating men and return them to their units.

Neither General Johnston or Beauregard ordered a concerted pursuit, each side had not realized until the end who was to prevail in the first serious battle of the long war. And at the end of it all both sides were too exhausted to put closure to the conflict.

On the day of the 22$^{nd}$ of July, General George McClelland would receive a telegram from President Lincoln appointing him to overall command of the Army. The very next day, President Lincoln would sign an order authorizing 500,000 troops to serve 3 years. The following day he would sign yet another order calling for 500,000 more. General McDowell was sacked and reduced to a minor command.

Henry Hunt arrived at Fort Albany in Arlington in the morning of the 22$^{nd}$ of July. He personally returned the body of Lieutenant Preston

O. Craig to his grieving family. Immediately following this sad task, he received a summons to see General Winfield Scott at the War Department for a personal interview and some well earned praise. There were not many good news stories about the battle, his was one of the few.

Major Hunt was summoned again to Washington when General McClelland arrived in town to take command of the shattered Army of Northeastern Virginia. Having been mentioned in dispatches McClelland offered him the deputy position assisting Colonel Barry as the overall artillery officer for the Union Army. McClelland would shortly thereafter recommend a Colonelcy for Hunt.

The command of M Company was transferred to Captain Benson, whom sickness had prevented his participation in the battle.

The Army would rebuild and inculcate a new professionalism within it's formations. The battle at Bull Run demonstrated that enthusiasm was a poor substitute for discipline and drill. George McClellan would build a professional Army from the vast mass of manpower that Mr. Lincoln's call summoned.

Colonel John Barry, nursing his guilt in regards to his failure to properly support Captain James Ricketts and his battery set about rebuilding the Artillery of the Army. Captain Ricketts had been wounded and captured and was recovering as a prisoner of war in Richmond. The two would hold a lifetime grudge.

At General McClellan's directive a camp was established in Rockville, Maryland. It was called Camp Barry where concentrated artillery training would be conducted for newly fitted and equipped volunteer artillerymen. Joshua Timmonds and the noncommissioned officers and men of M Company, 2nd US Artillery would play a crucial role in the training and preparation of a new generation of artillerymen.

Billy Cross would recover from his wounds and receive promotion to Corporal in B Company 5th South Carolina Infantry.

Louis Markley and Jacob Timmonds rode into Manassas on the night of the 22$^{nd}$ of July and were reunited with Colonel Hampton and the Legion became an all arms brigade again. Soon they would become an integral part of a cavalry division that was being formed under J.E.B. Stuart.

As the armies of both sides applied the lessons learned from this first encounter, the next great chess move of the conflict came about through the actions of the United States Navy. "The Anaconda Plan" that had been the brainchild of General Winfield Scott would be adapted and put into operation by Admiral Farragut. The economic starvation of the South would be its objective. Crucial to the success of this plan would be retention of Fort Monroe and Fort Pickens, which would serve as crucial future staging bases for the isolation of the South through naval blockade. The failure of the South to produce a meaningful counter to this naval power would prove to be her undoing.

# Acknowledgements

There are many that aided me in accomplishing this project. The first is my maternal grandmother Inez Dennis Evans, who at my earliest years taught me to respect my history and to remember. Her daughter, Maxine Lytle, carried on the tradition and has provided me with innumerable letters and papers that enabled me to capture the spirit of the South.

I thank Dr. Norman Sinkler Walsh, MD whose book *Macbeth, South Carolina, People and Places, 1811-2011* provided essential data on the origins of my protagonist. History that was difficult to grasp as much of the land that made up Macbeth disappeared under a large lake in the 1930s.

Special thanks go to the Idaho Military History Museum and Mr. Ken Swanson, the curator. Ken is one of the foremost experts of Civil War artillery technology in Idaho. Due to his dedication to history and its preservation, the museum has obtained and maintains two complete and functional M1857 Napoleon guns. With his support the Idaho Civil War Volunteers maintains a public presence with these pieces and provide frequent firing demonstrations and salute firings and great personal expense. The cover art for this first book is courtesy of the Idaho Civil War Volunteers who were firing a salute over Idaho's Dry Creek Veterans Cemetery to commemorate Veteran's Day. They perform this task every year.

I owe a debt of gratitude to Mr. Harry Smeltzer and his excellent blog site on the Battle of Bull Run at bullrunnings.wordpress.com. This site was essential towards visualizing the details of the battle and reading the official reports from the Official Records of the War of the Rebellion in an organized form.

Other Special thanks go to James Mace, author of multiple books about military books at Legionary Books LLC. James provided me with invaluable advice and consistently makes writing look easy.

I am indebted also to the men and women who watch over our history in the National Park Service for the National Battlefield Parks. Their helpful assistance has been invaluable in my research trips. No matter how many times I visit, I always hear something new from them. Hopefully we will retain the wisdom to keep their labors funded, lest we forget.

I thank the soldiers I have known and served with through my career. They made me want to write of and honor soldiers as the uniforms and equipment may change, but the soul of the soldier never changes.

Finally to Jana, my wife, whose constant support and encouragement greatly aided me in this endeavor.

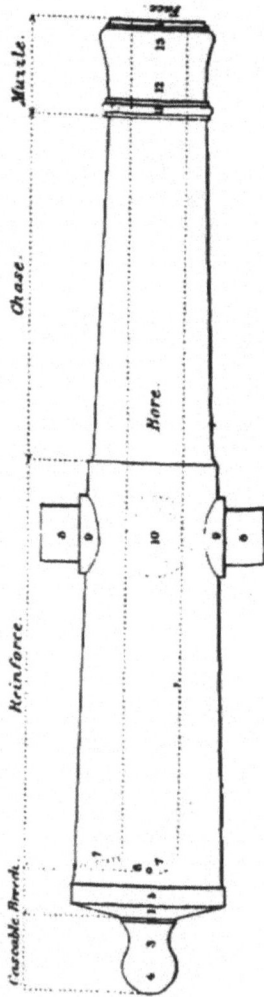

Cascable
1. Base of breech.
2. Fillet.
3. Neck.
4. Knob.
5. Base ring.

6. Bottom of the bore.
Reinforce
7. Horizontal and vertical projections of vent and vent-piece.
8. Horizontal projection of trunnions.
9. Da    do.
10. Vertical    do.

Muzzle
11. Astragal and Fillets.
12. Neck.
13. Swell of Muzzle.
14. Muzzle mouldings [Lip Face.

Rimbases.
Trunnions.trimbars.
Face.

# ABOUT THE AUTHOR

Robert K. Lytle is a 30 year veteran of the United States Army.
Born in Columbia, South Carolina he received his college education
at The Military College of South Carolina and was commissioned as
an Armor officer in 1982. He is a veteran of the Cold War in
Europe, the First Gulf War and Operation Iraqi Freedom.

www.ingramcontent.com/pod-product-compliance
Lightning Source LLC
Chambersburg PA
CBHW060229050426
42448CB00009B/1366